Science of
COACHING
TENNIS

Science of COACHING TENNIS

Jack L. Groppel, PhD
Harry Hopman/Saddlebrook International Tennis

James E. Loehr, EdD
United States Tennis Association

D. Scott Melville, PhD
Eastern Washington University

Ann M. Quinn, MS
Exercise Physiologist and Fitness Consultant,
Blackburn Station, Australia

Leisure Press
Champaign, Illinois

Developmental Editor: June I. Decker, PhD
Copy Editor: John Wentworth
Assistant Editor: Robert King
Production Director: Ernie Noa
Typesetters: Sandra Meier, Cindy Pritchard
Text Design: Keith Blomberg
Text Layout: Jayne Clampett, Kimberlie Henris, Denise Mueller
Cover Design: Jack Davis
Cover Photo: ALLSPORT/Brian Spurlock
Illustrations By: Raneé Rogers
Printed By: Braun-Brumfield

ISBN: 0-88011-337-5

Library of Congress Cataloging-in-Publication Data

Science of coaching tennis / Jack L. Groppel . . . [et al.].
    p.   cm.
  ISBN 0-88011-337-5
  1. Tennis—Coaching. 2. Tennis—Psychological aspects.
  3. Tennis—Physiological aspects. I. Groppel, Jack L.
  GV1002.9.C63S35 1989
  796.342'.07'7—dc19   88-28196
                                                     CIP

Printed in the United States of America

10 9 8 7 6 5 4 3 2 1

Leisure Press
A Division of Human Kinetics Publishers, Inc.
Box 5076, Champaign, IL 61820
1-800-342-5457
1-800-334-3665 (in Illinois)

Contents

Foreword

Today we understand more than ever that sport science is vital to the development of our young tennis players. I believe research being done in this area is the foundation not only for tennis but for all sports worldwide. Much of the newest research is discussed in *Science of Coaching Tennis*.

Authors Jack Groppel, Scott Melville, Ann Quinn, and Jim Loehr write about their specialties concisely and informatively. I believe any coach or player and even parents will be equipped to make better decisions about tennis after reading this book. We all—whether coaches, parents, or players—should be open to learn, no matter what our age or experience.

Jack Groppel reminds us, first, that there is no one right way to play the game, and, second, that although statistics are important, application of statistics is the key. I found the section on tennis facts and fallacies fascinating. I am sure we all have a few misconceptions about the game—I know I did.

Jack hits the nail on the head when he says that the fun of coaching is deciding exactly *what* to say and *how* to teach the various movements. This is a challenge to all of us who coach, and I think Jack's advice can make this challenge easier.

Scott Melville gives great practical coaching advice on how to actually demonstrate, guide, and analyze the game. He makes a good point that we should drill more than scrimmage during team practices, for most players do plenty of scrimmaging outside of practice. He also tells us that reaction time can be decreased, which is good to know when working with less gifted kids. Another informative concept from Scott is that we should get kids to accelerate forcibly through the ball for the best long-term results.

Ann Quinn's section on exercise physiology in tennis contributes a great deal of useful information. She describes physical fitness as the key for muscle endurance, strength, flexibility, and cardiovascular endurance. If I had known this years ago, I could probably have avoided some of the injuries that have sidelined me off and on. Ann explains the benefits of training and provides training guidelines specific to tennis. The sections on stretching and nutrition also offer a practical basis for improving long-term performance.

Jim Loehr delves into the mental side of tennis with real clarity. I enjoyed the section on qualities of a champion and Jim's assertion that problem solving during a match is normal and a sign of a good player, but it is not just automatic. He encourages coaches to know their players' mental strengths and weaknesses so they can design mental training programs just like they do physical nutritional programs.

These authors are leaders in their fields of expertise, and I recommend this book to all coaches. Some coaches know the techniques of the game very well, but every coach can apply the guidance and advice about sport science that is covered so well in *Science of Coaching Tennis*. Our young tennis players deserve the best and most complete advice available.

Stan Smith

Preface

The application of science to sport is a rapidly expanding field. With the advent of the research-oriented United States Olympic Training Center and of research-designed training regimens for many athletes, it is appropriate to begin applying scientific information to tennis. An abundance of valuable information exists for coaches who know how to interpret and properly apply it. This book presents usable methods through which tennis coaches can effectively incorporate the available information into their programs.

All coaches should strive to keep up with contemporary applications of technology. Although most prevalent in equipment design, technology is increasing in the realm of coaching techniques. With the help of computers, coaches can compile statistics on athletes' patterns of play, shot-effectiveness percentages, competitive strengths and weaknesses, and other characteristics not immediately apparent through observation from the sidelines.

By scientifically evaluating players in game situations, coaches can better design training methods to strengthen weaknesses, can more accurately scout future opponents, and can develop specific competitive strategies. Admittedly, however, technology has its limitations. The computer can help coaches analyze specific information, but the coach must know how to best utilize the information to help each player achieve optimal performance.

The specific application of sport science to tennis shares the benefits and limitations of technology on sports in general. The area of biomechanics, for example, enables coaches to understand the difference between muscular force and ballistic action. Without a basic grasp of biomechanics, skeptics who consider physical strength an automatic advantage are hard pressed to explain how Rod Laver (5 feet, 8 inches tall) could serve as hard as Stan Smith (6 feet, 3 inches tall), or how Jimmy Connors and John McEnroe, neither of whom were physically dominating, ascended to the pinnacle of success.

Biomechanics is but the first of four areas of sport science this book examines in relation to tennis. In Part 2, Dr. Scott Melville, assistant professor of physical education at Eastern Washington University, discusses how coaches can use motor-learning research to become more effective teachers of tennis. In Part 3, Ann Quinn, an Australian sport science consultant and presently exercise physiologist of Wimbledon champ Pat Cash, examines the importance of fitness to successful tennis and specific ways coaches can get players to enjoy conditioning drills. Finally, Dr. James Loehr, considered by many to be the pioneer in mental toughness training for tennis, explores the athlete's mind, the last frontier of sport research, and suggests strategies for improving the mental skills of players.

No book can purport to be an all-purpose guide to teaching skills or developing physically and mentally superior players. Each athlete represents an individual coaching challenge, and the effectiveness of your approach lies both in your ability to teach the principles of competitive tennis and in your motivational creativity. We hope that this book will convince you of the advantages of a comprehensive scientific approach to coaching, and that the specific ideas presented will help you introduce a degree of variety into your practice sessions that will keep your players alert, eager, and involved in the ongoing process of learning.

Jack L. Groppel, PhD

Director of Player Development

Harry Hopman/Saddlebrook International Tennis

PART I

BIOMECHANICS OF TENNIS

Jack L. Groppel, PhD

CHAPTER 1

The Complete Tennis Coach

A classic tennis confrontation took place between Martina Navratilova and Steffi Graf in the 1988 Wimbledon final. Trading shot for shot, the women sprinted back and forth in a superb exhibition of movement and form. Spectators, awed by how these two athletes played the game, undoubtedly wondered what it takes to be that good. There is only one answer: It takes a lot of talent, combined with years of practice and great coaching.

Since tennis originated, players, coaches, and most recently, sport scientists have examined aspects of the game, always trying to improve how it is played. An area of particular concern has been the teaching of technique. As various methods of teaching technique exist, each thought to optimize student learning, it's no wonder that students are sometimes confused as to which method is best. Two questions emerge: Does the perfect technique exist and, if so, how is it best taught?

Before we consider these questions we should note that coaching has recently entered a technological era with innovations ranging from the highest-performance sports equipment ever to unique methods of stress management related to performance. These concepts have burst upon our age from a relatively new body of knowledge called the *sport sciences.*

How can a coach become aware of and ultimately employ (to optimize athletic performance) the principles of sport science? Over a century ago a wealthy golf enthusiast, Sir Ainsley Bridgland, developed one of the first research teams in all of sport, consisting of anatomists, engineers, and physiologists. Their goal was to discover the hidden secrets of the perfect swing. But after much research, the conclusion at which they arrived was that there is no such thing as a perfect swing. They found that a variety of swing techniques could achieve an optimal outcome and that there would probably be several ways to teach the various techniques.

The same is true for tennis: There is no perfect or best way to play the game. Many different grips and swing techniques are required to hit shots of different speeds and with different spins. Look at the game's greatest players: Becker consistently strikes the ball hard, but uses spin well; Agassi uses a two-handed backhand; Navratilova rushes the net with abandon; and Graf is one of the world's best baseline players. These players play very differently from one another, but they have one thing in common: They all play very well.

Similarly, there are a variety of good ways to teach tennis skills. No single best way exists. For optimal performance, each player must be instructed individually how best to swing the racket. Some players respond well to a sophisticated, scientific approach; others do better with a kinesthetic approach to movement and stroke production. An explanation of torque and how the length and mass of a racket can affect strokes may be most appropriate for one player, whereas another may learn more readily through imaging techniques and using psychological cues. With this in mind, let's examine what it takes to be a skilled tennis instructor and coach.

ATTRIBUTES OF A SKILLED TENNIS COACH

Most good tennis coaches are easy to identify. Many were good players at one time (and often remain so). Usually they have interest in the tennis business, good personalities for relating with people, and sound understanding of stroke mechanics, conditioning methods, and strategy. These competent coaches contribute to the game and affect the lives of their students. However, if these coaches neglect to study ways to improve their coaching skills, they may never rise in the ranks of coaching or help the number of players they possibly could.

The skilled coach is literally a student of the game, a high achiever who strives to excel by learning about all the factors involved in competitive tennis. The outstanding teaching professional is a jack of all trades who tries to be master of all as well.

An ambitious goal, but it is amazing how weaknesses can be discovered and improved. And there is *always* room for improvement. For example, a teaching professional considered to be one of the best in the business asked me if I could suggest how one of his players could hit a more forceful serve. After watching the player compete and studying a video tape of his serve, I concluded that he needed more hip rotation to transfer additional force to the service motion. "That's what I thought," responded my colleague, "but I wasn't sure I was recommending the right thing."

He had coached all levels of players, including world-class professionals, but despite his success this coach always questioned and analyzed to verify his conclusions. This is precisely the attitude a good coach needs to continue improving his or her effectiveness.

BECOMING A COMPLETE TENNIS COACH

It is said of any business that there is no substitute for experience. Experience means much more than simply having been a great player. In fact, great players do not always make great coaches. In a recent television interview one of the world's top players was asked what he would charge to give private lessons. Most people probably expected him to quote a healthy fee, but the player admitted he would never try to teach anyone the game. "I would leave that up to the teachers because they spend so much time studying the game," he said. "I really don't know very much about stroke mechanics and things like that."

This player showed a great deal of character in so responding, but he may have short-changed himself by underestimating his coaching potential. He may not know much about how he actually hits the ball, but he knows a great deal about competition—when to hit which shot, how to handle the psychological stress of a match, how to control the tempo, how to handle the opponent's psyching attempts. No professional achieves world-class status without understanding these and other elements of competition.

On the other hand, a coach who has never played the game competitively will find it particularly difficult to coach successfully at the world-class level. However, such a coach, if he or she has studied the game and experienced the pressures of tournament tennis at some level, should be able to work successfully with skilled players.

No matter how scientific their methods of analyzing skills, all coaches go through a certain amount of trial and error to isolate which experiences were negative and to be discarded and which were positive and to be remembered, used, and built upon. Through years of working with athletes, they accumulate a vast amount of information about performance.

A SPORT SCIENCE APPROACH

The sport sciences are becoming increasingly involved with the game of tennis and can play a significant role in developing complete tennis coaches. All aspiring coaches can benefit by learning from the fields of biomechanics and motor learning just how skills are performed and learned. A coach with years of playing experience might want to improve by learning about the concepts of stroke mechanics. A coach who loves the game but has limited experience playing tough matches might want to learn about competition and pressure from sport psychology. This book presents many useful applications for all coaches who wish to expand their knowledge and skills.

THE SCIENCE OF TENNIS

All sport research has increased dramatically in the past decade. The East Germans are renowned for their research in swimming, the Soviet Union for its track and field research, and Bulgaria for its focus on weight lifting. Unfortunately, tennis has only recently begun reaping the benefits of research, but there is definitely an increasing involvement of scientists and engineers in the study of our game. Recent research has made a positive contribution to the coaching and playing of tennis by developing better rackets, devising better performance techniques, improving conditioning of players, and producing more mentally tough competitors.

However, the expectations of research must be realistic. Research will not produce a single best way to play tennis. But scientific research can determine which instructional methods are most efficient and effective in the teaching of strokes. A baseline player whose matches tend to last more than 3 hours must be well conditioned aerobically, whereas the inveterate serve-and-volley player whose matches finish in less time may need to train differently. Some types of imagery may not benefit a particular athlete, but some form of relaxation training might. Research helps us understand coaching alternatives and in which cases to employ them.

There are problems associated with research, however. First, some research adds no useful knowledge. Coaches are not interested in the fact that Boris Becker can serve harder than Jimmy Arias. That knowledge is intuitive. A second problem is that research is often not presented in usable form. Without reasonable interpretation by the sport scientist, some research fails to convey to the coach or player what the findings imply. Even to a world-class player, the information that the ball is only on the racket face for 4 milliseconds is meaningless. The importance of such a statistic is depreciated by trying to fathom that time in a practical sense.

However, such information is valuable if interpreted in usable form. The coach could persuade the player that, because the time of contact is so incredibly brief, it is impossible to roll the racket over the ball when trying to hit with a topspin. This helps the player visualize that topspin can only be produced by brushing the back-side of the ball with an upward stroke from a vertical racket face.

From this one example of the significance of proper interpretation and communication among sport scientist, coach, and player, you may wonder if tennis research is really all that helpful. Figure 1.1 illustrates how some people view the role of tennis research. At the top of the diagram is the outcome of a match that is extremely important to both player and coach. Consider what goes into a match outcome. Obviously, the psychological and physical conditions surrounding the match play a big role. Added to the pot is the large population of athletes with various forms of genetic skills and limitations. Below this area of the figure are three important factors: improved facilities, improved coaching knowledge, and scientific research.

This diagram was not developed by this book's authors but was prepared several years ago by Professor Mitsumasa Miyashita of the Faculty of Education at the University of Tokyo. It offers an idea of how another country looks upon the application of tennis research and its importance to the outcome of a single match. As Professor Miyashita has shown, research plays a role in training and can provide incredible insight into the performance attributes of a sport skill. Research is here to stay, and it will have a lasting influence on tennis.

Many areas of science have played an important role in developing the game of tennis. The fields of engineering, medicine, physiology, physics, psychology, and sociology all provide information that can expand our understanding of tennis. In one book it is not possible to provide a complete treatise of all aspects of science that

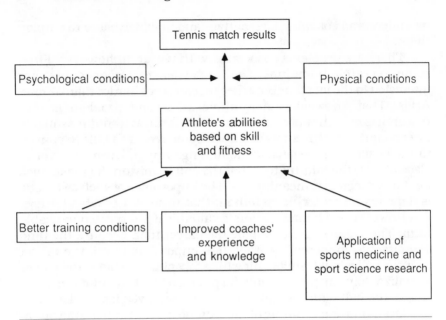

Figure 1.1 The role of tennis research.

are relevant to tennis and coaching. This book examines applications of prime importance to tennis from four subdisciplines of the sport sciences. These areas are biomechanics, motor learning, exercise physiology and sport psychology.

In *biomechanics*, scientists examine the forces that cause motion, forces that might cause injury, and the efficiency and effectiveness of stroke production. Experts in *motor learning* examine how skills are acquired and what teaching methods are most effective in successful tennis coaching. *Exercise physiologists* examine the importance of such things as conditioning, flexibility training, and nutrition; they are concerned with physiological changes that occur during competition as well as those that may occur during leisure play or in practice settings. *Sport psychologists* study what goes on in players' minds to make them want to play the game and play it well. They consider the pressures of this individual sport and are interested in the aggressive tendencies of players, how they handle stress, and to what extent imagery plays a role in training.

Today's coaches want to learn more about sport science research and its applications to tennis. As we investigate such applications, we must be sure to put research in proper perspective. Research is not easy to conduct; sometimes it takes years to develop a method to study a problem, conduct the proper research protocol, analyze the data, interpret the findings, and relate them to the public, whose reactions range from scoffs to cheers.

Many people look to research findings as an end-all to their problems, but the majority of research is really a starting point. Rarely does a research project give a conclusive answer to all problems associated with a specific question. Research applications may be confusing; they may create differences of opinion among experts. Controversy can be constructive if handled in a positive manner. Communication is the key word in understanding research. All too often self-proclaimed interpreters of research disclaim findings without understanding everything that was involved.

The coach's own experience and judgment play the lead role in how he or she interprets and utilizes the findings of a research project. Knowing that research is not the ultimate answer, consider what you can use in coaching and what might be the best application for your athletes. If some findings do not make sense or appear usable, ask questions. If you still do not see an acceptable application, disregard the findings until something you *can* use becomes available. Keep research in its proper perspective, and the rest of this book can be extremely valuable to you.

CHAPTER 2

The Biomechanics of Tennis

Throughout the existence of their profession, coaches have had to address problems in human movement. This is true in all sports, but especially in tennis, as few sports involve as many physical actions. A tennis player must move quickly to get positioned where impact will occur, keep the body under control, synchronize all the body segments, generate an optimal racket head acceleration, and coordinate the eyes with the point of impact, all while preparing to strike the ball with the proper velocity and control. Meanwhile the player must be aware of the opponent's actions and position on the court, of the type and amount of spin on the approaching ball, and of external conditions such as sun and wind. On top of all this, the player must be deciding how hard to hit the ball and how much spin to use.

The difficulty of the game, however, is part of its beauty. To excel in tennis an athlete must be proficient in many areas, several of which are addressed in this book. One of the most important areas is the biomechanics of stroke production.

Biomechanics is the study of the internal (or muscular) and external (wind, gravity, etc.) forces affecting human performance. Simplistically stated, it is the study of human motion. In biomechanics it is important to understand the efficiency and effectiveness of movement, the sports-medicine implications of performance, and the effects of various equipment designs on performance, and on the performer's body.

Efficiency and effectiveness of movement involve proper form. Good form is not a set pattern of movement, but rather movement that accomplishes the purpose with the least expenditure of energy. The coach must teach how to properly use the body to conserve energy and explain how to expend energy with the greatest efficiency.

Identifying proper form can be difficult, however, because good form is unique to individuals and does not necessarily follow norms. For example, when Bjorn Borg began playing world-class tennis, his unorthodox strokes became a major topic of discussion. Some experts felt his technique would be his downfall. Borg proved them wrong. Although his mechanics were not aesthetically pleasing, they were outstanding at the right moment—at impact.

Impact is the crucial point of any tennis stroke. The objective of the coach must be to teach players how to get to that point of impact efficiently and effectively, through good form. Form must be "good" not necessarily from the standpoint of aesthetics, but in terms of developing optimal force and control within each player's capabilities.

Efficiency of movement in tennis has specific implications for a second area of biomechanics: preventive sports medicine. Proper form plays a large role in the prevention of either chronic (occurring from overuse or extended misuse) or acute (sudden trauma) injury. For example, if an athlete uses the lower body incorrectly when positioning for a shot, the arm is forced to work much harder than it should, often resulting in tennis elbow. However, by coaching players in proper technique through the use of practical drills, coaches will decrease players' injury potential and increase their longevity in the game.

The third area of study in tennis from a biomechanical viewpoint involves equipment design. Rackets and shoes significantly affect players' performance, both physically and psychologically. Skilled players must be able to dash about, confident their shoes will provide cushioning, traction, and support. Similarly, they must know a specific racket will perform well. Mechanical engineers and design specialists in sporting goods companies strive to create innovative, high-performance products, so it behooves the progressive coach to keep up with the entire industry, new equipment technology as well as new coaching methods.

GRAVITY

When hitting tennis balls, most players do not consider the important role of gravity. In volleying from a position about 10 feet from the net, for example, players (being much taller than the net) often feel the shoulder-high volley must be hit downward to keep it in play. The usual result of downward ball projection is a netted shot, or one so shallow it invites an offensive return. If volleyers realize that gravity pulls the ball downward, coaches can more easily persuade them to hit the shoulder-high volley horizontally across the net (not downward) so that the ball falls deeper in the opponent's court and reduces the chance of an offensive return.

Gravity also plays a role in serving and hitting an overhead smash. Because serves and overheads require ball contact high above the head, most players think they must hit the ball downward to get it in the court. But the only players who need to hit downward are those who reach 11 feet (with the racket) and hit the ball 100 miles per hour. Even tall (6 foot, 3 inch) Stan Smith hits his serve so that the ball travels horizontally from his racket, *not downward*. Considering the effect of gravity, players should be coached to serve the ball horizontally, or even slightly upward from the racket face at impact.

BALANCE

Without good balance, a tennis player is doomed to mediocrity. Balance is controlled by the position of the *center of gravity*, the central point slightly above the center of the pelvic region about which the body mass is distributed. Interestingly, the location of the center of gravity changes with limb position and with extra weight added to the hand. By simply placing a racket in an athlete's hand, the center of gravity shifts slightly in the direction of the racket. If the athlete lifts an arm, the center of gravity moves in this same direction. Consider then how the center of gravity fluctuates during the countless maneuvers that take place during a match: Every time the positions of arms and legs shift, so does the center of gravity. The athlete must maintain body control or lose balance.

To picture how balance is maintained, imagine that a plumb line is dropped from the athlete's center of gravity to the ground. The *line of gravity* should fall to the ground somewhere between the feet. The feet and the area between them form the athlete's *base of support*. With the athlete standing at attention, the base of support is fairly small. As the feet are spread, the base of support expands and the player becomes more stable, but the line of gravity remains unchanged. Optimal balance occurs when the line of gravity falls within the boundaries of the base of support; the nearer it falls to the center of the base of support, the more stable the player.

To demonstrate to yourself the interplay of the line of gravity and the base of support, assume an erect balanced position with your feet comfortably spread. Without moving your shoulders, lift one foot. As soon as your foot leaves the ground, your base of support becomes the size of the one foot remaining on the ground. Unless you shift your shoulders, your line of gravity is immediately outside the base of support, and you begin to fall.

It is this falling action created when the line of gravity gets beyond the boundaries of the base of support that enables a tennis player to accelerate to run. As the body shifts from a state of balance to one of imbalance, a sprinting action is initiated. The imbalance forces the player to move his or her feet to keep from falling, but clearly a sprinting player would not want to become too stable, as that would slow the player down. Instead, a continual push-off from the hind foot in a sprint moves the line of gravity beyond the base of support. The alternative leg swings ahead, catches the body before it falls, and then becomes the push-off leg for the next stride.

Balance is also important when the player is set. Because the center of gravity is a locus about which all body mass is centralized, any time a body part moves (such as an arm swinging upward to toss the ball for a serve), the center of gravity automatically moves in the same direction. Therefore, during almost the entire serve, the center of gravity is higher than usual. An external weight (such as a racket) added to the body becomes part of the body mass and affects the location of the center of gravity, displacing it in the direction of the added weight. Therefore, as a player swings the racket in preparing to make a stroke, another body part (usually the other arm) must move far enough in the opposite direction to counter the motion of the racket arm so that the athlete keeps the center of gravity over the base of support and retains control of the body.

Just as the position of the center of gravity rises when the arms are raised, it lowers when the body crouches. The lower the center of gravity, the more stable the body. The ready position of some players involves slightly flexed knees with the trunk inclined slightly forward, causing a lower center of gravity. However, if the crouch is excessive, stability is increased to the point that it becomes difficult to respond quickly to an opponent's shot.

LAWS OF MOTION

Aside from gravity and its effect on human movement, Newton's three basic laws of motion, plus some other principles of physics, describe how control and force are gained or lost by the tennis player.

The *law of inertia* states that an object at rest or in motion will remain at rest or in motion at the same speed until affected by an outside force. When a player is in a ready position, for example, the body and racket are not moving and have a certain amount of *resting inertia*. When the player reacts to an opponent's shot, resting inertia must be overcome by creating sufficient force against the ground to move. Muscular contraction from the legs causes movement to occur.

A tennis player playing a point has *inertia of motion* and will keep going until some force stops the movement. Think of an athlete in full sprint running to hit a wide forehand return. Once the ball is hit, the player must get to a strategic part of the court in anticipation of the return. A recovery step often stops the player from moving in one direction and reverses him or her to the opposite direction. After the ball is hit, the trail leg swings around, applies the brakes to stop the moving inertia, then generates force to overcome resting inertia so that the player can return to an advantageous court position.

The law of inertia also affects ball flight. If it were not for gravity, the ball would continue its flight until it struck something. One external force that influences a ball's flight pattern is air resistance. This effect is most visible on a windy day when gusty air currents can drastically alter the ball's trajectory.

A more subtle effect of air resistance occurs when the ball is spinning. Topspin, underspin, and sidespin affect the travel of a tennis ball. High-pressure zones created at various points on the ball's surface cause it to behave differently than when it has no spin. For example, a ball with no spin encounters equal air pressure around it and, as long as there is no wind effect, follows a normal parabola (gravity effect) on its flight to the opponent's court. A ball with top-spin has a thin boundary layer of air rotating around it in the direction of the spin. On the top of the ball, air flow in the boundary layer encounters the static air head-on and a violent intermixing creates a high-pressure zone atop the ball (Figure 2.1), forcing the ball downward in the looping trajectory of topspin. The opposite occurs with underspin (Figure 2.2). The high-pressure zone is created under the ball, causing it to "float" or suspend longer in the air.

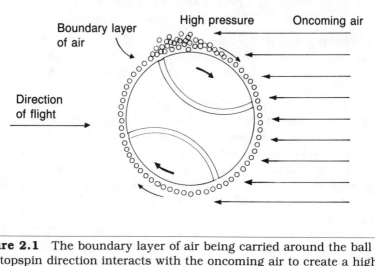

Figure 2.1 The boundary layer of air being carried around the ball in a topspin direction interacts with the oncoming air to create a high pressure zone above the ball.

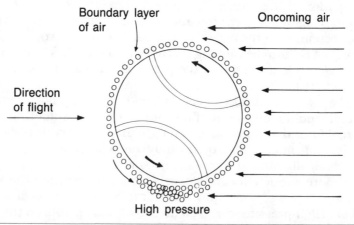

Figure 2.2 The boundary layer of air travels around the ball in the direction of the underspin and interacts with the oncoming air to create a high pressure zone below the ball.

The *law of acceleration* states that as a body is acted upon by a force *(F)*, its resulting acceleration *(A)* is directly proportional to the force and inversely proportional to the mass *(M)* [*(M)*: $A = F/M$]. Therefore, given an object of specific mass, such as a tennis racket, the greater the force applied to move the object, the greater its acceleration. The faster the racket head is travelling at impact, the greater the force applied to the ball.

Sounds simple enough, but the skilled coach must bear one important thing in mind: the speed-accuracy trade-off. As Melville discusses later, an optimal speed of stroke production exists for each athlete that enables him or her to maintain excellent shot control. However, the faster the racket head moves beyond that optimal speed, the more difficult it is to control the accuracy of the shot. Tennis is unlike baseball, where a home run may be hit over any part of the fence between the foul poles. Tennis is first and foremost a *control* game. A service ace is typically struck with high velocity, but must also be accurately placed. A high-speed serve can be relatively easily returned if it is not well placed. The aim of the skilled player is to hit the ball very hard with control. Hitting the ball hard is easy, but hitting it with speed *and* accuracy is difficult. Therefore, the law of acceleration should be applied within the context of shot control.

The law of acceleration helps us to understand another phenomenon in tennis that receives a lot of attention: arm injuries. With force directly proportional to acceleration, we know that more developed force means greater racket head acceleration, resulting in a powerful shot. However, the law of acceleration also entails that the greater the force used to swing the racket, the greater the force impacting the arm of the player. This helps explain why so many of today's young players develop sore arms, as they are taught to hit punishing topspin ground strokes from behind the baseline. The body can handle only so much, either in the acute sense from one excessively forceful stroke, or in the chronic sense from many repetitions of forceful strokes.

Probably the most important of Newton's laws of motion to the tennis coach is the *law of action and reaction*, which holds that for every action, there is an equal and opposite reaction. This law provides the foundation for almost every tennis stroke, because a *ground reaction force* is required to overcome inertia and initiate movement. When the player in a ready position pushes against the ground to move, the ground pushes back with an equal and opposite force. Likewise, in a ground stroke, when the hind foot pushes to initiate the forward weight transfer, this ground reaction force initiates the body's total generation of force to hit the stroke. The ground reaction force also influences shot control because its direction of application against the ground determines the direction of body movement.

The law of action and reaction also affects the serve (Figure 2.3). Once the ground reaction force has been created and the force is being transferred up through the body, the trunk begins rotating with extreme speed. In a normal throwing motion (as in serving), the opposite arm comes across the trunk in the opposite direction from trunk rotation just as the swinging arm initiates its forward action (Figure 2.4). The other arm's action acts as a brake (because it's moving in the opposite direction) and abruptly slows the trunk rotation, causing the swinging arm and racket to accelerate toward impact.

Figure 2.3   The law of action and reaction in serving.

The law of action and reaction also helps explain the sports-medicine implications of tennis performance. The racket imparts force to the ball, sending it over the net. Simultaneously, the ball creates an equal and opposite force against the racket that is often felt in the hand and arm. This is especially true of off-center impacts because of the torsional effect of the twisting racket as it responds to the off-center contact. The forces encountered by the body can create trauma (i.e., tennis elbow) if the athlete continually hits improperly or is not strong enough to withstand the impacts.

Figure 2.4   Opposition of the arm action in the serve.

However, as far as tennis success is concerned, the force transfer from racket to ball is elemental to optimal performance.

OTHER BIOMECHANICAL PRINCIPLES

Besides the effects of gravity and the laws of motion, other physical principles play large roles in understanding the game of tennis. *Linear momentum* is one such factor. Linear momentum is equal to mass *(M)* times velocity *(V)*. It applies when a quantity of mass and velocity from an implement transfers its momentum to an object having another mass and velocity. For instance, to return an oncoming tennis ball, the player must impact enough force on the ball to stop it and start it traveling at a predetermined velocity in the opposite direction. The greater the oncoming momentum, the greater the force required to stop it and reverse its direction. Since the ball's mass remains the same, the two factors that determine how much force must be imparted are (a) the speed of the ball at the moment of impact, and (b) the time (how long) the force is applied to stop it and send it back.

The speed of an object is directly proportional to the quantity of force × time (or impulse) applied to it. Increasing the impulse increases the velocity of the departing ball. The velocities of the ball and racket are the only velocity factors that can be changed by the player.

Apart from ball speed, direction must be considered in controlling the shot. If the ball hits the racket face off center, causing the racket to rotate while the ball is in contact with it, the ball will leave the racket in an errant direction, resulting in either a poor or a lucky shot. If the ball contacts near the hitting zone of the racket, and the racket is gripped firmly to minimize racket rotation, the shot can be controlled.

Linear momentum also plays a role in the initiation of the body's total force to hit the ball. If the player elects to hit a shot involving a forward step (i.e., from a closed or semiclosed stance), the step forward should occur in a straight line. The mass and velocity of the individual moving in a straight line toward the desired direction of the shot transfers linear momentum to the shot.

Before further describing the mechanical aspects of stroke production, we need to consider one more concept, the *moment of inertia*, which is defined as a body's resistance to rotation. A good example of how moment of inertia affects rotation is when a player hits a two-handed backhand. With arms fully extended away from the body, a player will rotate his or her trunk slowly, but when arms are drawn in nearer to the trunk, he or she can rotate quickly. The moment of inertia (I) is equal to the individual's mass (M) multiplied by the individual's radius (R) squared $(I \approx M \times R^2)$. The tennis player's mass does not change when hitting the two-handed backhand, but the radius is significantly shortened when the arms are pulled closer to the trunk, decreasing the resistance to rotation and allowing the player to rotate quickly. The lower the I factor, the faster the player can rotate the trunk.

There are other applications of the moment-of-inertia factor. A tennis racket may feel cumbersome to some people, so they choke up on the handle. Choking up enables them to more easily swing the racket because the radius, or length from the racket head to the hand, has been shortened. Another example is when players try to hit very hard from the baseline. If they use improper technique and initiate the swing with a fully extended arm, attempting to increase leverage against the ball, they extend the radius (or arm length from the body) and increase the resistance to rotation (I), which makes the racket more difficult to swing.

Coaches should teach players to swing from inside out on ground strokes. At the beginning of the forward swing the arm should be positioned fairly close to the body, lowering the moment of inertia, promoting faster body rotation, and generating a higher racket head velocity. As the arm extends into the shot the resistance to body rotation increases, but at this point the racket already has a high velocity and whatever deceleration occurs just prior to contact will be offset by the increased leverage.

Body rotation is an important consideration in developing a skilled tennis player. The rotation generated by the hips and trunk during many strokes actually creates *angular momentum*. Angular momentum is equal to the moment of inertia *(I)* of a body multiplied by its angular, or rotary, velocity *(I* × angular velocity). When hitting a ground stroke, a player's linear momentum is initiated by striding forward and is then transferred into angular (rotary) momentum in the hips and trunk. Both types of momentum are applied when hitting ground strokes, serves, or overhead smashes: Linear momentum, generated by the legs, transfers to angular momentum in the hips, trunk, and upper limb to bring the racket head into proper hitting position.

To summarize, then, tennis coaches must be cognizant of the physical factors that affect performance. The external forces of gravity and air resistance dictate the flight path of the ball once it is struck. As a player moves to hit a return, body control and balance are crucial to the efficiency and effectiveness of the motion. Once in position, the player must combine linear and angular momentum to hit the optimal return.

The key point for the tennis coach to bear in mind is that control is of ultimate importance and should constantly be emphasized as the student's first priority. Students tend to work on maximizing their physical potential for power, but any coaching for increased power should always be within the context of shot control.

CHAPTER 3

The Science
of Technique

As noted, there are many approaches to teaching the game of
tennis. Some coaches prefer teaching only parts of a stroke at first,
leading up to the whole motion; others prefer to teach the whole
movement from the start. Some teachers begin their students on
tracking drills, whereas others work on positioning. Some coaches
like to start a beginner at the net, teaching the volley instead of baseline ground strokes. Regardless of your personal approach, the principles in this chapter can serve as a foundation for improving the
skills of your students.

TRACKING SKILLS

Because tracking (visually following the ball movement) is so
important in tennis, coaches must be sure that players know how
to properly identify ball movement and position their bodies relative to the ball. Although advanced tournament competitors have
probably mastered tracking, intermediates often have problems
with it. Tracking principles and a few basic drills can help a student improve this skill.

To teach a student tracking principles, it is necessary to explain
speed and accuracy trade-offs. The faster a ball travels toward a

player, the more difficult it is to track. Balls flying at a very low or very high trajectory are also difficult to track. A beginning player can improve tracking skills by learning to follow a ball moving slowly in a small arc (usually slightly above the player's hand). Various catching drills are effective in teaching players how to properly track.

For example, stand 5 to 6 feet from the student and toss balls to him or her slowly in a short arc. The arc can be increased gradually as the player learns to follow the ball and catch it. Once this simple task is learned, toss the ball a few feet away from the student, causing him or her to move to catch it. Teach no specific footwork, just instruct the player that his or her body must be in front of the ball before catching it. Again, the ball should be tossed slowly in a small arc. The goal is for the player to recognize the position and velocity of the ball and respond by moving to the proper position, similar to the way a player must in a match.

As skill develops, toss the ball farther away from the student, always trying to make him or her move quickly to get in position for the catch. Next, change the catching drill to one that follows a bounce. Separate yourself from the student by 15 to 20 feet and toss the ball so that it bounces before he or she catches it. As skill develops, increase the speed and arc of the toss.

At higher skill levels (this drill can be used even with tournament players) use one ball and toss wide, short, and deep, each time asking the student to hurry, catch the ball, toss it back to you, and then recover a starting position. An adaptation is to bounce or roll the ball to different areas of the court, which improves the student's tracking and body positioning. The aim of these drills is to teach the student to respond to the velocity and trajectory of the ball, training him or her to move quickly to the position where the ball will be *before* it gets there.

PROPER POSITIONING

Once athletes learn to correctly track and position their bodies in response to the tossing drills, it is time for them to learn movement with the racket. A good way to begin is to practice shadow drills, where the students imitate a coach's movements. The coach stands in front of the students, usually facing away from them, and demonstrates lateral movement and how to ready the racket to imitate a stroke. Students learn how to move in balance with an external weight in their hands.

One problem some players have when developing stroke technique is how to position themselves relative to the ball to strike the ball effectively. As they run to hit a return, they find themselves either too far from the ball or so close to it that they are jammed and cannot swing effectively. It is important to continually emphasize arm position relative to the body and how the body needs to move to the ball for stroke efficiency. When your players have stroking problems, start by tossing a ball toward them, allowing them to hit from a stationary position. Then gradually move the ball away from them so that they must adjust their bodies. As they practice these adjustments, players learn how to move to get away from a ball traveling toward them and how to approach a ball that is a distance away. The key is to gradually move the ball away from them, so that these movements can be learned progressively and correctly.

Even when a student's tracking and movement skills develop to an advanced level, the coach should never let him or her relax on drills involving footwork. The fitness and conditioning section of this book presents detailed agility drills that help footwork, which is among the most overlooked aspects of world-class players' movements. Many players work diligently on perfecting their strokes, but for some reason avoid working on responding to the opponent's actions with footwork and efficiency of movement. Great strokes mean little if players are not in the right place at the right time in competition.

HITTING THE BALL

In teaching stroke technique, coaches' philosophies vary as to what backswing to use, what spin to hit, and what movement patterns to use from certain parts of the court. This section provides physical principles that dictate the mechanics of stroke performance; these concepts should play a role in your instruction regardless of your teaching philosophy.

A simple rule to use in teaching the backswing is that the lower the skill level of the student, the simpler the movement must be. Because the less-skilled player often has poor timing or rhythm, a straight-back backswing is usually preferred, as it lets the player line up the racket in a proper position for a forward swing. Accuracy is improved at the beginning level when the straight-back backswing is used, but often at the expense of velocity. It is difficult to hit a ball with high velocity using the straight-back backswing because the racket must stop before it is swung forward. Resting inertia must be overcome to swing the racket forward, making high racket velocity difficult to achieve.

Very few professional players use a straight-back backswing. Many people believe Vitas Gerulaitis used one in his forehand drive, but film analysis shows otherwise. As his former coach Tommy Thompson explains, Gerulaitis took the racket straight back to a stationary position, but at the initiation of his forward swing he dropped it slightly, making a small loop. This loop helped him overcome resting inertia to generate a higher racket velocity and maintain rhythm.

The small-loop backswing is the most common backswing on the professional tour. It requires a racket position slightly higher than the straight-back backswing. Just prior to swinging the racket forward, the player drops it a small distance vertically. This vertical drop adds several miles per hour to the swing, as gravity plays a role in overcoming the resting inertia of the stopped racket.

The large-loop backswing is also seen on the circuit, but not as frequently as the small loop. The large-loop backswing brings the racket back very high, leading to a significant vertical drop before the racket moves forward for impact. This big drop allows the large-loop backswing to generate high velocity, but the extra movement may create timing and rhythm problems and cause loss of control of certain shots. For example, if a player misreads the spin on a ball or if the ball hits a small pebble on the court, the large-loop backswing makes it more difficult to adjust the stroke suddenly to the change in ball position.

Regardless of the backswing method used, the body should prepare by rotating into position (Figure 3.1). The foot on the racket side turns outward while the hips and shoulders rotate into a preparatory stance. This coiling effect prepares the body to generate its angular momentum as it unwinds into the shot.

Again, the initiation of a stroke, be it a ground stroke or a serve, occurs in the form of a ground reaction force. The hind foot pushes off against the ground, giving the body a slight linear momentum in the direction of the step forward. Immediately after the step is made, the generated force is transferred through the legs to the hips, which begin rotating in turn, transferring the force (angular momentum now) to the trunk. The rotating trunk then transfers its velocity to the arm and racket. Figure 3.2 depicts how this transfer of force and velocity occurs. The sequence of events is commonly called the body's *kinetic chain* and is elemental to effective stroke production in tournament tennis.

Played correctly, tennis is a lower-body sport. The power mechanism should come from the ground reaction force, legs, hips,

Figure 3.1   The body rotates into preparatory position.

Figure 3.2   Transfer of body force and velocity.

and trunk, whereas the controlling mechanism of the stroke should come from the upper limb. Since the impact of a racket on the ball lasts only 4 to 8 thousandths of a second, it is vital that the arm and racket achieve their velocity before impact occurs and that the arm does not try to muscle the ball at the point of impact.

Some experts have suggested that follow-through is of no consequence. After the ball is gone, they argue, what further effect can the finish of the stroke have on its flight? Actually, their rationale is correct if we consider the human body to be a perfect machine, capable of going from high velocity to zero in an instant. Of course, this is impossible. The body consists of a series of bony levers attached by connective tissue and moved by muscular contraction and ballistic actions. The body is not designed for sudden stops. If a body segment generates a high velocity and suddenly stops, that body part and its respective joints are endangered. Just as the body must accelerate to create force, it must decelerate to slow a movement. An athlete who swings at a tennis ball and immediately stops swinging at impact will likely lose control of the shot and possibly suffer injury. So, the need for a good follow-through is twofold: (a) to allow the racket to complete the impact phase with velocity adequate to an effective shot, and (b) to avoid injury to the athlete by allowing normal racket deceleration.

Tennis coaches should spend time discussing with their players the goals of certain shots. For example, a forehand hit from 8 feet behind the baseline requires quite a bit of racket head acceleration. To accelerate the racket, the body's entire linked system must come into play. However, a forehand from just inside the service line requires much less acceleration of the racket. Also, if a player is inside the service line and wants to hit a drop shot, he or she will have to decelerate the racket instead of accelerating. This concept is extremely important in demonstrating the goals of certain movements on the court and the requirements for the racket head and the body when hitting different strokes. The less acceleration required, the less of the linked system that needs to be used. When a player decelerates to hit a shot, the controlling mechanism (upper limb) alone might be sufficient to slow the racket head.

RECOVERY AFTER A SHOT

Once athletes have learned to hit different shots from different parts of the court, they must learn how to recover to a strategic part of the court. The geometry of court positions need not be discussed, as coaches know where an athlete should finally be positioned to facilitate the quickest possible recovery. However, many athletes focus so hard on returning quickly to an optimal court position that they sacrifice the effectiveness of their return by attempting to recover before they have completed a proper stroke. Therefore, the coach's first consideration is to be sure the ball is hit properly, and only afterward to examine how well the athlete recovers. For example, at ball contact the player should be balanced and in total control of his or her body. There should be no extraneous movement that might impede stroke execution. Once the ball has been hit (and *only* then), the athlete can recover to anticipate the opponent's return.

After an aggressive forehand drive, for example, it is common for the trail leg to rotate around to square the athlete's body to the net. Immediately upon attaining the squared position, the athlete brakes his or her body with the trail leg and generates a ground reaction force that enables a return to a strategic court position. What the coach needs to watch is the timing of the trail leg rotating around the body and how wide it is placed when squared to the net. If the trail leg comes around too quickly (i.e., before or just as the ball is hit), balance is lost and the shot is poor. On the other hand, too slow a rotation of the trail leg leads to a poor recovery. Also, if the trail leg comes around and splits very wide, the athlete will have trouble generating a sufficient ground reaction force in order to push off effectively. Because the trail leg determines the effectiveness of both shot and recovery, the coach needs to always be aware of the timing and placement of that leg during the stroke.

FACTS AND FALLACIES

There are many myths associated with tennis that coaches often use as cues to try to improve a player's skills. Although these myths might mean something in the coach's mind (and may serve as effective teaching cues), they do not necessarily mean anything to individual athletes. This section discusses some of these common concepts and examines their physical accuracy, thereby explaining some of the less-apparent phenomena of tennis.

Fact: *The fewer body segments involved in a movement, the less chance for error.* Using enough of the body to generate an optimal amount of force is necessary, but maintaining control over a specific stroke is also important. Players at times exaggerate their movements, using many segmental actions in an attempt to develop more force or disguise a shot. Take as an example the ball toss when serving. Using all three joints of the upper limb (shoulder, elbow, and wrist) when tossing increases the number of body parts that must be used accurately. Three joints in action decrease the chances of placing the ball in the exact position to hit the best serve because a movement error could occur in any of the three joints. It is better to toss the ball with the upper limb moving only at the shoulder, thereby maintaining fairly rigid elbow and wrist joints and increasing the likelihood of an accurate toss. The coach's first objective is to determine how much force is required and what body parts must be involved to perform the movement effectively. Then he or she must examine how the specific performer is using those body parts.

Fallacy: *Keep the ball on the strings as long as possible.* During a 1985 French Open quarterfinal between Jimmy Connors and Stefan Edberg, television commentator Donald Dell described one of Connors's maneuvers as his "best shot of the tournament." Connors had hit a crosscourt approach shot as he went to the net. Edberg lobbed over Connors on the forehand side (Jimmy's left) and followed his lob to the net. Connors then hit an unbelievable winner past Edberg, which Dell described this way: "Jimmy ran back, *held it,* waited for Edberg to commit himself and then passed him."

Such commentaries are common, and such phrases are also used in coaching. When coaches talk about holding the ball on the racket, they intend to assist the student in lengthening the hitting zone of a stroke or lengthening the follow-through. It is, of course, impossible for any player to "hold" the ball on the strings during a stroke. Considering the acceleration of the racket head and the velocity of the oncoming ball, there is little a player can do to vary contact time. Besides, the longer a ball stays on the strings, the greater the chance for a mistake to occur.

The phrase has become common probably because some athletes seem to control their strokes so well that they give the impression that the ball is being held on the racket face, as Dell described. In a situation where a player is attempting to pass an opponent who is in an attacking position at the net, he or she wants to wait until the opponent commits (by shifting center of gravity), and then hit the passing shot. Rather than the player holding the ball on the strings, what apparently occurs is that he or she holds the backswing a bit longer, letting the ball drop a little, thereby placing extreme time limitations on the opponent, who will usually move or lean in one direction or the other. Once detecting this directional commitment, the player simply strokes the ball in the opposite direction.

Fallacy: *Roll the racket head to produce topspin.* Although it seems that some players actually roll over the ball to hit topspin (e.g., Bjorn Borg), it has been repeatedly demonstrated that this does not occur. The only way to produce topspin is to initiate the forward swing below the impact point and brush the backside of the ball in an upward manner, completing the stroke with a high follow-through. The more vertical the swing, the more topspin that can be applied. A rollover appears to occur because of the internal structure of the shoulder joint. As the arm comes across the trunk in the follow-through, the shoulder rotates (Figure 3.3), giving the appearance of a rollover that is meant to maximize spin, but this rollover does not even begin until the ball is about 3 feet off the player's racket.

Figure 3.3   Shoulder rotation during a topspin stroke.

Fallacy: *Keep your eye on the ball.* Athletes should track the ball when competing, which is as close as they can come to keeping their eyes on it. It has been scientifically shown that once the ball is 5 to 6 feet away from a player it becomes a blur, and vision usually remains focused at that point, 5 feet away. The better the player, the easier it is for him or her to utilize a mental motor program (or image) of a stroke, anticipating where the ball will be, based on projectile motion. This procedure is more difficult for intermediates, who usually have not yet developed a proper motor program. The risk in telling intermediates to keep their eye on the ball is that they actually try to do it. Some rotate their heads to maintain eye contact as the ball approaches. If it is true that the ball becomes a blur near the player, head rotation creates a useless imbalance. Also, if a player develops the bad habit of head rotation, he or she will have a more difficult time constructing a proper motor program for stroke production. Better the coach use the cue *concentrate on the ball*, which will not prompt players to practice turning their heads and training their eyes on the oncoming ball.

Fact: *Most of the force in tennis comes from the ground.* From the law of action/reaction we know that for every action there is an equal and opposite reaction. The initiation of force to effectively swing a racket must come from the ground reaction force and be transferred through the body's linked system of legs, hips, trunk, and upper limb. The only shots in tennis where ground reaction force does not apply are the punch volley (drive volleys usually do require force from the ground) and the touch shots (shots requiring more control than force). Ground strokes, serves, and overheads all require an optimum ground reaction force to generate racket speed.

Fact: *The racket face must be near the vertical to achieve optimal impact.* In almost every shot attempted, the racket face, at contact, must be nearly perpendicular (within 5 degrees) to the flight of the ball. The only time the racket can sway farther from the vertical is when underspin is being attempted. Then the racket can open more than 5 degrees (but not much more) because the racket head's action is from high to low. The high-to-low swing accommodates a slightly open racket face and usually keeps the ball in the court.

Fact: *Force in tennis comes from both linear and angular momentum.* Regardless of the shot being attempted, the body uses both linear and angular momentum to produce force. When players step into a shot, they create momentum in the linear direction of the step. Angular momentum occurs from the rotation of the hips and trunk to bring the racket head into position. Even in serving and in striking open-stance ground strokes there is both linear and angular momentum. In the serve, the legs extend to produce a linear ground reaction force, transferring this momentum to angular momentum at the hips. For the open-stance ground stroke, force generated from the ground in a linear direction is transferred via the hips and trunk in the form of angular momentum. The more important of these two types of momentum is the angular momentum obtained from hip and trunk rotation, as it provides impetus to the upper limb.

Fact: *Larger-headed rackets have a larger hitting zone and also absorb vibration better than conventional rackets.* Recall the discussion on moment of inertia: There are two ways to increase a racket head's resistance to rotation in the hand. The first is to increase the radius of the racket head (make it larger); the second is to add small weights to the perimeter of the racket head. Both serve the basic function of increasing the resistance to rotation by creating a larger effective hitting zone. Also, both ways tend to reduce the amount of torque from off-center impacts better than conventional rackets.

Fact: *Changing grips in the volley as a beginner facilitates skill acquisition.* Changing grips in the volley has been widely debated. The only study on this topic indicates that beginning tennis players taught to change grips from an Eastern forehand to an Eastern backhand acquired greater control of the volley than beginners taught to use only the continental grip. Some of the players taught to change grips when volleying later tried the continental grip, which, again, seemed to help them improve more quickly. They were able to hit forehand and backhand volleys more readily without taking time for grip changes. These findings suggest it is advisable to initiate a beginner in volleying by teaching the grip change, then switching him or her to the continental grip at a later date.

Fallacy: *Feel the ball on the strings.* When impact occurs on the racket face, the signal (or vibration) must travel through the racket, hand, forearm, upper arm, shoulder, and neck before arriving at the brain where the sensation is felt, a trip that takes about 50 milliseconds. As mentioned previously, the time of impact of ball on racket lasts between 3 and 5 milliseconds. The time lag between impact and the sensation of impact is at least 10 times longer than the impact itself. Consequently, by the time a player feels the ball hit the racket, the ball is about 3 feet off the strings on its way back across the net.

Some instructors have used this cue to help their athletes change movement patterns at the last second to hit a better shot. This task is not only impossible to do, it is also unhelpful. It will only hurt a player's chance of improvement. Once the forward swing is initiated and acceleration of the racket is occurring, a player should not change the intent of the stroke. Any change should occur prior to the initiation of the stroke.

The one time when the cue "Feel the ball on the strings" can be effective is when providing feedback to a player on what was wrong with a certain shot. If a coach encourages a player to feel how a bad shot felt, the player might subsequently be able to avoid that feeling in future shots. Used this way, this cue could be a helpful coaching tool.

Fallacy: *Run with the racket back.* The human body was not designed to run with an arm extended or while holding a long implement weighing several ounces. If an athlete's goal is to sprint into position, he or she must learn to use the arms in the normal pumping action associated with sprinting. This facilitates balance and allows the athlete to generate the proper rhythm for quick sprinting actions. When the racket is held back in position for the swing, balance is precarious.

Because running with the racket is an advanced skill, however, beginners and intermediates may be better off moving toward a shot with the racket held back. Although they will not be able to run their fastest, early racket preparation will enhance stroke accuracy. When a less-skilled player tries to run toward a ball and swing, timing is usually poor. To assist these players in proper movement and racket position, this cue may be effective in helping them produce an optimal combination of movement and stroke. As players develop, however, it is strongly urged that coaches teach them to move with the arm and racket held in a way that allows for optimal speed and balance.

Fact: *Don't jump when hitting ground strokes.* Leaving the ground is common in serving. In fact, it has been demonstrated that the higher an elite player is off the ground, the more effective the serve is. However, it should be recognized that a player never intentionally jumps when serving, but that his or her body is actually pulled off the ground by the leg action and body rotation. Movement off the ground is all right when hitting the ball. The primary concern is not that the player is off the ground but *at what point* during the stroke he or she is off the ground.

When elite players leave the ground just prior to hitting a ground stroke, all the force they generate is in the small body parts (the upper limb). If any of these players leave the ground when the force they generate is in the hips or trunk, the law of action/reaction will take effect. For example, if a player leaves the ground when all the force he or she has generated is in the trunk, that force will travel back down through the hips and the subsequent stroke will be poor. If a player leaves the ground when the force is in the upper limb, there is still a reaction of the upper limb against the trunk (a small body part against a large), but the loss is negligible. Teaching this movement of leaving the ground during a ground stroke or serve is unnecessary because it occurs naturally as optimal and forceful stroke development occurs.

Fallacy: *Hit down on your serve.* The height of the extended racket during a serve often gives a false impression of the necessary trajectory for a serve. As mentioned earlier, many players develop a feeling that they must hit down on the ball to keep it in the service court. However, computer simulation proves that a player must have a reach of about 11 feet with the racket and hit the ball approximately 120 miles per hour to be able to hit downward 3 degrees from the horizontal. As few tennis players meet these physical requirements, it is important to instruct them to let gravity work for them. It is much better to hit the ball straight out from the racket or even to hit up when serving. From another perspective, it is much easier to learn the serve by hitting the ball beyond the service line and then working on bringing it back in than it is to hit serves into the net and then working on getting it over.

Fallacy: *Turn sideways to the net when hitting ground strokes.* Although it is necessary to rotate the shoulders to the side, it is not necessary to turn the whole body sideways to the net, which only serves to fix the athlete in one position and limit flexibility. The open-stance forehand requires hip and trunk rotation to develop optimal angular momentum, and the feet must be positioned to allow necessary rotation when stepping into the shot, but seldom is a player's body completely sideways to the net. It may be helpful to teach beginners sideways movement to enhance skill acquisition, but as their skills progress, teach them flexibility of movement and be sure they understand how the hips and trunk must rotate.

Fact: *The one-handed and two-handed backhands have a similar reach.* Up until the late 1970s, tennis instructors felt that the one-handed backhand was the preferred stroke because of its ability to reach further in stroke production. A 1978 study of this question found very little difference in reach between the one-handed and two-handed backhand drives when the player gets to the proper position for swinging the racket. There are the obvious problems of extremely wide shots or low approach shots for the two-handed backhand, but players using a one-handed stroke had similar problems on very wide shots. Few offensive ground strokes occur when the player is stretched out, even with the one-handed backhand. Players using the two-handed backhand can be taught defensive maneuvers to use with one hand when pulled wide. Consequently, limited reach is not a valid reason to avoid teaching a two-handed backhand.

Fallacy: *Bevel the racket to hit underspin.* Although the racket is slightly open to hit an underspin drive, coaches should avoid teaching this racket position. True, the best underspin players have the racket extremely open in the backswing and also in the follow-through, giving the impression that the racket is extremely open on contact. What actually occurs is that the racket is open in the backswing because of the internal structure of the shoulder. As the forward swing is initiated and impact is near, the racket actually becomes nearly vertical (Figure 3.4). Then, to maximize the follow-through, the shoulder again rotates giving the impression of the open racket face.

Figure 3.4 The racket should be nearly vertical during the forward swing.

Fallacy: *Roll the ball crosscourt or hit the ball early to go cross-court.* This common instruction gives the player the false impression that this is the only way to hit a ball crosscourt. When a player is hitting with direction (down the line, to midcourt, or crosscourt), the position of the racket face determines where the ball goes. A ball does not have to be hit early or with heavy topspin to go cross-court. An athlete can actually go crosscourt with a ball that has gotten behind him or her simply by correctly positioning the racket face. The same holds true for the old teaching adage, "Hit late to go down the line." Because the orientation of the racket face determines the flight path of the ball, these instructions are only successful when they happen to result in correct racket position. Impact timing is not the determinant.

Fallacy: *Keep the racket head above your wrist when volley-ing.* The intent of this teaching cue is to minimize the amount of joint freedom in a controlled stroke like volleying. Unnecessary joint activity in a stroke increases the chance of a mistake. With the wrist held fairly rigid, players can produce effective and penetrating volleys. In its literal sense, however, this cue is incorrect. If the angle at the wrist is static, the upper limb and trunk actions can position the racket head in various locations relative to other body parts. The racket head can even be positioned *below* the wrist with the same wrist angle as when held above the wrist (Figure 3.5). Therefore, key your coaching cues on the wrist angle and not necessarily on the racket head position.

Figure 3.5 Wrist angle is more important than racket head position during the volley.

This discussion of facts and fallacies might be useful in teaching, depending on your interaction with the players. In the purely physical sense, phrases such as "Feel the ball," "Drive through the ball," and "Keep your head down" have little meaning. When used in the proper context, however, they may help players improve skill. Coaches must decide which cues will be helpful to skill acquisition and which will be detrimental. Part of the fun of coaching is the challenge of deciding what to say and how to teach the various movements. Use your imagination to generate cues tuned to the goals and expectations of your players, always bearing in mind the facts of biomechanics.

GOAL SETTING WITH MECHANICS IN MIND

Regardless of skill levels, set the same goal for stroke production for all players. The goal involves four concepts crucial to skill acquisition and competitive performance: control, consistency, depth, and power. The key point for almost any player of any skill level is that power is the last phase of stroke development and control is the first. Players must learn to control movement patterns to achieve optimal stroke production. This includes the ability to hit down the line, crosscourt, and to specific areas of the court. Control does not necessarily mean being able to hit a dime on the court, but players must work to achieve some measure of accuracy.

The second part of the stroke-production goal involves consistency. Once control is attained, the player must learn to hit consistently with accuracy to various parts of the court. This requires that the athlete maintain balance and properly use his or her body to enhance shot effectiveness. For players at lower skill levels, try teaching the unarguable strategy that the last player to hit the ball in the court wins the match. This sounds simple, but the more balls your athletes keep in play, the more pressure they place on the opposition, and the more confidence they gain. At higher skill levels they must combine control and consistency along with a third factor, depth.

Stroke depth is crucial to upper-level tennis performance. If your athlete can keep every shot within 5 feet of the baseline, then the opponent is kept behind the baseline, from where attack is difficult. Many athletes tend to forget the importance of depth and go directly to power. They hit very hard offensive strokes, but end up hitting them into an area around the service line. Regardless of the force behind a shot, its lack of depth allows the opponent to move in, using forward momentum to take the offensive during a point. At most skill levels it is much more effective for the athlete to take some power off the ball and hit it deeper into the opponent's court. The more consistently deep your player's strokes, the more effectively he or she will take advantage of the opponent's court position and any other match situations.

The final factor in stroke development is power. To be able to hit with control, consistency, and depth is marvelous; adding the element of power puts the player near world-class ability. The problem is that most players do not wait to develop the first three elements—they want to go immediately to powerful strokes. This is probably the biggest mistake they will ever make in their tennis careers.

As we have said, if you merely hit powerful strokes without control, consistency, or depth, you are asking for trouble. Never coach your players to hit powerful ground strokes or volleys. Coach them to penetrate the opponent's court or to attempt heavy strokes. This advice gears their mentality to a goal of placement in the opponent's court and not to swinging hard. As soon as they start swinging hard, they tend to disorganize the body's linked system and the arm is overworked. Remember that although it contributes to the force of a stroke, the upper limb is above all a controlling mechanism, whereas the legs, hips, and trunk are the major force producers. You are advised to coach your athletes to consistently deliver solid, controlled shots that penetrate deeply into the opponent's court. Power will take care of itself.

CHAPTER 4

Using Biomechanics to Improve Performance

It is generally accepted that the point of impact is absolutely the only time in a tennis stroke when perfection must exist. This may seem oversimplified, but bear in mind that many different ways of holding and swinging the racket give good results. The second most important part of stroke production is footwork and positioning. A player must be in the right place at the right time to hit the ball well. Approximately 70% of all errors in the game stem from problems with footwork and positioning. Of course once an athlete performs the proper footwork, the body's linked system can still perform incorrectly, producing a stroking error. How do we define an error in tennis?

Obviously, a stroking error is a missed shot; if the ball is hit long or into the net, it is clearly a mistake. But what about a weak shot? The ball may have landed in the opponent's court, but without the penetration a skilled player wants. If the opponent continually takes advantage of a certain stroke, that stroke may as well be termed an error. If your players tend to make shots that are less than forceful or lack control, it may be beneficial to analyze various movement parameters in more depth.

When analyzing a tennis stroke, the skilled coach must know what to look for. Many physical actions of the body in sport performance are misleading. Some are symptoms of an error, others merely idiosyncrasies. An idiosyncrasy is a movement peculiar to a certain individual. For example, on public courts one commonly sees young women hitting forehands with their free hand held out as though they were patting a baby's bottom (Figure 4.1). This position of the off hand when hitting a forehand is an obvious imitation of Chris Evert. However, Chris's hand position is an idiosyncrasy and in no way influences her excellent forehand drive. What players should be observing and emulating is the rhythm and rotation of Chris's shoulders as she rotates her trunk to position the racket head.

Figure 4.1   Chris Evert's forehand.

Another famous idiosyncrasy often imitated is the starting position of John McEnroe on his serve. After McEnroe's first national television appearance, I was observing young boys taking a serving lesson. During the lesson, about half the children began imitating McEnroe. They did not understand that McEnroe's starting position is an idiosyncrasy. His impeccable timing allows him to get tremendous hip and trunk rotation from this position; it is not the position itself that creates his great serve.

Once a coach sorts out error symptoms from idiosyncrasies, the next concern is identifying the actual cause of the error. The coach needs to make sure not to respond merely to a symptom of the error. A symptom is a movement that may seem to be causing the error, but is actually not the root of the problem. Rather, the error causes the symptom, and the skilled coach must not be misled by this. Examples of symptomatic problems are (a) a leading elbow on the one-handed backhand, (b) a low ball toss on the serve, or (c) a rushed stroke.

The leading elbow is common in beginners and intermediates. Many causes may exist, such as the lack of coordination to move all three upper limb segments at once. One cause seldom considered is poor body positioning. Sometimes a player who leads with the elbow is actually too close to the ball. The closeness forces the player to hit inefficiently. The most common end of poor positioning on the one-handed backhand is to cramp the upper limb by leading with the elbow to strike the ball. The cause of the poor backhand appears to be the leading elbow and lack of coordination, but in fact may be caused by poor positioning.

The low ball toss on the serve can also be misleading. Obviously, it is possible to simply have a low ball toss, but other factors could be involved. For example, a player who lacks sufficient hip rotation must forcefully flex the trunk forward to hit an effective serve. Because this forward flex occurs too quickly for the eye to note, it appears that the ball toss is too low, when in fact if the player had a better throwing motion with the hips and trunk, he or she would be able to hit a higher ball toss. If you tell this player simply to toss the ball higher, the player will only wait for it to fall to his or her preferred (and inefficient) position.

Many coaches might feel that a rushed or hurried stroke is a sign of a player playing in a panic. They tell the player to relax and not to rush. The problem could actually be the result of poor footwork. Instead of timing their stroke to the ball, many players time their body to the ball. In so doing, these players must swing immediately upon arriving at the spot on the court, appearing to rush the shot. If they would time their stroke to the shot, they would be in place before they had to begin the swing.

Skill coaching will improve if we avoid looking at starting positions and body configurations during a movement and begin examining body segment speeds and the exertion of force. We waste time looking at idiosyncrasies or trying to change the symptoms of errors. A 1975 study showed that correcting the cause of an error will usually correct the symptom, but correcting the symptom will not necessarily correct the cause. Error detection based on symptoms only leads to frustration for both coach and player. Coaches must study the *causes* of errors, which requires an understanding of human movement mechanics—what is efficient and what is not regarding specific tennis actions.

To improve error detection skills coaches must understand the goal of a good tennis player (often before the player understands it). The tournament tennis player must try to hit each stroke forcefully, yet with control. This means the athlete should avoid using maximum force, instead using only enough force combined with optimal control to keep the opponent on the defensive. This combination of force and optimal control is the skilled player's goal. How is it achieved?

As stated earlier, the body is a linked system. If an athlete swings the racket as hard as possible using only the upper limb, a great amount of force can be developed, but with less than optimal control. If the athlete swings the racket with the efficient, synchronous movement of the legs–hips–trunk–upper limb linked system, optimal force and control will result.

The linked system is the basis of generating force in tennis, and the amount of force exerted in a specific stroke depends on three factors: (a) how many body parts are used, (b) how much force exists at each segment, and (c) the timing among these segmental actions. Errors result from body parts being left out of the movement and body parts being used without optimal force and timing. Consider the two-handed backhand drive with no trunk action. If the two upper limbs must generate the entire force in hitting this stroke, the shot has a limited chance of being well hit. The player has a weakness for the opponent to exploit. Likewise, if there is not enough hip rotation when serving, the player may compensate by flexing the trunk forcefully forward, but the serve will never be as good as it could be with balanced, synchronous interplay of all segments.

How, then, does one evaluate the amount of force generated by a certain body part? First, force cannot be seen, but velocity can be. To see the interaction and timing among body parts, you must learn to be specific—a veritable Sherlock Holmes—in error detection. Try these guidelines as you practice detecting and analyzing errors in your players' movements.

1. Establish the purpose of the movement. This may seem simplistic, but it is crucial to the analysis of tennis performance. For example, two forehands from behind the baseline may have the same general goal (forcing an error), but the backswings and the amount of ball spin may differ depending on the specific intent. Be sure you know this intent before critiquing the stroke motion.

2. Observe the specific motion several times and confirm that something is wrong. If the shot is missed, something is clearly

wrong; if it is less forceful than desired, or lacks control or penetration, this also indicates an error. You should decide exactly why the shot is ineffective before proceeding.

3. Attempt to assess the cause of the problem and localize it (i.e., upper half or lower half of the body). After observing a stroke several times, you should be able to localize a specific body part that is the likely source of the error.

4. Continue to observe the movement, watching only the identified part, and pin down the problem to a specific body segment. Limiting the error-correcting alternatives by localizing the cause to a specific part of the stroke is a key in determining the cause of an error. Furthermore, never cut off your analysis too early. If you feel the error is in the trunk, continue your analysis all the way to the footwork to be sure. You have no time to waste correcting symptoms instead of causes.

5. Correct performance errors. The biomechanical information used to detect errors is also helpful in correcting them. A problem with the linked system can be detected by systematically evaluating how each link contributes to the outcome. A similar systematic approach can be used to correct the problem. Once you have determined the cause of the problem, there is one very important step to follow before trying to correct the motion. That step is to create a mental image of the model performance—exactly how you think the player should look during the movement. Once you have this perfect model in your mind, compare it to the movements of your player. Determine what your player must do to perform like the model. Then it is time to consider how to change the player's movement pattern accordingly.

6. When coaching a player to modify a stroke, take care to give only the amount of information necessary to effect the change. Too much information can create circuit overload, resulting in paralysis by analysis. Try to develop briefly stated performance cues that will elicit the movement pattern desired. If you explain to an athlete how each segment of the body's linked system must reach its optimal rotational velocity before the subsequent segment gets involved, the player might begin thinking too much about how the hips and trunk interact and not enough about hitting the ball. Instead, have the player throw a ball normally (for example), then have him or her throw again while restricting movement by not rotating the trunk. The player should sense or feel the difference when the throwing pattern is altered. Now you can draw analogies between

the throw and the way the player is using his or her body in the stroke motion.

Explanations should be neither too technical nor too lengthy. Try to correct linked-system problems by using common illustrations and developing performance cues that help players acquire proper motion patterns without delving too deeply into the scientific basis. Providing the players with too much information can cause performance decrements. Keep the cues simple to help the players develop a mental image that will help them effect the change.

Consider now the following biomechanical applications pertinent to errors and possible performance cues. These are not the only cues that can be used, but they are representative.

Relax on the serve. It is amazing to see all the muscular contraction in the forearms of athletes preparing to serve. This contraction means that the grip on the racket is very firm. In addition, one sees all sorts of contortions at the wrist. Excessive contraction creates muscular fatigue and a loss of rhythm. Preparing to serve, the player should assume a relaxed position, free of muscular contraction. The hand and forearm should be straight, with no strange contortions. Remember, the power supply is initially in the legs, hips, and trunk; the upper limb finally receives and adds to the power, but more from whip-like action than from muscular contraction. A relaxed server allows gravity to initiate the backswing, thereby attaining rhythm much more easily.

Maintain rhythm on the serve. Many players tend to forget the importance of hip/trunk rotation when serving. They go through idiosyncratic rituals of bouncing the ball, putting on their shirt, and so on, but they then rush the backswing and the serving motion turns out hurried and cramped. The usual cause of a hurried backswing is poor hip/trunk rotation. The movement occurs so quickly that no rhythm is attained and the athlete ends up hitting a poor serve. Servers should use a rhythmic and deliberate backswing, just as in golf. That is not to say they should be so slow in the backswing as to cause a loss of timing, but they should be deliberate enough to generate proper hip/trunk rotation. In a more deliberate backswing more coiling is likely to take place, usually in the trunk area.

Thrust and throw when serving. When teaching intermediate players to use their legs on the serve, emphasize the sequence of events in the body's linked system—the timing between the extension of the legs, rotation of the hips and then of the trunk, and finally the throwing action of the upper limb. Try having players dip their center of gravity (flex their knees) as the tossing arm goes up. Combined with the rhythmic backswing, this knee flex enables them to prepare adequately. The optimal amount of flexion depends on the individual and the coach must determine how each player's service motion is affected by various amounts. When the backswing of the serve reaches the top of its action, the body "explodes" out of its preparatory stance. This explosion consists of a thrusting action of the legs and then a throwing action by the hips, trunk, and arm. Thus the cue, "thrust and throw."

Point the line between your shoulders at the ball on the one-handed backhand. A skilled player will often try to overhit a one-handed backhand and lift the front shoulder, causing a loss of racket control. To minimize extraneous body movement and maximize control of the shot the athlete should reduce movement of that front shoulder. Tell players that each shoulder represents a dot and that they should mentally connect the dots with a straight line and extend the line forward. As they turn in preparation for the one-handed backhand, they should point the shoulder line at the ball and keep it straight until the ball has been hit.

There will always be some movement of the shoulders in a stroke like the one-handed backhand, but this cue localizes one cause of problems and minimizes excessive shoulder movement. The cue also helps athletes use their legs to get under the one-handed backhand rather than varying the arm action to get the racket head under the ball.

Crowd the ball a bit to hit a topspin forehand. Tim Gullikson had always wanted to hit a heavy topspin forehand. One day when Tim was hitting with Tom, his twin brother, it became apparent why he was having so much trouble developing this shot. As he swung to hit his topspin forehand drive, his arm extended so quickly that his racket was far from his body early in the stroke. To understand how Tim solved his problem, consider a figure skater and our friend, moment of inertia. When figure skaters are spinning with arms held close, they spin very quickly; when their arms are extended, they spin much more slowly. The same principle applies to a tennis player hitting a heavy topspin forehand. The only way to hit topspin is to accelerate the racket head low to high, brushing the backside of the ball. Tim's racket head was extended so far away from him that when he tried to accelerate it he lost control. By crowding the ball *a little* he decreased the moment of inertia (resistance to rotation), enabling him to rotate his trunk faster and rip his topspin forehand.

Knife the approach shot with a long follow-through. Many players tend to have a short follow-through on the approach shot, which opens the racket face too early in the shot. This causes the ball to have a trajectory higher than normal and to "sit up" when it bounces in the opponent's court. Obviously, this is not an effective approach shot. There are two things to consider when working on this stroke. The first is to be sure the player accelerates the racket head through impact to *drive* the approach shot rather than *guide* it. Although the word *knife* suggests that the racket head is parallel to the ground, it is not. Few players realize that the racket head is only slightly beveled at impact or the ball would go straight up in the air. It is not necessary to explain the exact mechanics of the stroke, but merely to use a cue that enables the player to accelerate through impact. A long follow-through will not allow the racket head to open too much prior to impact and enables the acceleration to continue through impact so that the ball clears the net like a line drive and approaches the opponent's court at a low angle. The ideal result is that the ball skids low, forcing the opponent to hit up to clear the net.

Use a balanced hop forward when returning serve. At the 1983 U.S. Open, Tom Gullikson was preparing to play Chip Hooper, who stands 6 feet 7 inches and has one of the biggest serves in the game. Tom felt if he could return Hooper's serve effectively, he had an excellent chance of winning. Tom felt he could not wait on Hooper's serve, but that he had to attack it, similar to the way Bjorn Borg returned serve. Borg always began his service return by standing about 7 to 8 feet behind the baseline. As the opponent served, Borg moved forward and usually made contact with the ball about 3 to 5 feet behind the baseline. In so doing, Borg created a lot of forward momentum and forced his body to attack the opponent's serve every time without having to muscle it. The key, however, was his balance.

Gullikson thought it necessary to examine where he should stand when returning a heavy serve like Hooper's. This was done by having his brother, Tim, serve flat (no spin) balls to Tom, who took a stance about one yard behind the baseline. He was then instructed to move back 3 more feet so that he was 2 yards behind the baseline. As soon as Tim began the forward swing on his serve, Tom was to take a *small* hop forward, landing as Tim contacted the ball. Identifying which side the ball was coming on as he continued his forward body momentum, he could use proper footwork and body rotation to get the racket head prepared correctly. Keeping his shoulders level and using his forward momentum properly, Tom was able to hit an incredibly penetrating return of serve. He felt confident he would succeed against Hooper. During the match, Tom had lost the first set 6-3, and a spectator remarked, "How in the world is that guy ever going to beat Hooper by attacking every serve that way?" Well, it took Tom one set to get his timing down and realize exactly how far behind the baseline he should stand to be in the proper position to hop, read, and react to Hooper's serve. Tom won the next three sets and advanced to the fourth round.

Cut off balls on ground strokes whenever possible. Many players have excellent ground strokes that weaken when hit on the run. When stationary, a player's effective ground strokes come from force produced through the legs, hips, and trunk. However, stroke effectiveness when hitting on the run is not as dependent on the various body parts as it is on the direction of the player's movement.

Take as an analogy a third baseman in baseball. When a ground ball is hit between the third baseman and the shortstop, the third baseman moves forward and on an angle toward first base. If the third baseman cuts off the ball, linear momentum carries him or her toward first base, providing the third baseman with a better first-base throwing position than the shortstop, who is angling away from first base in case the ball gets past the third baseman.

The same thing happens in tennis. If players develop the mentality to cut off balls when hitting on the run, they can hit penetrating ground strokes without swinging too vigorously. The key is using the body's forward momentum and staying balanced. One caution: Players who get too cocky might sometimes find themselves too far inside the baseline and be caught in no man's land. Part of the coach's job is to help players identify when they can and cannot cut off a ball successfully.

Squeeze the racket grip when hitting shoulder-high volleys. The Gullikson twins' success in doubles attests that they are among the best volleyers in professional tennis. However, like all professionals, they always work to improve. They felt they needed to transfer more energy to the ball ("Get more stick on it") on the high volley. Films and video tapes of both players revealed that on volleys when the ball was below net height they tended to "dish" or "fold" the racket head. What happens is that the racket head stays firmly positioned until the ball has left, then reacts to the impact by dishing. In so reacting, the racket is absorbing some energy from the ball and thus hitting a more controlled shot than might be expected. However, the same type of dishing was seen on balls Tim and Tom hit above net height, shots on which they wanted to impart maximum energy to the ball.

The cue, then, became "Squeeze the grip on high volleys," which reduces racket reaction to impact and maximizes the transfer of energy to the ball while still maintaining control. Before recommending the use of this cue with less-skilled players, we must raise a huge flag of caution. By squeezing the grip, the player increases the interaction between racket and body, which could lead to a serious case of tennis elbow if the player is not strong enough to withstand repeated impacts. As always, coaches must use discretion and employ a cue only when their players are capable.

Developing cues on your own. To create your own performance cues, consider various analogies or phrases easily understood by players. The analogy you select can be from everyday life or from the court. Say, for example, your player is having trouble flexing his or her knees during the serve and is consequently not serving well. As the player releases the toss, your cue could be "Sit down!," encouraging him or her to bend the knees. Then, at the right instant, the cue, "Explode up!" might effect extension and proper delivery of the serve.

Another example could stem from your concern about a player who does not rotate his or her hips properly during the service motion. Instructing the athlete to toss the ball a little farther into the court could correct the problem without ever mentioning the lack of hip rotation. When the ball is tossed a little farther into the court, the player is forced to go not only up but also forward, which demands more rotation.

Try to develop cues that players can easily interpret and react to. Be cautious with the phrasing you use. I know of one nationally ranked junior who, after complaining of tennis elbow, was observed excessively pronating his hand and forearm during his service motion. His coach had instructed him to do so. This was disconcerting because pronation during the serve is actually a release or follow-through mechanism. As a release mechanism it serves to protect the body, but if the athlete tries to forcefully pronate, there is no release mechanism available and the elbow absorbs all the shock from that action. Thus, the old standby cue, "Snap the wrist toward impact," still seems to be the best when teaching upper limb action on the serve.

Depending on the personalities of your players and how you interact with them, the number of appropriate cues are limitless. Try to be innovative. Don't overload circuits by giving athletes too much information; develop simple cues that they can easily implement. It will make their acquisition of skills easier and your job a lot more enjoyable.

PART II

MOTOR LEARNING AND TENNIS

Scott Melville, PhD

CHAPTER 5

How Best to Teach
Skills to Tennis Players

Of all the sport sciences, motor learning is probably the least understood and applied. Most tennis players and coaches are beginning to realize that biomechanics experts can provide invaluable information about court movements and stroking techniques. The sport physiologist's knowledge of such things as the circulatory system and musculo-skeletal system is now recognized as having great potential for conditioning athletes for tennis. And people are increasingly recognizing that the sport psychologist's understanding of motivational and emotional factors can greatly help players achieve their maximal performance. However, few coaches would be able to explain in any detail what is going on in the field of motor learning, or to give examples of how this area of research can be useful to them.

For our purposes, motor learning refers to the study of defining the best ways to teach people to learn and perform physical skills. How does a coach explain and demonstrate skills? Give feedback to players? Design drills? How much practice time should be devoted to drills and scrimmages? These and many related questions fall under the science of motor learning and importantly affect how well players acquire and execute skills.

Until now coaches generally have had to answer the previous questions on the basis of intuition and experience. These two attributes are valuable, of course, but they alone will not likely lead to optimal educational choices. A great body of recent motor research has practical implications for tennis coaches. This chapter applies some of this knowledge to address a foremost concern of tennis coaches: how best to teach skills to players.

Experienced coaches know that teaching people to properly swing a tennis racket is not as easy as it might seem. Perhaps you have experienced the situation where you have worked diligently with a player on a technique, yet failed, partially or utterly. I once worked extensively with a player who had a fairly effective underspin backhand and wanted to develop a topspin backhand ground stroke. He was pleased with the instruction and vociferously praised my aid everywhere he went. The disheartening truth was that the results only confirmed my inability to communicate with the player. He still sliced the backhand as much as ever, only now he had a fancier follow-through.

Motor researchers have identified a concept that serves as a very helpful guide whenever we attempt to teach physical skills. This concept is that when people are learning a new skill, or making changes in an old one, they need to know two things: (a) what the correct form is supposed to look and feel like, and (b) how they are actually performing the skill. In research, knowing what the correct form looks and feels like is called the *image of correctness*. How they actually perform is referred to as the *image of actual performance*. In learning new techniques, players improve their skills by comparing the two images. They adjust future attempts to achieve a correspondence between the two. If either image is not clearly known, players will not learn at an optimal rate.

Making performers aware of what form they are trying to achieve and what they are actually doing might sound easy. Some coaches assume that all they have to do is explain the movement or skill, demonstrate it a few times and then, as players practice it, critique performance. In reality, successfully communicating this information is difficult, and it is precisely for this reason that many attempts to teach a stroking technique fail.

Fortunately, teaching skills does not have to be as difficult as it once was. Substantial research has investigated how communication of this kind is best accomplished, and we will relate how this information can be usefully applied to help players learn new techniques. For clarity, our discussion will be divided into the following sections: Explanations and Demonstrations, Guidance Techniques, Verbal Feedback, Using Checklists for Feedback, and Using Videotapes for Feedback.

EXPLANATIONS AND DEMONSTRATIONS

The purpose of explaining and demonstrating a tennis skill is to get learners to store a clear image of correctness in their minds. Research indicates that explanations alone are not particularly effective in accomplishing this. You can prove the point to yourself by trying to verbally explain a sport technique to someone totally unfamiliar with the skill. Even if you go to great length in explaining the skill, the student will be able to make only crude approximations of it.

The complexity of motor skills, which require a rich interplay of many body movements, makes it difficult to convey images of correctness by explanation. It would take much time and extremely good elocution skills to precisely describe these diverse movements and their relationships to each other. Adding to the difficulty is that learners must take in all this verbal information, translate it into a visual picture, and accurately remember this image as they practice.

The point is, lengthy explanations alone are not a very good way to teach tennis techniques. Demonstrations of the techniques much more effectively create visual images. Demonstrations can easily present a wide array of movements to learners, which relieves them of the difficult mental task of translating words to visual images.

Although demonstrations have built-in advantages, they are not a magic means of communication. Verbal information can effectively promote the storage of images. Explanations, when used to cue aspects of demonstrated movements, can greatly contribute to the development and retention of the image of correctness. We will set forth some ways in which you can improve the quality of your demonstrations.

Research has shown that observers are immensely better at both noticing and recalling aspects of a demonstration when verbal phrases or words are used to cue their attention. Without verbal cues, most aspects of a demonstration go virtually unnoticed. Tennis strokes involve such complex movements that learners, even when they are trying very hard, can easily be distracted by unimportant parts of the swing and fail to see the most important aspects.

Verbal cueing also dramatically improves the retention of movement aspects by attaching labels to them. Just as you cannot bring an image of a dog to your mind without first thinking *dog,* so do tennis players fail to remember an aspect of your demonstration if they have not given it a name. For instance, even though you have demonstrated the weight shift that should accompany a ground stroke, the observer might not be able to recall that concept without a name tag such as *shift weight, step forward,* or *lean into it.*

So, there is good reason to supplement demonstration with verbal cues. Before demonstrating a skill, think of one or two movement aspects you want the observer to notice. When demonstrating, have ready concise, vivid cues that will rivet the learner's attention to these aspects. Short, colorful expressions are more easily coded and retrieved from memory. For example, when demonstrating a topspin backhand ground stroke you might say, "Notice how my arm is moving as if I were drawing a sword." This cue should focus the student's attention to how your stroking arm moves low-to-high and inside-out rather than flat or around the body as is so commonly done. Later, the player thinking about or practicing this new technique can mentally rehearse *draw sword* and be easily reminded of this critical movement aspect. If you do not provide such ready-made cues, you are taking the chance that players might not generate personal ones and thus images will quickly slip away.

Another vividly memorable cue for the topspin backhand is one Vic Braden uses. He thinks that the follow-through position is an important part of this swing and exuberantly tells his students to "air the armpit." This cue is effective as well as colorful because it accents an end position. Beginning and ending positions are the most easily remembered aspects of movements and thus serve as good guideposts for future attempts. Coaches should give particular attention to trying to cue the starting and follow-through positions of the strokes they are correcting. Stress that players "pose for the picture" when preparing to hit an overhead, and "reach for the net" on the follow-through of volleys. With a little imagination you can undoubtedly improve on these cues.

One last comment on using verbal cues to remember a movement: If you want your players to remember cues, they must review them. Without review, even vivid cues may be forgotten, particularly in the case of very young athletes. Ask players frequently the cue words for the shot they are practicing. Evidence is accumulating that a less-developed motor system is not the primary reason children generally learn motor skills more slowly than adults. Their motor systems *are* somewhat less developed in terms of reaction time and strength, but children also often fail to rehearse the verbal cues you have given them because they have not learned the importance of doing so.

Probably one of the worst errors tennis teachers commit is failing to demonstrate often enough and effectively enough. Tennis swings consist of a multitude of movements, subtle and gross, occurring simultaneously or in close order. It may take many demonstrations before the observer achieves a well-digested image of correctness. Bear in mind that both the image of correctness and the image of actual performance are elements critical to learning, and coaches must allot significant amounts of time to each.

Coaches and players are typically impatient and begin practicing before they are ready. Players often get a few short minutes of demonstration and then are cut loose to practice for days and weeks without benefit of additional demonstrations. It is essential to demonstrate repeatedly in the beginning, and periodically thereafter, employing your movement cues as the player practices the skill. Memory images are not indelible and will assuredly fade if not occasionally reinstated.

In addition to encouraging repeated demonstrations, research findings suggest the best ways to demonstrate skills. We will consider two specific suggestions, not only because they have been found to importantly improve the learning process, but also because they are so seldom used by tennis coaches.

The first is to make sure that the learner observes the demonstration from a variety of angles. Tennis is a three-dimensional game; viewing from a single angle does not present a complete, working image of a tennis swing. As you repeat your demonstrations, move the observers around you to view some executions from the sides and from behind you. Even observations from the front are worthwhile.

The second suggestion is to demonstrate how the technique is used to handle a wide assortment of shots. If you are coaching a player in a new volleying technique, not all your demonstrations should be of shoulder-high volleys played at medium speed unless your purpose is to change the player's technique for only this one kind of volley. If you work with the player to form a good image of how to handle low and high shots, floaters and hard drives, midcourt and net shots, you must model how the new technique you are advocating adjusts to these different demands. This holds true even if you plan to have the player initially practice only shoulder-high volleys. Having seen different versions of the shot, the player will form a more thorough understanding and a better image of how to make shoulder-high volleys as well as higher and lower ones.

Varying your demonstration should not make assimilation more difficult for the learner, whom you have instructed to cue on one or two movement aspects that occur throughout. For instance, you might demonstrate three or four shoulder-high volleys while cueing the player's attention to how you reached for the net on follow-through. Then you might hit three or four knee-high volleys, still cueing the player to note how you reached in this shot variation. The same process would be repeated for volleys above the head.

Similar variation procedures work for all the strokes. You can instruct players to notice the sideward posing position as you demonstrate overheads while moving forward, moving backward, and standing still. You may illustrate a serving technique while following some serves in and staying back on others.

GUIDANCE TECHNIQUES

Even the best verbally cued demonstrations are not always sufficient to create a complete understanding of the image of correctness. Although they have heard it and seen it, some players will not accurately grasp what the swing should look and feel like when they themselves do it. Another way to increase players' understanding of the correct movement is to actually manipulate their movements. Teaching strategies that physically regulate learners' movement patterns are called *guidance techniques*. We will separately consider two types of guidance techniques as they apply to tennis instruction.

The Coach Physically Guides the Movement

One type of guidance technique involves the coach's moving a player's body segments into prescribed positions or routes. Tennis coaches should probably use this technique more frequently and sooner in the learning process than is commonly done. Some coaches either do not use it at all or they use it as a last resort.

For example, a player might be cued to watch to rotate the shoulders when serving or to air the armpit on the ground stroke follow-through. When it becomes apparent from performance that the player has not grasped the idea after repeated explanation and demonstration, the instructor steps forward, manually rotates the player's shoulders or lifts the player's arm as if "airing" the armpit and says, "There—this is what I mean," and, magically, the player understands.

This is not to recommend that coaches correct every player's technique by physical manipulation. In many cases, explanations and demonstrations will quickly communicate the message. But sometimes physical manipulation is just what the player needs to grasp the image of correctness. A coach familiar with the temperament and mental acuity of players can foresee which ones might have difficulty translating explanations and demonstrations into action. Young players or slow learners have particular difficulty with this. In such circumstances, try manual manipulation early in your instruction.

A by-product of this manual technique is that it communicates to the player that the coach is sincerely interested in his or her learning. The touching and animation involved is educationally positive in that it enhances an earnest, enthusiastic learning environment.

Finally, this technique is exceptionally good for accenting verbal cues, which we suggested earlier as valuable aids in the retention of skills. This technique involves placing the player in a position and giving *location* cues: "This is where you should be meeting the ball," or "Here is the backswing position you want to strive for." Granting its limitations in emphasizing *movement* cues, physical manipulation is still useful to at least show directions in which movement should be occurring. For instance, we can move the server's arm and racket in the manner that produces topspin. Or we can move the arm and racket in an elongated swing pattern to counter the around-the-body swing tendency of some ground strokers and volleyers.

Using Equipment to Guide Movement

The second type of guidance technique, using equipment to restrict movements, has not been extensively studied in skill acquisition. Much of the research that has been done on other motor skills suggests that using equipment to guide performance does not seem to be effective when used for extended periods. Apparently, performers do not fully concentrate on the activity because it is being done for them. With extended use, the technique becomes a crutch that encourages dependency. However, the research indicates that equipment guides may be useful in the initial stages of teaching a skilled movement. They can help convey the idea of what the movement should be like, thereby helping performers get started on the right track—much as manual promptings do.

The successful tennis coach should know some ways to use equipment in the early stages of teaching skills. Presented next is a list and brief description of some specific examples of instructional aids. Although players should not use them for other than brief practice sessions, and coaches may not find them useful for all players, they may prove beneficial for certain players with whom you are having communication problems. If nothing else, reviewing these examples of using equipment may spawn some more and better ideas of your own.

1. Use elbow devices to restrict elbow bend. This may reduce the problem of elbow leading and overuse in ground stroking.
2. Have players practice their volleying motion with a wall immediately behind them. The wall serves as a limiting boundary to keep players from taking an excessive backswing.
3. Require volleyers to sit on chairs when fielding half volleys to encourage knee bend and getting down to the shots.
4. Suspend balls at different heights and positions above servers. The purpose is to encourage a high contact point for flat serves and a slightly lower, more over-the-head contact point for topspin serves.
5. Use a wall diagram of the path the racket should make during topspin ground strokes. This technique is helpful to many, but not all. Even with the marked guide some players will inscribe a different racket path. An idea for some dedicated coach would be to cut a racket path in a plywood board—a kind of template. A player could grasp the handle of a racket placed through the groove and then practice swings that would necessarily be channeled in the desired upward direction. Moving around to the other side of the board could train the player in the racket path of the top spin backhand.

VERBAL FEEDBACK

Let us assume that with impeccable explanations, demonstrations, and guidance techniques, we have succeeded in providing a player with a good, retainable image of correctness for a new stroke. The next step is to have the player practice and make comparisons between this image of correctness and actual performance. Because players cannot see themselves performing, they have trouble making this comparison accurately. Our actual movements are often far different from what we think they are. The coach must play the key role in helping players realize exactly how their actions correspond to what is correct. We call this information provided by the coach *feedback.* The most common instance of giving feedback is where the coach verbally comments on players' performance.

This section offers suggestions on how coaches can best use feedback to teach stroking techniques. Keep in mind that research has consistently found feedback to be one of the strongest factors influencing the learning of motor skills. Accordingly, any improvement in the quality of feedback coaches provide to their athletes will likely have a pronounced effect on how quickly and well new skills can be achieved.

Frequency of Feedback

The first thing to consider is how frequently feedback should be provided. When the player first begins practicing the new technique, it is critically important that the coach be present to offer fairly constant feedback. Comments after every four or five swings or so should be enough to ensure that the player will practice with a good understanding of how actual performance is comparing to the desired model, or image of correctness. Less frequent feedback might result in incomplete understanding.

On the other hand, more frequent feedback can be counterproductive. When feedback is given after every trial, some learners begin to rely too heavily on it. They tend to use the coach's constant feedback as a crutch and do not think enough about what they are doing (as in the case of long-term guidance techniques). Some trials without feedback force the player into analyzing the situation, and this is necessary because, ultimately, performing the skill is the player's responsibility.

As the player continues to practice the new skill through subsequent days, weeks, and months, feedback remains very important. With the passage of time both the image of correctness and the image of actual performance may fade or become distorted. Also, the reassertion of old habits and the pressures of competitive situations often lead the player's performance to drift from what was so assiduously taught. The coach must not allow this drifting to occur. His or her role in teaching skills is not over until the player shows mastery of the new skill. And the skill is not mastered until the player demonstrates automatic use of it in important match play.

Clearly, the effective coach will have to hustle every practice session, because at any given time there might be a number of players in various states of practicing new techniques. Every day, the coach should circulate about the courts to provide continual follow-up feedback. A number of interesting research studies have shown that coaches who move about the practice area giving feedback are much more successful at teaching skills than those who lean against the net with their arms folded.

Precision of Feedback

Realizing the importance of the frequency of feedback, we will now examine how to improve the quality of feedback. An extremely important element of feedback is the degree of its precision. We can divide feedback into the categories of general and specific. *General feedback* is not very precise. In general feedback, the coach watches a player's performance and says "Good," "Not bad," "Your backswing was wrong," "Almost," or "Could be better" without ever pinpointing what it is, exactly, that is good or could be better.

Specific feedback is much more precise. "You definitely lowered your racket to knee level on the backswing"; "Your weight is still on the back foot"; "Make that toss an inch or two lower"—these are examples of specific feedback.

Not surprisingly, research shows that specific feedback is much more effective than general. After all, specific feedback provides learners with more information as to how their swings do or do not conform to the proper model. The unexpected aspect of this same research is that even though specific feedback is much more effective, most coaches seldom use it! In monitoring coaches, it is common to find that the majority of their feedback is in the general category. We do not know why. Maybe some coaches are not aware of the powerful importance of specific feedback. Maybe others do not really know the proper stroke techniques well enough to identify specific errors. And perhaps others have fallen into the habit of not making the extra effort that precise feedback requires. Insidiously, they find it easier to say "good" or "bad" and to permit some errors to go uncorrected.

Undoubtedly we can all improve our coaching by increasing the specificity of our feedback. If you have not been sufficiently specific in your feedback because you did not fully realize its importance, you do now. If your reason at times is an uncertainty as to what the technique should really be, keep working at your knowledge of tennis and mechanics. And finally, check your present use of specific feedback and then monitor your progress in increasing it. Consider having an assistant record the number of times you give general and specific feedback during practices. Or collect your own data by strapping a tape recorder to your waist. Such aids have produced good results in studies designed to improve coaching and teaching effectiveness.

Simplicity of Feedback

The old acronym KISS ("Keep It Simple, Stupid") is a good reminder when it comes to providing feedback to your players. Consider the following example. A coach intent on correcting a player's service motion says the following things during 10 minutes of instruction: "Square up your stance. Drop your tossing hand down more. Rotate the shoulders more. Toss the ball lower and farther in front of you. Have the racket moving upward when you contact the ball. Keep your eyes on the ball all the way this time. You did not transfer your weight into the shot."

It seems absurd to expect the player to take in, remember, and translate all this feedback into images and then to produce a movement that incorporates all of them. This is an especially unrealistic expectation when we know that each of these new movements may require changes in old techniques that the player may have practiced for years.

It is easy to fall into the trap of trying to make too many corrections too quickly. The errors players make are sometimes infuriating to coaches; as a result coaches may become too eager to correct them. It is imperative for teachers to fight this tendency. The key is to be precise with feedback and to aim at only one or two mistakes at a time. Until the player solves these mistakes and can perform the stroke or movement almost automatically, do not address other aspects. Only when the player has achieved this automatic degree of mastery will he or she be able to sufficiently concentrate on correcting other mistakes. Failure to follow this step-by-step procedure may discourage the player because of his or her inability to successfully accomplish the needed changes. The coach will likely be discouraged, as well.

Another danger sometimes associated with giving players too much feedback is a phenomenon known as "paralysis by analysis." The player is so overwhelmed by information that he or she freezes and does nothing. Once in a doubles scrimmage I "helpfully" instructed my net man to keep his racket up in the ready position, to stand further from the sideline, and to try using a continental grip. Shortly afterward one of our opponent's moderately paced ground strokes caught my partner right between the eyes. If he blinked it was the only movement he made. He was unable to move, he said, because, "I was trying to figure out all those things you were laying on me."

Positive Aspects of Feedback

Coaches who establish a positive learning environment are immensely more successful at teaching skills than coaches who work in a negative environment. Teaching/learning environments have been monitored by recording the verbal comments of coaches and classifying them as either positive or negative. When these recordings were examined, we generally found that coaches who gave about a four-to-one ratio of positive remarks to negative were the most effective. The most negative coaches achieved the worst results. Apparently, under negative conditions many players did not enjoy practices and developed low levels of confidence in their abilities. In contrast, coaches who made *only* positive statements were somewhat ineffective because the players perceived such coaches as insincere. The players knew their performances were not always deserving of praise; as a result the totally positive responses lacked credibility.

Because perhaps the greatest role the coach performs in practice is to provide verbal feedback, the tone of the feedback in large part sets the overall tone of practices. Coaches should therefore strive to be more positive than negative. Perhaps they might wish to set a slightly higher than four-to-one ratio of positive to negative responses for those players they are coaching in major technique revisions. After all, these players are especially susceptible to discouragement because their performance is impaired over long periods of time. This is a heavy burden to impose on young athletes without providing additional support.

The question is, how do we achieve a high level of sincere, positive feedback when working with players who must be made aware that they have major problems? One procedure found very effective is called *the sandwich principle*. In it, the coach provides negative verbal feedback sandwiched between comments about what the player is doing right. Example: "You had a low-to-high swing, but it's still a little too flat. Keep up that good concentration." Here the coach actually tells the player the swing was wrong, but because the feedback was sandwiched between encouraging comments the overall tone was positive. And the coach's credibility was preserved because everything said was true.

Effective coaches can employ the sandwich principle in the majority of situations. It may be harder to find good things to say to some players than to others, but there is usually something positive you can point out. Although important aspects of a player's swing are not right, he or she may still be making a good effort, getting into an effective ready position, showing early racket preparation, or meeting the ball out in front of the body. If any of these are occurring, be sure to reinforce them.

One final point concerning positive feedback: Do not always use the same expressions. Avoid repeating "Good try," "Good follow-through," or "Your racket preparation was good." This constant repetition of "good" is called the "global good," and is an extremely easy habit to develop. "Good" is but one example; you might be guilty of overusing some other word or phrase. Variation in your verbal comments will make them much more powerful reinforcers. Monitor whether your expressions are varied or limited to a few favorites.

CHECKLISTS FOR FEEDBACK

Although verbal feedback is one of the best ways of giving players an image of how their performance compares with ideal performance, it is not always completely effective. One of the chief problems with verbal feedback is its forgetability. Consider this analogy. During a trip to the grocery store you might forget some items. You might forget them even if your spouse repeatedly told you what to get and warned you not to forget. If you wished to remember everything on the shopping list, you would probably repeat the items to yourself as you walked along, or, better yet, write them down.

Tennis coaches present players with a similar problem, repeatedly and emphatically pointing out mistakes in their movements and swings. The players must remember these lists of failings over long periods of practice. Coaches can promote fuller retention of their instructions by periodically questioning the players. Questioning players forces them to rehearse the points of the swing. Or, even better than questioning them, coaches can give players written lists of instructions that they can use as checklists in monitoring their games.

The rest of this section explains how to use checklists in the teaching of tennis swings. Checklists are effective in helping performers remember verbal feedback and, when careful thought is given to their use and design, they can be worthwhile tools for helping players compare actual with ideal performance.

Individualizing Checklists

The first step in a sample checklist procedure is to place on three-by-five notecards a complete list of common errors that players commit on a given stroke (Figure 5.1). Then observe each player performing this shot and note any deficiencies. The size of the cards makes them easy to use on the courts; they can be carried in the pocket. After practice, transfer these notes onto a more detailed checklist (Figure 5.2). At some later time, perhaps prior to the next day's practice, meet with each player and give him or her a copy of the notes (keeping a copy for yourself). Discuss the reasons a technique change may be needed and how best to go about it.

		TOPSPIN BACKHAND GROUNDSTROKE			
NAMES	READY POSTION	LOW TO HIGH SWING	TRANSFER OF WEIGHT	HIGH FOLLOW THROUGH	COMMENT
TOM					
MARY					
JOE					
MARIE					
KAREN					
CHRIS					
PETER					
JAMES					

Figure 5.1 Sample form for recording tennis stroke errors.

These detailed checklists should provide more than just a written list of errors. In addition, they should contain drawings depicting correct form alongside drawings of the common errors that players make. When the subject player is deficient in an area, a check is placed next to the verbal description and the drawing depicting that error is circled. You might write a comment about the error checked.

(Cont.)

Figure 5.2 Sample detailed checklist for analyzing errors.

Figure 5.2 (Cont.)

The drawings make it easier for players to clearly see how their swings deviate from the correct model. If the drawings were not there, players would have to perform two mental exercises. First, they would have to translate each checked verbal statement into an image of the error. Second, they would have to match those error images with the correct images. They might not be able to accurately make this comparison because the ideal image has faded from memory. With drawings of the two images presented next to each other, these problems are resolved.

Drawbacks to Checklists

Of course there are limitations to the checklist system. Not everyone's errors can be accurately represented in drawings. Movement and timing errors are especially difficult to depict. However, there is some truth to the old expression that a picture is worth a thousand words. The important location cues *can* be presented in drawings and can convey information that players could not always obtain from written lists alone.

The accompanying figures offer many drawings that represent different aspects of good technique, as well as the stroking mistakes associated with each. Some of the drawings should usefully reflect the visual concepts you wish to present to your players. It should be easy enough for you to make additional tracings and drawings from books and magazines that portray other images to include in your checklists. Over the years, if you continue to revise them, your checklists will become increasingly valuable instructional tools.

One final caution about the use of these detailed checklists. This relates to the earlier discussion about keeping feedback simple. Remember how overwhelming a player with excessive feedback can lead to discouragement and paralysis by analysis. The detailed checklist system proposed does not have to violate this principle. During chalk-talk sessions you may indeed be showing that a significant number of problem areas exist in a player's swing. However, the checklist examples are limited to four or less aspects; thus they address a manageable number of things.

In situations where as many as four aspects require remediation, make it clear during your talk with the player that you need to zero in on one or two aspects at a time. The determination of which error to target first is easier when the coach has a biomechanics background. Generally it is wise to begin work on errors that occur early in the swing. Poor preparatory positions lead to subsequent mistakes. For example, correcting a backswing position might improve the player's foreswing or follow-through.

Conversely, it may prove difficult to correct the position of contact if the swing is being incorrectly initiated.

USING VIDEOTAPES FOR FEEDBACK

Videotapes are one more effective way of providing feedback. We have several times made the point that performance improves when players can make a visual comparison between their performance and correct performance. Perhaps no aid is better suited for providing simultaneous images of actual and correct form than the videotape. However, given the manner in which the videotape is generally used, it is not realizing its potential. Typical use of videotapes shows players their own performance, but does not show them the image of correctness. They are left to visualize the image of correctness either on their own or with the help of the instructor's verbalizations. For example, a player views his or her performance and the coach points out how the swing is inadequate with comments such as, "See what you are doing on the backswing? Remember where I told you your racket is supposed to be?" The player may or may not accurately remember where the racket was supposed to be.

The problem of recalling the correct image is remedied by having the correct form modeled in juxtaposition to the player's performance. It is easy enough for instructors or other players with excellent technique to position themselves, mindful of the camera, in the background diagonally behind the learner and exhibit the desired form for all shots. During playback the student simultaneously sees his or her own performance and that of the model.

Although videotapes may show both images, it does not follow that students will detect the important differences between them. They may have forgotten the important things to look for. One of the recognized difficulties in using videotapes to provide feedback is getting people to pay attention to the important aspects of performance. Players are often distracted by such things as their dress, appearance, or idiosyncratic movements. Experts recognize this problem and recommend that videotaping be accompanied by verbal cues and be used repeatedly. Once players become accustomed to seeing themselves on tape, the novelty wears off and they can better concentrate on technique concerns.

Using checklists in coordination with videotapes is a superb way to get players to focus on the key aspects of performance. The checklist gives players specific objectives when viewing the playback. They can evaluate themselves either during practice time or outside of practice. An in-practice procedure found effective is to tape various players during a practice, then edit the tape for playback during the next practice. Players are individually pulled from activity when their segments of the recording are ready for viewing. They watch themselves (with the model in the background) a number of times and are asked to identify the checklist items in which their performance deviates from the correct form. This individual format reduces the distraction problem and allows everyone to keep practicing except for that short period when viewing his or her section of the tape.

Another effective procedure is to have the self-evaluation of the playback take place outside of practice time. In a test case, players were assigned to visit a media room and evaluate their performance along checklist guidelines. This method, of course, saves practice time and players generally respond well. Many have analyzed their performances much more fully than would have been possible in practice. It is particularly good if some of the players can view the tapes just prior to practice so that those images are floating crystal-clear in their minds' eye.

CHAPTER 6

When to Teach New Techniques

Chapter 5 addressed the issue of how to teach skills to tennis players. An equally important issue is when—and when not—to teach new techniques. Some coaches will plunge ahead to correct a weak backhand ground stroke or a pushed, flat second serve. Other coaches witnessing the same errors might judge it better to leave well enough alone. In this chapter we will critically consider what conditions should exist before a coach attempts to teach a new technique and how coaches can create those necessary conditions if they are not present.

No hard and fast rules exist regarding which particular techniques require changing at a given stage in a player's development and which do not. The complexity and diversity of situations and individuals dictates otherwise. However, there are three questions to consider when deciding whether or not to correct a player's technique; we should begin corrections only when we can answer yes to each of them.

DETERMINING IF ANOTHER TECHNIQUE IS BETTER

The first question to ask is, Is the technique currently being used less effective than another technique for this individual? Sometimes the answer is clearly yes, and other times it is not. For instance, if a player is not bending his or her elbow during the backswing of a serve, the coach knows that an alternate service motion will most likely help the player hit with more power. However, when a player has a service motion in which he or she bends the elbow to a slightly lesser extent than do most good servers, the issue becomes clouded. If the coach is not certain a new technique would be significantly better, it would be foolish to disrupt the player's game.

Is there anything coaches can do to enable them to answer yes to the first question? Indeed there is. Knowledge of the bio-mechanical principles of tennis can provide a solid basis on which to evaluate the extent of helpfulness or harm in teaching different techniques. When coaches maximize their understanding of ten-nis mechanics, they have the tools to resolve most of these clouded situations that deter many skill-correction procedures. In the previous example, the coach knowledgeable in mechanical principles would recognize the critical importance of elbow flexion in the generation of racket head speed and could judge that another technique would improve the player's skill.

It is easy to improve your ability to mechanically analyze tennis skills. Become familiar with the writings in this area. In addition to the biomechanics section of this book, I recommend Groppel (1984), Hay and Reid (1982), and Plagenhoef (1970) as other excellent sources. They make interesting reading and I have found them invaluable.

ACCEPTING SHORT-TERM DECREASES IN PERFORMANCE

Having decided that a better technique exists for a player, the coach must then be able to answer yes to a second question: Can the player afford to accept an inevitable short-term decrement in performance? Performance inevitably suffers when players try to learn new ways of executing skills. This is true even when the technique adjustment is small. Such a minor adjustment as a slight grip change will likely require days, weeks, and sometimes months of drilling before performance begins to match and surpass the precorrection ability level. And just because the new adjustment has been mastered in practice drills does not mean it will be operational in a match. During competition the player must have mastered the skill to the point where it is automatic, and that takes even more time.

The more major the changes required of players, the longer it will take them to utilize the new skills in matches. When we switch players from a two-handed to a one-handed backhand, teach them to hit a kick serve, or make a major grip change, we may very well be facing a transition period of months or years before they reach a more advanced level of performance. Consequently, there will be situations when the timing is not right for correcting a faulty technique. When a match of great importance is coming up, we must be especially careful about instigating changes. In fact, most in-season technique changes (including relatively minor adjustments) will often result in performance impairment rather than improvement.

What can we do to make short-term decrements in performance more acceptable to players? The best solution is to plan ahead so new techniques can be practiced at times other than during the season. Decrements in performance are most affordable during postseason and early preseason when there is time to accommodate any technique changes into the training regimens. Table 6.1 lists the different tennis seasons and the appropriateness of initiating technique corrections during each.

**Table 6.1 Tennis Seasons of the Year
When Technique Corrections Might Be Initiated**

Tennis seasons of the year	Appropriateness of initiating corrections in technique
Preseason	Good time to initiate corrections; no match pressure; some time constraints
Regular season	Poor time to initiate corrections; match pressures; time constraints
Immediate postseason	Excellent time to initiate corrections; no match pressure; weaknesses fresh in mind
Off season	Not normally a good time to initiate corrections because the coach often is not available for instructional feedback.

Recognizing that in-season attempts to change techniques will impair the present season's performance at least as often as they will help it must not lead coaches to discontinue in-season technique changes altogether. Many technique changes require a great length of time and necessarily continue into and through the heart of the tennis season. We must never forget that teaching sound skill techniques is perhaps the greatest service we can provide to our players. Even getting the maximal performance out of players during their final year under our charge may not be the best goal when we consider their entire tennis lives.

Let me use an example from my own experience. When I was a young player I realized I had an ineffective backhand. Although I attempted to make minor adjustments, I did not attempt a complete revamping because I was reluctant to suffer the short-term consequences. I did not relish the prospect of a year or more of poor match play. Winning matches seemed all-important, and a year or two represented an eternity. Now, looking back with a more mature and philosophical perspective, a year or two of depressed performance seems insignificant in my overall tennis life. I wish I had had a mentor who would have taken the time and interest to work on my weakness even at the cost of some of my victories.

CONVINCING THE PLAYER
OF THE NEED FOR CHANGE

Assume the coach is assured the player is using an inefficient technique and that a temporary performance decrement is worth the long-term gain. One final question must be answered positively before embarking on a correction program: Can I fully convince the player a change is needed and worth a difficult transition period? We cannot overemphasize the point that successfully changing a player's technique is no easy task. The player has probably executed the wrong technique thousands of times, establishing neuromotor patterns to the degree they run automatically. Overlearned patterns will stubbornly remain an interfering factor as we attempt reeducation. If the coach and player cannot agree on a concerted effort to correct the error, the instructional intervention is doomed to frustration and failure.

Defend Your Case

What can a coach do to convince the player a technique change is needed? First, the coach can help the player realize that the particular flaw is a detriment to his or her game. Sometimes a simple conversation with the player will suffice. However, the coach should do some homework before approaching the player. Armed with a planned attack and supporting data the coach, like a good salesperson, will more likely be able to get the player to see the problem in the same light.

The kind of data used to support your position can vary. Use every kind of support information available to you. Charting game performance is one method of obtaining data to support your case. For example, if a player has a faulty overhead you could chart a few matches to document the percentage of overheads he or she misses, the percentage hit for winners, and the percentage that were merely returned. Confronting the player with black and white evidence that 50% of his or her overheads are missed carries more weight than the less specific, "Your overhead needs work." Charting becomes even more effective when you can compare your player's performance percentages with the higher norms of teammates and opponents.

Other kinds of data include videotaping and the presentation of biomechanical facts. The videotape can probably shock a player into awareness of a problem better than anything. For maximal effect, videotape the player while he or she is competing in a serious match, where any existing stroking weaknesses will be accentuated. If time permits, edit the tapes so the player can repeatedly see the weakness free of other match distractions.

Do not be reluctant to present biomechanical data. Because athletes are not usually schooled in the fundamentals of biomechanics, their basis for evaluation is not on the soundest of footings. For instance, if a player has a pronounced pause in the service backswing, you might discuss the mechanics section of this book that deals with timing problems. You can avoid scientific terms and hold thorough chalk talks in player's language. When the player realizes your recommendations are supported by biomechanical evidence, your advice gains credibility.

Set Goals

The second thing the coach can do is to convince players that technique changes are needed to help them set tennis goals. One method is to show players how current techniques might limit their future performance level. Not all players have well-thought-out goals for their tennis futures. Their goals often start and end with winning tomorrow's match. When they do have longer-term goals they may not have progressively planned objectives for meeting them. They might want to win the league championship, but may not have thought of precisely what they must do to accomplish this. Players with well-organized plans for 5 or 10 years down the road are rare.

Much interesting research has been done in recent years in the area of goal-setting in sports. This research strongly suggests that by helping athletes formulate goals, coaches can get them to work long and hard at major adjustments in their games. In the next paragraphs, I will briefly examine the key steps in effective goal setting and explain how to apply them to tennis players. (For a complete review of work done in the area of goal-setting for sports you may wish to refer to O'Block and Evans, 1984.)

Personal Choice

The first step in effective goal-setting is to attempt to get players to select their own goals. Research clearly indicates that players will work most diligently to achieve goals that they perceive to have set themselves. Coaches should begin by sitting down with each of their players and asking, "Where would you like to see your tennis game in the future?" The coach's role is not to dictate long-term goals, but rather to stimulate players to think of their own.

When asked to state long-term goals, some players will already have good ones in mind or will be able to develop some in response to the question. Other players will have trouble in thinking of goals, or will put forth unsatisfactory ones—unsatisfactory because they are well below the ability of the player and will not function as worthy challenges. Or (and this is often the case) goals may be unrealistically high, and attempts to achieve them will be futile.

Coaches can help players who have difficulty formulating good goals by making suggestions. The coach might ask one player if she would like to develop her game to the point of effectively hitting spin serves. Another player might be asked if he wants to try to become adept at an aggressive, attacking style of tennis. Such suggestions might strike a responsive chord with some players, who will then willingly spend many hours practicing new techniques the coach prescribes. A coach who finds it necessary to lead players in the formulation of goals must make sure to allow the players to make the ultimate selections themselves. Ascribe to them the credit for doing so. You want them working for themselves, not just for you.

Time Frame

Once the coach has helped the athletes verbalize some goals, the next step is to help them realize that achieving these goals may necessitate adoption of new techniques that will require long periods of practice time and initially lower their present level of play. Players sometimes do not realize the true amounts of hard practice time necessary to perfect the motor skills of tennis. If the coach does not make these realities known, the players may easily become discouraged when their performance suffers and they seem farther than ever from their adopted goals.

Do not underestimate the importance of coaching players to defer short-term gratifications in the interest of pursuing their goals. The ability to unflaggingly endure tough times is likely one of the most important attributes that separates great athletes from the not so great. Coaches can help players accept delays and endure difficulties by showing sincere enthusiasm and confidence that the players will ultimately achieve their goals. It helps if coaches can persuade players that they are engaged in a joint effort. The players are buoyed by the knowledge that the coach is anxious to do all he or she can to support them in pursuit of their goals.

Enabling Objectives

After the players have been advised of the difficulties and time frames associated with the achievement of their goals, the third critical step is for the coach to guide them in the establishment of what researchers call *enabling objectives*. These are nothing more than short-term goals—stepping stones leading to or enabling the achievement of long-term goals. Enabling objectives provide a blueprint of the specifics that need to be done.

Consider a player who has already set the goal of making next year's tennis team. The coach can involve the player in the process of selecting enabling objectives by asking, "What things do we need to accomplish to get us to our goal?" Listing the player's strengths and weaknesses will help stimulate discussion about which phases of his or her game require the most work. If the major obstacle is an inconsistent serve, this area is targeted for enabling objectives. If the inconsistency seems to be a function of inexperience rather than poor technique, an enabling objective might be to practice an hour of game-simulated serves 5 days a week for 6 months. (For this to be a reasonable objective, thought must be given to practice facilities. If for some reason sufficient court space is not available, use of a wall target might need to be arranged. For some excellent ideas on constructing wall targets, refer to Hoyle, 1985.)

Another objective for a server with proper technique might be this: "Within 3 weeks I will score _____ on a serving test." Serving test scores can provide good objective evidence of gradual performance improvements. (Although there are many tennis serving tests available, I suggest the one developed by Hewitt [1966], which provides a measurement not only of service accuracy but also of speed. Speed is determined by court markings that evaluate the length the balls bounce.)

If the player's service inconsistency is attributed to faulty technique, such as an extraneous loop in the backswing, enabling objectives must be designed to correct the fault. Here are some examples: "I will practice for _____ hours my new serve in which I do not loop my racket in the backswing." Or, "I will achieve a score of _____ on a serving test while using the new, loopless technique." Or, "I will get _____ % of my first serves in during my scrimmage matches while using the new technique."

For any of the above objectives to be effective, it is critically important to monitor whether or not the new technique is being faithfully followed. This checking should be done on a planned schedule by the coach, an assistant, or by the player viewing videotapes.

Note an important characteristic about the enabling objectives given as examples. They are not directly concerned with defeating this week's opponent, winning a particular tournament, or beating a certain record. Objectives that concentrate on win-loss outcomes are risky because they are not always achievable. Players who unswervingly practice skills and adopt the technique changes that have been set will not always win. Luck and a player's adversaries will play significant roles in the number of matches he or she wins. Needless to say, the sincere coach must sometimes subordinate his or her own won-lost record to the long-term welfare of players.

Failure to achieve goals is a discouraging experience that can lead to decreases in perceived ability and motivation to continue striving to develop skills. Consequently, research suggests coaches get their players to concentrate on performance rather than on winning. Coaches must help players see winning as a by-product of improving performance. Players can lose matches and yet be happy about achieving objectives. Conversely, players also need to realize they can win matches without achieving objectives. The setting of objectives geared to performance is a good way to develop such an orientation.

Making Goals Stick

The final step in the goal-setting process is to actually write down the jointly selected goals and enabling objectives. As the saying goes, if you want someone to display commitment to a goal, you should "ink it, don't just think it." A goal in writing serves as a contract. The coach can increase the extent to which the contract functions as a reminder by making a copy for the player to hang where he or she will frequently see it. Sometimes, depending on the personalities of the team members, these individual goals can be effectively posted for the whole team to see. Posting may enlist cooperation of other players and thereby produce additional social incentives for a player to achieve his or her objectives.

Whether or not you post individual goals, it is usually wise to make it public when players achieve their goals and objectives. This can be done by announcing such achievements to the rest of the team, posting achievement charts, and relaying these accomplishments to reporters and publicists. Think how encouraging it would be for a player who has lost a number of matches to read the following quote from in the newspaper: "I am very proud of this player for showing courage in working at a new technique that will eventually improve her game. Her present losses do not truly reflect her ability."

REFERENCES

Groppel, J.L. (1984). *Tennis for advanced players: And those who would like to be.* Champaign, IL: Human Kinetics.

Hay, J., & Reid, J. (1982). *The anatomical and mechanical bases of human motion.* Englewood Cliffs, NJ: Prentice-Hall.

Hewitt, J.E. (1966). Hewitt's tennis achievement test. *Research Quarterly,* **37**, 231-240.

Hoyle, J.E. (1985). Targets for practicing tennis serves. *Journal of Physical Education, Recreation and Dance,* **56**(3), 60-61.

O'Block, R.R., & Evans, F.H. (1984). Goal-setting as a motivational technique. In J.M. Silva III & R.S. Weinberg (Eds.), *Psychological foundations of sport.* Champaign, IL: Human Kinetics.

Plagenhoef, S. (1970). *Fundamentals of tennis.* Englewood Cliffs, NJ: Prentice-Hall.

CHAPTER 7

The Best Tennis Drills

There are thousands of tennis drills. Some coaches and players adamantly recommend certain drills, whereas others advocate different ones just as strongly. How can coaches judge what tennis drills are best? In the last 10 years researchers have extensively investigated the effects of different types of practice drills on the learning of motor skills. This research has produced two very interesting findings that can help coaches make wise selections.

One of these discoveries is that how well a skill is learned is greatly affected by the extent to which performers must vary their practice performance. For example, players who wish to develop a good forehand ground stroke could spend a large part of practice drills fielding moderately paced, waist-high balls. And all the balls could be hit, for example, to the same crosscourt target so that players would not have to make big stroke adjustments. Researchers call this a *low variability* type of practice because players do not have to significantly vary their shots. On the other hand, players could attempt to develop good forehand ground strokes by organizing drills that require them to make rather extensive adjustments in their shots. In a *high variability* form of stroke, players must play low- and high-bouncing shots and hit balls both down the line and at short angles.

Which of the two approaches is the more effective? Based on research, high-variability practice appears much superior. The research suggests that players who practice a wide variety of forehand ground strokes would be much better at hitting high- and low-bouncing balls and more able to accurately hit down-the-line and short-angle shots. Also, such players would be able to adjust to types of forehand ground strokes that have not been practiced. They would even be able to hit waist-high crosscourts as well as (or better than) players who spent most practice time drilling only on waist-high crosscourt shots.

The other finding regarding practice drills is that the sequence in which a performer practices different motor skills, or variations of a motor skill, pronouncedly affects the quality of learning. One possible order of practicing different shots is to hit several overheads, then some volleys, then some ground strokes. This is called *blocked* sequencing because all shots of one type are chunked together in a practice block. An opposite way to practice the same shots is to switch from one shot to another—an overhead, then a volley, then a ground stroke, and so on. This method of practice is called *mixed* or *randomized* sequencing.

Players practicing only serves can also choose between blocking practice trials or mixing them up. They could hit only flat serves first, then only spin serves, which would be blocking. Or they could practice flat and spin serves in mixed or random order, frequently switching between the two.

Motor-learning research strongly supports randomized sequencing practice trials that require players to frequently switch from one skill (or skill version) to another. Although players have been found to perform better during practice when they are allowed to block their trials, this type of practice does not well prepare them to handle game-like situations, which usually call for a highly random order of shots (Figure 7.1).

The balance of this chapter is divided into two main sections: practice variability and sequencing of practice trials. Each section is an in-depth discussion of the practical applications research in these areas can have for the selection and design of better tennis drills.

PRACTICE VARIABILITY

As stated, practice variability research indicates that the more variable the practice experiences, the better players learn to make needed adjustments in motor skills. Because tennis demands constant adjustments, it follows that coaches should minimize the time

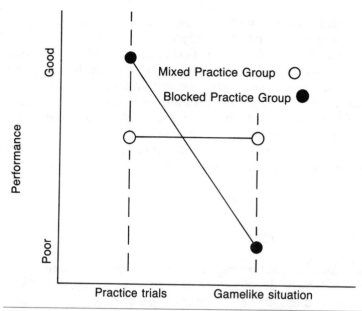

Figure 7.1 Performance levels are high when coaches allow players to block practice trials.

allotted to drills that do not require much response variability. Wise coaches design drills and manipulate environmental conditions to demand a variety of stroking adjustments.

Drills designed to *groove* a swing are typically the ones that elicit relatively low response variability. A grooving drill has a player standing in one place on the court repeatedly hitting the same shoulder-high volleys to the same spot under the same environmental conditions. The popularity of such drills is due in part to the fact that players perform them well. Consequently, players (and some coaches) believe that such drills are the best way to learn. Players and coaches who defend these kinds of drills use terms like *consistently* and *automatically* in reference to making the shot. "I can refine this shot," they say, "to the point of never missing it," and "If I can handle this easy shot, the more difficult ones will take care of themselves."

But will they? This kind of reasoning might sound good, but research simply does not support it. The results of many studies clearly suggest that spending a lot of time on low variability practice does not best prepare a player for a match. Repeatedly hitting the same shoulder-high volleys will not prepare the player to cope with low volleys, balls that stretch or jam the player, balls that approach rapidly, or balls that float. And, importantly, repeatedly hitting the standard shoulder-high volley is not even the best way to learn to make shoulder-high volleys.

The argument applies to all drills that require minimal stroke variation. These drills are not *bad* for a player's game, but they are not nearly as effective as drills that demand a diversity of swings. Prudent coaches take a close look at all their drills and make sure that most of them do not fall into the grooving category. In their place, they develop drills that foster greater practice variability.

Now let's consider some high-variability drills and how they can be coordinated with environmental settings to promote a better practice session.

Drilling With a Partner

When teammates are drilling together they should intentionally hit shots that require a wide spectrum of responses from each other. This is true regardless of the stroke they are primarily practicing. Two example drills will illustrate how to maximize shot-making variability. Once we have shown how to vary partner volleying and overhead practice, you will readily see how to apply similar techniques for other shots.

A volleying drill begins with a feeder and a container of balls. The feeder is instructed to hit shots that require all types of volleys. The feeds should include soft and hard shots, topspin and backspin, low and high balls, and shots both down the line and crosscourt. The volleyer adds further variety to the drill by moving around, so that some of the shots are hit from no-man's land, others from just inside the service line, and others from very near the net. The volleyer should also attempt to vary the direction of his or her shots so that some are crosscourt, some down the line, and some are stop volleys. The speeds of the volleys should vary, as well.

A partner drill for overhead smashes starts with a feeder dropping and hitting lobs of diverse trajectories. The lobs should range from extremely high ones to those on the borderline of being high volleys. Similarly, some lobs should be deep and others short. Some should be directed over the backhand side and others should require a rapid shift to the forehand side.

Meanwhile, the smasher's job is to mix spinning defensive returns with forceful kills. The returns should be attempted crosscourt, up the middle, and down the line. Another means of maximizing variability is for the smasher to begin the drill from different positions. An initial position virtually on top of the net will force the player to field shots while moving back. A deep starting position will require forward movement and a different kind of overhead execution.

These two example drills differ from most partner drills commonly used by coaches in one fundamental way. In these drills the players do not attempt to hit the ball back and forth *to* each other. It is fair to say that most traditional partner drills emphasize keeping the ball in play, which usually means players will have long rallies with low shot variation. In these drills, variety is not planned and happens only by accident. The players seldom have to perform unorthodox movements. They do not have to adjust their swings to nearly the degree that playing a match requires. In some drills players are not even expected to attempt the more difficult shots when they present themselves. It is as if they are coached to work hard at the shots within their immediate range and not worry about the unusual ones—which is hardly what occurs during a match.

Rallying drills have their place. They are appropriate during warm-ups and can be an important part of everyday practice drills. Sometimes you simply may not have the court space or adequate balls to implement the high-variability drills. Besides, keeping a ball in play has an exciting, challenging element. It can be great fun, it permits the concentration of many shots in a limited time period, and players derive satisfaction from the evidence of skill improvement in the form of longer rallies. Coaches are rightfully reluctant to cause players to miss out on this kind of morale-boosting experience.

Perhaps I can clarify my partner drill recommendations by outlining four specific suggestions.

1. Have a preseason talk with your players about how practice variability can improve their games. Your coaching prestige will be enhanced when you show them you have invested the time and effort to learn how skills are best learned and have developed some practice plans to help them. When players are aware of the potential benefits, they will enthusiastically work at new variability practice drills both during and outside of practice.
2. Incorporate some high-variability drills into most of your practices. The examples posed earlier should guide you in your planning.
3. Continue to use rallying drills. Although these drills may not provide highly variable experiences, they offer other benefits. Having both types of drills in your playbook will enable you to change drills frequently, which helps avoid motivational problems associated with stale practice sessions.

4. Use compromise drill versions of the above types of drills. For instance, use rallying drills in which the players consistently hit shots right to each other and only occasionally throw in a zinger. The zinger does not have to be an attempt at an all-out winner, just a shot a bit harder or wider than normal. In such a drill the challenge might be in attempting to get the ball back under control.

Lastly, there may be a need to address those coaches who find high-variability partner drills or compromise versions unacceptable. You love rallying drills and are reluctant to instigate anything that might terminate rallies sooner than necessary. I urge you to at least consider discouraging your players from always assuming the exact same rallying positions. Do not always allow volleyers to belly up to the net; demand that sometimes they volley from deeper in the court. Encourage your ground strokers to sometimes play their shots from inside the baseline and sometimes from well behind the baseline. These kinds of slight changes can painlessly be added to your drills and will interject some valuable variety.

Another painless procedure is to frequently rotate rallying partners. Different players hit different kinds of strokes and demand different response adjustments. Keep one caution in mind when rotating partners. Although rotation is desirable, some degree of skill-level matching should be maintained. A mismatch in partner skill will likely result in less variability for stronger players. Weaker players will either not be able to return shots or will hit shots poor in diversity (they might not have the ability to hit hard shots with various spins). Such situations cheat the more talented or more experienced players of opportunities to learn to handle different shots. Also, in mismatch situations the better players sometimes feel obliged to limit their shot variety to avoid overwhelming the weaker player.

Drilling and the Environment

In our discussions to this point we have considered two basic ways of increasing the variability of players' swings. One way was to change the flight characteristics of balls hit to the players by varying speeds, spins, and directions. The other way was to have players hit balls with different speeds, to different targets, and from different court positions. This section explores how environmental conditions can be used to foster swing alterations, placing different task demands on players.

One environmental factor is the wind. Hitting into the wind as opposed to with the wind causes a diversity of responses. Whereas hitting into the wind requires big, forceful swings, playing with the wind calls for shorter, more controlled shots.

Although no studies have been done on the effects of practicing in windy conditions, practice variability research would strongly support players' doing so. Stroking adjustments demanded by a strong wind prepare players to compete under such conditions—and with spring schedules, wind-blown matches are more the rule than the exception. Coaches probably err in assuming that because player performance suffers in the wind they should move practice inside or postpone it. Adverse conditions that require major stroke adaptations are probably ideal learning experiences.

I am so convinced of the importance of practice variability that I believe coaches should actually seek opportunities to practice in the wind. If players are properly attired and warmed up as prescribed in the physiology section of this book, occasional practice in even strong wind is justifiable for those players with good swing mechanics.

Playing in the wind is one way of taking advantage of the environment to change the swings of your players. Other ways are playing on different surfaces, playing with different types of balls, playing indoors and out, and even playing with different types of rackets. Because changing environmental influences are valuable learning experiences, coaches should expose their players to them.

This is not to suggest that coaches subject their players to such controllable environmental variables immediately before or during a match. Assuredly athletes need to become accustomed to the balls, the playing surface, and so on. But usually one day's practice or less is sufficient to readjust to playing circumstances. Players with a limited range of experiences need to practice adjusting to various circumstances and to changes in the environment. Many young players fall in love with a favorite kind of racket and marry it. Or they develop an early aversion to playing either indoors or outdoors and avoid doing so with a passion. Some players will not stoop to playing with balls more than an hour old. Coaches surely recognize the types.

The time will come when these people must compete under unfamiliar conditions. Tournaments will be moved inside, racket strings or frames will break, balls will not be promptly replaced when they become light or fuzzy. Even if players miraculously avoid such unexpected occurrences, variable practice experiences produced by environmental factors still make sense. The variety improves players' overall ability to make the shot variations that will be required of them.

The world's finest players are highly competent on all types of surfaces and in all kinds of wind conditions. Granted, the Navratilovas and Lendls play better on a surface suited to their styles, but they win on *all* surfaces. Of course these players have great innate ability, but isn't it conceivable that their varied experiences of playing under all conditions contribute to their greatness?

Take as an example the strong 1984 U.S. Davis Cup team that lost on clay in the finals. Some might suggest that the loss stemmed from Sweden's specialized practice on clay and the lack of specialization by the American team. Motor research fully supports the idea that training drills should be designed to closely approximate game conditions. As we know, clay courts favor a groundstroking style of play, whereas hard courts place a premium on aggressive attacking and volleying. To be successful on clay, players must spend a large part of their practice on that surface.

However, concentrating the majority of practice on the conditions to be encountered in a tournament is one thing—limiting virtually all practice to those conditions is something else. Adherence to the principle of practice variability suggests that players benefit from experiencing conditions dissimilar to those they will most likely encounter. In actual practice, the vast majority of American players grow up almost exclusively on fast courts. Until the time comes when Americans have a significantly larger amount of practice on clay and still lose to those who have specialized more, we have no good reason to believe that variability should not be planned into our practices.

Drilling and the Beginner

I have suggested incorporating various procedures and environmental factors that require players to make adjustments in their swings. Coaches might assume that practice variability and playing under different conditions is fine for players who already possess excellent swing mechanics and are good enough to handle and learn from these more difficult kinds of drills. But in regard to weaker players, or players revamping a technique, coaches might consider high-variability drills too difficult, thinking the drills might cause the players to become more frustrated and that their techniques could suffer.

Such thoughts are sound and need to be addressed. My stance is that a beginner (or an old hand revamping a stroke) needs drills that produce response variations. Research shows practice variability is an important ingredient for people just beginning to learn a new skill. Coaches simply cannot afford to ignore this.

Agreed, coaches must be careful not to overwhelm beginners with unrealistically difficult tasks. We cannot have beginners participating in a drill where they are completely unsuccessful and correct form is unattainable. Avoid the problem of undue task difficulty by systematically introducing variability into practice. For example, assume you and a player have agreed that his or her backhand drive needs a major change. Perhaps you have read about the mechanical advantages of a two-handed backhand and have decided a switch to it is in order.

Do not have this player engage in the normal procedure of spending lengthy practice sessions standing in one place, receiving consistently paced balls, and trying to return them down the center of the court. Neither have the player immediately running, hitting severe slices, and trying to spin short-angle passing shots. Instead, introduce just one of the elements of variability that we have discussed. For example, keep everything relatively constant except the height of the ball bounce. The balls could be tossed so that one must be played at shoulder height, the next at knee height, and the next somewhere in between. Then, in another practice session, manipulate the speed of the delivered balls. Ask the player to try different shots, such as soft crosscourts or hard down the lines. Or introduce a moving element into the drill. All these variations should be introduced *singly*. Eventually, you can start altering a couple of variables at a time. Untimately, the player should have to deal with multiple variables that begin to resemble match environment.

You can see that the idea is systematic progression. Do not overwhelm the player with too much at once, but do immediately begin teaching how to make adjustments. Some coaches have done players a disservice by not progressively introducing them to coping skills. Players who have been trained to hit waist-high, moderately paced ground strokes will have their form break down in competition and consequently become discouraged. Suddenly they are not hitting the shots they thought they had mastered. The swing they developed for the standard shot no longer serves them well. The range of their experience proves to be too limited to allow them to figure out how to generate different shot adjustments. As a result, they are unable to cope.

The primary requirement tennis places on us is the need to adapt shots to a changing array of demands. The strokes of tennis contestants must undergo constant adjustments to balls approaching at different speeds from different directions. Furthermore, players have to hit those uniquely approaching balls in different directions with various degrees of speed and spin. In short, with the possible exception of some serves, no two swings players make in a match can be exactly the same if they are going to succeed. When we keep a player from experiencing shot variations, we are only postponing the inevitable. There is no royal road to tennis success. It's better to systematically introduce practice variability from the start. By doing it this way, we facilitate the transition to the real tennis world.

Drilling With the Ball Machine

Unlike live opponents, ball machines cannot deliver balls in a highly variable way. Although some machines project balls with different speeds and oscillate to vary the direction, the speeds and directional changes they achieve generally vary much less than what players will encounter in matches. Furthermore, ball machines do not produce the dramatic spin variations of match play, an inability that reduces the swing variations required of players. Consider how much players must adjust their groundstroke swings to play low-skidding, sliced drives and high-bouncing topspin shots. Or how much they must adjust their overheads to hit topspin lobs rather than defensive, backspin lobs.

Because ball machines call forth relatively low response variability, their effectiveness in teaching players to make stroke adjustments is limited. For that reason, nonmachine drills are better for developing the adaptability skills of players. In most cases, coaches would be better off having people assume the role of the machine. Armed with a basket of balls, coaches, assistants, or teammates could be trained to efficiently feed balls to a performer in great variation—low skidders, exaggerated topspins, short balls, etc. This variability could be suited to each hitter's unique needs and abilities.

Even partner rallying drills, previously criticized for not producing enough stroking variety, are probably better than ball machines for teaching swing adaptability. Watch the different swing variations one of your players makes during a rallying drill. Then watch this same player hitting against the machine. You will see that the machine results in a swing that does not change much from ball to ball.

Again, however, this criticism does not mean that coaches should relegate the ball machine to the storage bin. Ball machines can be an integral part of nearly every practice, and a scheduled check-out plan for off-day and off-season machine use would be beneficial. One advantage to ball machines is that they are available when trained coaches, assistants and teammates might not be. They are also good to have when you cannot find an evenly matched partner for a particular player.

Another reason for using ball machines is that they are an ideal practice aid for someone beginning to learn a new swing pattern. The machine consistently projects balls with virtually no variability—an ideal learning opportunity for beginning ground strokers. Smashers and volleyers could use the machine in a similar way, introducing an element of variability by attempting to hit both crosscourt and down the line.

Ball machines are also excellent for holding everything constant as they introduce limited variations for beginners. For instance, a setting that keeps everything standard except for a gradual increment in directional variability provides a good learning progression for a beginner. Likewise, shooting balls at different speeds provides a worthwhile beginning drill for all strokes.

Again, machines *by themselves* do not provide enough practice variety to prepare advanced performers for match situations. However, the third good reason for incorporating ball machines in practice is that, when used with ingenuity, they can create a reasonably varied practice experience—varied enough even for the advanced player. Most machines can be set at different intensity levels, a feature permitting application to numerous different types of shots. For example, the volleyer could practice hitting balls that are both rifled and blooped, the smasher could adjust the intensity to produce very high and very low lobs, and so on.

Directional settings should also be periodically regulated to produce more than just forehand and backhand alterations. By using different oscillating selections in conjunction with differing machine placement, players are forced to move different distances to hit returns. Although coaches sometimes set machines to create moving ground strokes, they seldom do so for other shots, which is strange considering most of the lobs, smashes, and volleys players must execute in match play will certainly be on the move.

Besides using different machine settings, players can augment swing variety by assuming different court positions to create different return attempts. We have already considered different starting positions and shots to create response variety, but here are some specific suggestions. A player might set up in a doubles net position as though his or her partner were serving. The machine is aimed to simulate down-the-line and crosscourt service returns. The player plays the crosscourt returns as if poaching in a match, waiting as long as possible before moving quickly to intercept and hit the ball. For the shots the machine directs down the line, the player will generally attempt to put the ball away by hitting crosscourt into the gap between envisioned opponents.

One final comment wraps up the discussion of ball machines. Accelerating advances in scientific technology will continue to affect tennis. We can envision the time when practice variability will be widely recognized as an effective practice strategy and when technology will respond by designing ball machines capable of providing much more variety than today's models. With the push of a button, the machine will deliver an assortment of ball trajectories; another push and it will produce a still wider range. Other buttons will propel balls with different spins. There are already some machines on the market with progressive settings. The extent of these progressions can only expand, based more and more on scientific research data. But until the day machines become this sophisticated, their limitations must be recognized. Coaches will have to use their intellects to get the most variability out of machines.

SEQUENCING OF PRACTICE TRIALS

Ball machines of the future will be programmable to deliver balls in a diversity of sequences—three balls to the forehand followed by three to the backhand, and so on. The reason for this is the contention of many experts that the order in which swings are made can profoundly affect how well a skill is learned. We have already seen that players learn motor skills best when practice sequences are mixed rather than blocked. Although performance levels in random drills are not as high during practice, these drills are much better at preparing players for game situations.

Why this is true is not entirely clear. Most experts believe the reason is related to the unequal amounts of effort required by the two practice schedules. Because the mixed practice is more difficult, players have to work harder and concentrate more intently on the skill required and the results produced, which results in a deeper learning experience than the automatic repetition of one specific skill.

Before applying the concepts I have described to the design of tennis drills, consider some recent related research findings. A few people have begun to wonder if completely mixed practice is the best way to learn motor skills. The documentation that mixed drills are preferable to completely blocked drills does not preclude that some intermediate level of blocking might be effective. Perhaps a player switching strokes every second or third trial would be better than the completely mixed procedure of switching after every trial.

Although few answers to this interesting question are available, current evidence hints that frequent switching (after every two or three attempts of a skill) is as good as and possibly better than switching after every trial. Not surprisingly, a strong confirmation of these new studies is that mixed and partially blocked practice sequences have definite advantages over completely blocked sequences.

To prepare for a tennis match it appears that a player should practice drills that are either completely mixed or predominantly mixed. However, this is not the case. It is safe to state that the vast majority of current tennis drills involve blocked practice for ground strokes, volleys, serves, etc. Many drills even go beyond the blocking of shot types. Sometimes coaches and players block within strokes, not only mass repeating ground strokes but actually blocking forehands and backhands. Still greater blocking is designed into drills where players are asked to keep backhand exchanges going, further narrowing the drill to consist of all backhand crosscourts.

Switch Strokes

The first specific drill suggestion is that players do more drills where they frequently switch from one completely different type of shot to another. For example, if they are fed balls, they should hit one or two ground strokes, come in and hit a couple of volleys, hit an overhead or two, then retreat a few steps and hit ground strokes again. This sequence should be repeated several times, perhaps varying the feeds to require both forehand and backhand shots. Serve-and-volley drills and drills in which players alternate hitting lobs and ground strokes are other examples of complete switching between shots.

It is not proposed that *all* drills be a mixing of completely different shot types. Good reasons exist for drills wholly devoted to serves, lobs, and so on. One reason is that players sometimes have a dire weakness in their shot repertoire that cries out for concentrated work. If a player's lobs are weak and important matches loom near, obviously he or she needs to spend time hitting lobs.

Another reason for using blocked drills is that they are highly manageable. When court space is at a premium, one court can accommodate four people working on one specific type of shot. Four servers can simultaneously practice, or two volleyers can work with two feeders. Switching from one shot to another necessitates more court movement and creates greater logistical problems.

Switch Skills Within Strokes

The second specific suggestion is that when using drills of one shot type it is best to avoid blocking within skill. Consider a situation where a player needs to concentrate on serving, either because he or she is having particular trouble with serving or because there is only court space to work on that shot. The player should continually switch between flat and spin serves. Serving actions might be staggered by serving and staying back, or serving and starting toward the net. Also, serves to the middle might be combined with wide serves. Instructing your players to visualize match situations as they practice encourages them to frequently change from one kind of serve to another.

Consider one last example. Just as there are different kinds of serves, there are different kinds of ground strokes. Coaches are better off using drills in which players frequently switch off among some of these variations rather than spending lengthy blocks of time on one stroke. Even when a player is weak in a specific area, continual switching is still the best way. For a player with a weak backhand, interspersed forehand shots are going to further improve the player's stronger forehand and make it more of a weapon. And the switching will increase the overall difficulty of the drill, forcing the player to concentrate harder when hitting the backhand.

CHAPTER 8

Drills Versus Scrimmage Matches

Once they have selected the best drills for their players, tennis coaches must decide how much practice time should be devoted to them. Coaches differ markedly on this issue. Some feel drills are all-important and have their players spend virtually their entire practice time assiduously working on drill after drill. Conversely, others view drills as being the obligatory salad before the meat of the meal. These coaches use a few drills to warm up, then go straight into scrimmaging.

To resolve the question of optimal drilling time, we need to realize that successful players must be able to do two basic things. First, they must be able to effectively execute the motor skills of tennis. We might think of these motor skills as sound mechanical techniques for the various strokes. The mechanics do not necessarily have to be identical for every player, but they must allow players to do a number of things. Players must be able to consistently hit the ball with a certain degree of speed and accuracy. They must be able to hit shots under a variety of conditions—that is, their swings must be adaptable. Finally, players must be able to perform these swings automatically; they are in trouble if they must think much about stroke technique during matches. Focusing on mechanics will interfere with attending to other important considerations, such as the ball, the opponent, and game strategy.

The second thing players must be able to do is consistently apply their motor skills to meet the needs of a match. To apply motor skills successfully, players need to do four things.

1. They must use court strategies. Proper court positioning and smart shot selections are important. Additionally, players must play those shots up to their capabilities.
2. They must adapt their strategy to the circumstances and the environment. Strategies cannot remain the same against different opponents with different abilities and styles of play. Types of court surface, wind conditions, temperature, and other environmental factors also need to be considered.
3. They need to quickly read the movements and anticipate the shots of both opponents and their own doubles partners. If players wait for events to occur before reacting, they will not have the opportunity to use their well-learned motor skills.
4. They must pace themselves both physiologically and psychologically. They must know when and how to conserve energy in matches and be able to recognize situations demanding peak effort. They must know their own body signs of fatigue and adjust their games accordingly. Psychologically, players must learn the important skill of maintaining concentration throughout matches and tournaments. Additionally, they must regulate anxiety and arousal to levels conducive to optimal performance.

Now that we see the player's task as twofold—motor skill execution and application of motor skills to match situations—we can better judge the relative importance of drilling and scrimmaging by analyzing how the two forms of practice contribute to improving tennis skills. We will first examine why drills have been found to be the most effective means of acquiring motor skills. Then we will consider how best to achieve the application of motor skills to a match.

DRILLS AS THE BEST MEANS OF DEVELOPING MOTOR SKILLS

Extensive research has clearly shown that performers learn motor skills much more efficiently by drilling than by participating in scrimmage matches. There are various reasons why this is true for all kinds of sports skills. It may be helpful to outline these reasons and consider some tennis examples.

One reason drills are effective for teaching motor skills is that they can easily be designed to suit the specific needs of the learner. For example, assume one of your intermediates hits poor topspin backhands. You know this player is going to have trouble developing a mechanically sound topspin backhand if he or she is simply thrust into a scrimmage and told to hit backhands with topspin. Even a scrimmage against a teammate of lesser ability will require the player to handle some difficult backhand shots that are by no means uniform in speed, spin, and height of bounce. The player will be attempting these shots from various court positions and will often be on the move or have little time to prepare. In short, the scrimmage will be too complex for this player. Unsound swing technique would be the likely and undesirable result.

A drill can easily be arranged to simplify the backhand task to match the particular stage of skill development of a player. For a less-skilled player this might mean his or her standing in one position and having balls delivered in a relatively consistent fashion. For a more advanced player some dimensions of the task could be made more complex while others remained constant. A drill might be designed in which balls are hit right to the player in a variety of speeds and bounces. Alternatively, balls could be hit with consistent speed but in various directions, requiring the player to move to make the shots.

Sometimes the value of a drill lies in its adaptability to systematically increase shot complexity rather than simplify it. You have probably witnessed practice matches that do not challenge a player with sufficient complexity to optimally develop a technique. For instance, a better player may not be challenged by a teammate's serve, which is likely less forceful than serves encountered in a tournament.

In such cases, drills can be designed to increase the challenge of the teammate's serves by allowing him or her to stand inside the baseline, hit over a lowered net, or use slightly worn balls (which bounce faster). These adaptations permit less-skilled players to get more serves in, hit harder, and swing the serves wider. Also, drill servers can stand on a platform to hit serves that simulate high-kicking serves.

If a player is a good service returner and has too easy a time hitting winners off a teammate's weak serve, you might find it necessary to restrict the area in which the return can fall, thereby providing the player with a challenge. Or you could tell the player his or her return must be hit under a line strung above the net or be successful at a high percentage rate. Obviously, with a bit of creativity, coaches can design drill conditions to meet the needs of all ability levels. There is never a need for a beginner to be overwhelmed or for an advanced player to be underchallenged.

Another reason drills are more conducive to motor skill acquisition than scrimmages is that during drills players can concentrate either on technique or on specific aspects of their shots, such as depth, spin, or crispness. Although players *can* think about these things while scrimmaging, the competition involved in a scrimmage often distracts them. Scoring points overrides the close monitoring of grip, follow-through, spin, and so on. Drills diminish this problem by establishing specific, tangible goals for players to achieve. Relieved of worrying about winning or losing a set, players are less apt to aimlessly bang the ball back and forth.

A third reason drills develop skills better than scrimmages is the obvious fact that, when properly designed, they provide much greater skill repetition in a given period of time. For example, if a player has a poorly developed overhead, the coach can organize a drill that has the player hitting 50 to 60 overheads in 5 minutes. Hours of scrimmaging might elapse before the player would hit 50 overheads. Coaches can design drills that concentrate practice time on any stroke that players need to improve.

SCRIMMAGES AS THE BEST WAY TO DEVELOP APPLICATION SKILLS

Now that we have established the importance of drills in the learning of motor skills, let us look at the other side of the coin. We have said that tennis success depends not only on motor skills, but also on appropriately applying those skills in match play. This involves court strategies, reading and anticipating, and pacing yourself physiologically and psychologically—all skills equally important to the motor skills. We all know players with good strokes who seldom win because they have not learned how to apply their skills in a match.

Not surprisingly, players generally acquire application skills more effectively from scrimmages than from drills. To teach players to apply motor skills in match situations, coaches must place players in situations that closely resemble match conditions. Players must experience these kinds of situations and discover what things work and what things do not.

By their very nature, drills create unreal, contrived situations. Such situations are good for motor skill development but tend to be detrimental to the learning of application skills. Consider the example of a doubles volleyer. First, from drills alone the volleyer may never learn such game strategies as the ideal volleying position in different match situations, when a volley should be played and when it should be left to the partner, or when it is strategically wise to direct the volley toward the net person and when it is better to hit it to the deeper opponent.

Second, drills may not prepare the volleyer to anticipate when an opponent might poach, lob, or volley down the middle. Drills either do not confront the volleyer with these situations or do so under altered probabilities. The point is that if the shots and opponent movements of the drill differ from what they will be like in the game, the player is not going to be trained to quickly react to particular situations when they occur "for real."

Finally, drills do not help develop the many psychological and physiological pacing skills players must learn. Maintaining concentration is a representative example. To successfully play volleys throughout a doubles match, a player must sustain a high level of concentration, and few of us are born with this skill. In fact, some players seem to have the concentration of a hummingbird. This ability to concentrate must be trained and the only way to do so is to have the player work at it through numerous long three-set matches.

DEVOTE A MAJOR PART OF TEAM PRACTICE TIME TO DRILLS

As it appears that motor skills and the application of those skills are of approximately equal importance to a player's match success, you would logically expect me to recommend a roughly equal division of practice time between drills and scrimmages. I do not.

Certainly we must ensure that the experiences of our players are not deficient in developing either motor skills or application skills. However, it does not necessarily follow that to achieve this balance we need to devote equal amounts of practice time to drills and scrimmages. Rather than a 50-50 time split, I advocate something in the range of 75-25. I have several reasons for tipping the scales in favor of greater emphasis on drills.

Drills Balance Scrimmages Outside Practice

Players typically get a lot of scrimmaging experience outside of practice. Practice time usually constitutes a relatively small percentage of the time a player spends on the court. More often than not, players are on the court after practice, on weekends, and during the off-season. They spend the majority of this time scrimmaging. Also, in the heart of your seasonal schedule one match or tournament seems to come tripping on the heels of another. These are fun, of course, but they cut into practice time that could be devoted to drills for the improvement of motor skills. A strong reliance on drills during the available practice time in part counters this imbalance.

Drills Provide Motivation and Variety

Motivation—of both players and coaches—is a second reason for spending more practice time on drills. At first this might sound strange. After all, most players enjoy the excitement of actual match play more than drilling. However, on closer examination we will see that a greater reliance on drills can increase the motivation of players.

Motor learning research clearly shows that changing, stimulating practice sessions are essential to optimal learning. When practice experiences are routine, people usually concentrate less on the job at hand and learn at a slower rate. The tennis coach who typically has players scrimmage for long periods of time risks having a degree of sameness creep into practice. If such a routine develops, the motivation of the players is likely to be mixed. Some players with good intrinsic motivation will be happy scrimmaging every day; others will not be motivated by constantly playing practice sets. Some coaches have difficulty understanding players in this second category. To these coaches it is inconceivable that anyone could tire of participating in a sport delightfully interesting as tennis. But it happens. In the eyes of many players the prospect of doing the same thing—any same thing—day after day, week after week, and even year after year can lead to flagging interest.

Heavy reliance on drills in practice serves to increase player motivation in a number of ways. If the coach keeps the drills short and snappy, they have the potential of adding variety to practice sessions. By using many different drills throughout the season, coaches avoid the same-old-thing syndrome. Also, players like the structure and the challenge of appropriately designed drills. Drills allow players to better see improvements they are making in their skills, giving them the good feeling that they are doing something worthwhile to improve themselves.

When drills are an integral part of practices, the motivation of coaches is improved for much the same reasons. Coaches also like variety. They like structured, purposeful practice sessions. They like to see tangible evidence that players are mastering skills. Furthermore, drills often involve coaches in active roles of interaction with players, where scrimmages tend to place coaches into passive spectator positions. As we saw in chapter 5, research clearly supports the effectiveness of active, dynamic instruction. Better learning results, and the prestige of coaches rises in the perception of the players.

Drills Supply Physical Conditioning

A third reason for allotting a large part of practice time to drills is that they serve to physically condition the players. Many coaches have not used tennis-related drills to condition their athletes because they believe fatigue interferes with learning of skills. Motor learning research has found this to be a baseless concern. High fatigue levels can produce decreases in skill performance, but, paradoxically, even in those situations where fatigue impairs performance, it does not normally impair learning. Performers benefit as much from practicing a skill when tired as they do when rested.

Such evidence suggests that drills can occasionally be used to simultaneously condition players and develop skills. Consequently, coaches do not have to feel that they must always schedule separate conditioning activities at the end of practice. Periodically scheduling conditioning activities earlier in practice adds variety and should not hinder the amount of learning. For many good tennis drills that can be effectively used to develop physical fitness, refer to the physiology chapters of this book.

CHAPTER 9

Improving Reaction Time

Tennis requires fast reactions. Players must constantly make quick decisions about where to be and what to do. The players quickest at making and implementing appropriate decisions will probably win. The great differences in reaction speeds of players are fairly evident. One players will see a ball fly by before being able to flinch. Another player will see the same ball in time to lean into it, meet it out in front of the body, and hit it into the open court.

Opinions differ as to why tennis reactions vary so greatly from player to player. There are basically two schools of thought. Some believe the differences in reaction speed stem primarily from variations in natural abilities. They view reaction time as an innate, fixed characteristic. Others put much more faith in the theory that reaction times can be improved with training. Whereas they concede that some players do appear to have intrinsically faster reaction times, they believe lightning-quick responses are not inborn but achieved mainly through hard work. To support their theory, they cite examples of how some players exhibit big improvements in reaction time over the course of years of practice.

Which school of thought is correct? Motor research supports the second view. Although research shows innate differences do exist, it also clearly demonstrates that, in all kinds of reaction-time tasks, practice can have dramatic positive effects. Changes that occur in reaction time over long periods of practice are typically *greater than* the differences we see existing among untrained people. Furthermore, the research definitely illustrates practice especially improves reaction times in situations where players must deal with a number of stimuli and choose from several possible responses. In these kinds of complex reaction-time tasks, it is not uncommon for people to learn to reduce their reaction times by more than 50%.

The fact that practice can significantly influence reaction time should be encouraging to tennis coaches, as it means nothing insurmountable is keeping your players from developing faster reaction times. The findings that complex reaction-time situations are especially susceptible to improvement through practice offer further encouragement, because tennis involves many complex reaction-time decisions. Indeed, the tennis player must sort through an incredible number of stimuli and choose one of many possible responses.

Although the research findings regarding the effect of practice on reaction time justify optimism, we must realize one critically important thing. Coaches cannot assume reaction times are always going to show big improvements just because players are practicing. They might not improve at all. The research simply indicates improvement is *possible*. This chapter discusses the three factors that affect reaction time. If we improve any of these factors, whether through practice or any other means, reaction times will also improve. However, if none of these factors shows improvement, no reaction time improvement will occur either.

This information raises the important question of whether or not the development of reaction-time skills should be left to chance. Should practices be planned as they traditionally have been in the hope that players will gradually, somewhat unconsciously, learn to improve those factors that affect reaction time? In the past, this is the way many have honed their reaction times and become excellent performers.

As you might suspect, I disagree that such an undirected approach constitutes the most effective way for today's players to develop their skills. We know much more today about what things affect reaction time. By acquainting themselves with these things, coaches should be able to make practices more systematic and purposeful.

To provide suggestions as to how to improve a player's reaction time, this chapter is divided into two main sections. The first takes a look at the factors motor research has found to affect reaction time. The second, constituting the greater part of the chapter, analyzes how coaches can use their knowledge about the factors affecting reaction time to help players learn to react faster.

We make no claims that by reading the chapter you will immediately be able to improve the reaction times of your athletes. Improvements come as the result of extensive practice. However, some practice procedures will contribute to better reaction times more surely than others. This chapter explains in no uncertain terms specific things tennis coaches should do to make practices as effective as possible. If your players want to evolve from court sloths to cats of the court, the work remains up to them.

FACTORS AFFECTING REACTION TIME

An early train of thought in reaction-time research was that delays in response were a result of the speed with which neural messages move through the body. It was known that neural messages had to travel from the sensory receptors to the brain and from the brain to the limbs before the muscles could respond. It seemed logical that this process might require a certain length of time, accounting for delays in reacting. Such thinking attributed innate differences in reaction time to the fact that some people have "better" neural pathways.

Improvements in reaction time as a consequence of practice could be explained by some type of refinement of the neural circuits; practice somehow cleared out the circuits so that messages could move more quickly.

Although the theory might appear credible, our current knowledge of the body's operation proves it wrong. Experiments have shown that neural messages move through the body at incredible speeds. In some human nerves the speed of conduction may be as high as 120 meters per second. Such speeds preclude neural transmission rates from affecting reaction time in any but the most minuscule, indetectable way.

If conduction speed, then, is not the cause of our delays in reacting to situations, what is? The answer lies in the brain. Marvelous as it is, the brain is responsible for slowing us down. When neural messages come from the eyes or other sensory source, the brain must process that information before it can send the appropriate command to the muscles. This processing of information in the brain requires valuable time that tennis players can ill afford.

Cleverly designed studies have shown there are three distinct things the brain must do. Because each of these processes requires time, we can henceforth think of them as the three factors affecting reaction times. They are (a) identification of what is seen, (b) selection of what response to make, and (c) organization of the messages to be sent to the muscles. We will consider these factors individually relative to tennis situations.

Factor 1: Identification of What Is Seen

To react, an individual must first be aware. The brain always requires some time to identify the stimulus received. The less clear the stimulus, the more time the brain requires. Visualize yourself in volleying position. Suppose you choose to concentrate on the type of backswing your opponent is making. Assume you know she tips off the type of passing shot she will play by taking different backswings. In this case, the type of backswing the opponent takes is the stimulus to which you must react. The brain requires some time after receiving neural impulses from the eyes to say, "Ah, she is taking a big looping backswing, which means a crosscourt return." The less distinctly characteristic the opponent's backswing, the longer it will take you to make the identification. For instance, the cue may be less apparent if the backswing differs only slightly from other kinds of backswings, or if it is disguised by other movements.

Factor 2: Selection of What Response to Make

After the brain has identified the stimulus, the next thing it must do is select the appropriate response. Suppose you are in the volleying position again and have already identified the stimulus as indicating a crosscourt passing shot. Is the correct response to backpedal, stay still, move toward the line, move diagonally forward, or none of the above? Research has shown that this selection process requires time, contributing to reaction-time delays, and that the more responses from which a player must choose, the longer it will take to decide.

Compare this to looking for a needle in a haystack. If the stack is big, the search will take a long time. If the stack consists of only a few strands of hay, the search will be brief. If you as volleyer do not *know* what response is appropriate, then your brain must choose from numerous possibilities. The list of possible responses just cited could be expanded to include ducking, jumping up and down, or any other physical movement your body can perform. On the other hand, if you have prepared yourself to choose between two or three appropriate responses, you will be able to react quicker when you see a volley taking shape. Reducing the number of possible responses from which you need to choose enables your brain to decide quicker.

Factor 3: Organization of the Messages to be Sent to the Muscles

After the stimulus has been identified and a response selected, the brain requires still more time to send neural messages to the muscles. Consider that for even a very simple movement like flexing a finger a large number of intricately timed messages must be sent to numerous muscles. Certain flexors must be instructed to contract in the right sequence and at the right intensity, while simultaneously extensor muscles must be receiving messages to relax in coordination.

Not surprisingly, research analyzing this organizing stage has found that the more complex a movement, the more time it requires. For example, hitting a volley requires the brain to do relatively sophisticated neural planning before sending messages to the muscles. Think of the elaborately timed neural impulses that must be sent to almost every joint of the body before it can move diagonally forward to intercept a crosscourt passing shot. Logically, of two tennis movements that vary in degree of complexity, athletes will take longer to initiate the more complex one.

APPLICATION OF REACTION-TIME FACTORS TO TENNIS

Knowing the three factors affecting reaction time provides a base from which we can systematically examine the ways players may be able to reduce reaction time.

Cues Causing Reactions

What can be done to reduce identification time? To answer this question, we must first determine what cues in the tennis environment cause a player to react. This is not an easy task because the stimulus environment is very complex. There are many cues that players can use, and players might use different kinds of cues in different situations. To simplify the issue, the cues used by athletes will be classified into three kinds: *ball cues, opponent cues,* and *game cues.*

Ball Cues

Probably one of the most common encouragements of instructors is to watch the ball. This advice is often justifiable when we realize that the cues derived from watching the ball are probably more reliable than all others. When a player sees the ball flying in a certain direction at a certain speed, he or she knows where and how fast to move.

Although ball cues are reliable, they do have one severe drawback. Players cannot utilize ball cues until the ball has been hit by the opponent. This presents a problem in situations where players have little time to react. Consider the situation where a player is close to an opponent and the ball is hit very hard at him or her. If the player waits to see where the ball is going, it will have passed before he or she can play the shot. In situations like this, players must learn to base their reactions on cues other than the ball. They must shift their attention to cues that give them earlier warning of what will happen. We will consider those cues later.

For now, we need to establish ball-cue situations. These occur mainly in singles matches, unless players are playing a very aggressive, attacking game. For example, when competitors are engaged in a baseline rally, they probably wait to see the ball coming before deciding where they should move. This waiting for the reliable ball cue will prevent them from being caught running in one direction as the ball goes behind them in the other direction. Only in unusual baseline situations will waiting for ball cues make it difficult for players to react quickly enough.

Tennis players also rely extensively on ball cues when returning serves. Service returners are not often seen moving in one direction when the ball goes in the other, which suggests that they wait to see the direction of the ball before moving. However, there are also certain service-return situations in which waiting for ball cues costs too much time, such as when a player is playing against a powerful server on a fast surface.

We have established that ball cues play an important role during groundstroke rallies, on service returns, and in other situations where time constraints are not severe. Next we will address what we might do to improve our players' reaction times to ball cues. Basically, there are two types of ball cues that players can use to react quickly: *trajectory cues* and *looming cues.*

Trajectory cues are those that players receive when watching the flight path of the ball. If they see the returning ball moving across in front of their opponent very rapidly with little dropping, they learn to interpret that the ball is coming crosscourt at a fast rate. If the ball is moving away from their opponent at a slow rate and with pronounced dropping, they interpret this as a shorter shot and react by moving toward the net.

Trajectory cues are the ball cues players most often rely on because they can easily pick up these cues during the earliest part of a ball's flight. This is important because only for slowly hit balls can players afford to wait for the ball to travel very far before responding. Obviously, if they can determine the ball's direction when it is only a few feet off their opponent's racket, they will be able to react faster than if they have to monitor the ball for 10 to 20 feet. Research has shown that skilled performers, by reading flight path cues, have learned to determine a ball's direction sooner than beginners. How can players best develop this early skill?

Unfortunately there is no trick to quickly learning to read flight path cues. Because ball trajectory cues are the ones players typically use in groundstroking and return of serves, coaches should instruct their players to concentrate on the first phase of the flight path. During these kinds of shots players normally do not need to be reading every move their opponents make, which might distract them from closely concentrating on ball trajectory cues. Nor should coaches have players identify the spin or fuzz of the approaching ball as early as possible. Some think doing this helps players pay closer attention to the ball. Looking for the fuzz might be good for players to do later in the ball's flight to keep them from taking their eyes off the ball too soon. But doing this as the ball comes off the opponent's racket may distract players from the real cues on which reaction time is based.

Providing players with as much experience as possible in reading trajectory cues can only serve to improve reaction time. This experience can best be achieved through drills in which players must respond to a wide assortment of differently paced and directed shots. Such practice will make them work at interpreting the different kinds of trajectories. Extended drills where players hit the ball at the same pace back and forth directly toward each other will not develop reaction time as well as a more scrimmage-like drill. Also, keep in mind that for *any* drill to optimally improve reaction time, players have to *try* to react as quickly as possible when making each return. Instead of just going through the motions, they should consciously challenge themselves to begin movements as soon as possible each time.

Whereas trajectory cues are undoubtedly the primary type of ball cue that performers use, they are not the only ones. The second kind of important ball cues are *looming cues*. Looming cues involve the player's ability to estimate the distance and rate of approach of objects by the perceived size of the object and the rate at which it appears to change. A good example of a looming cue is driving on a straight stretch of highway with a car approaching in the opposite lane. Although it is not always easy, people estimate the distance of the car based on its size. They also estimate its speed based on how fast its size seems to be changing.

Looming cues play an important reaction-time role in tennis when trajectory cues are not easily discernible, which happens in a couple of situations. One is when the ball is hit directly at the player. Such balls are the most difficult to judge because no trajectory cues are displayed. To the person toward whom it is coming, the ball appears almost stationary because it is not moving up, down, left, or right. In one sense this situation can be thought of as a trajectory cue indicating to players that the ball is coming straight at them. The problem is that this trajectory cue does not offer good information as to how fast the ball is coming. Consequently, players rely on a looming cue. If they can accurately gauge the changing size of the ball, players will know whether to move forward or backward and how quickly they should swing the racket.

Sometimes the background makes it hard for a player to judge a ball's trajectory. One case is movement in the background: It is very difficult to judge the ball when people, cars, or whatever are moving behind it. It is hard to determine whether the ball is moving in a certain direction, or if it just seems that way because something in the background has moved in the opposite direction. The second case of background complication is where there is nothing in the background. It is difficult and sometimes impossible to determine the direction of a ball when there is no reference with which to compare it. Hitting overheads and even high-tossed serves against a cloudless sky are prime examples of the difficulties in playing shots without good trajectory cues.

How can players effectively use looming cues in situations where trajectory cues are lacking? A practical first suggestion is to make sure some of your practice drills force your players to rely on looming cues. Because balls hit directly at players require the interpretation of looming cues, plan an occasional drill where balls are hit at players at randomly varied speeds. Random variation in ball speed is important because if players can predict the speed they will not be using the looming cues they need to develop.

Also, since some backgrounds cause problems with using trajectory cues, occasionally plan practices with these kinds of background conditions. Rather than avoiding hitting serves and over-heads on days when the sky is clear, take advantage of those days as unique learning opportunities. If any possibility exists that a player must play an important match on a court with a distracting background, coaches should plan some training under those con-ditions as well.

A final suggestion to improve the use of looming cues is to be sure that a player's eyesight is the best it can be. Many athletes in ball sports have pronounced visual defects; relatively few have 20-20 vision. This information seems to indicate that perfect vision is not essential to good performance in ball sports, as many players are still able to detect cues and react quickly. However, although visual acuity is not always necessary for reading trajectory cues, it may be critical in those special situations where looming cues make the difference.

Many players have experienced visual difficulties while play-ing during twilight hours or in a dimly lit indoor arena. Judging the speed of approaching shots under such circumstances is diffi-cult. As vast improvements have been made in glasses and soft con-tact lenses in recent years, there is no good reason for serious tennis players to take the chance of penalizing themselves a shot or two every match.

Opponent Cues

As discussed previously, situations arise in tennis where players cannot wait for ball cues to initiate reaction. This can be true for many situations, but especially for volleys and returns of volleys, smashes, and fast serves. What information do athletes use in these situations that allows them to begin preparing their reaction prior to the return of the ball? One cue could be opponents' movements, which tip players off about what shot is coming.

The usefulness of opponent cues varies greatly. Some players display many movements, "telegraphing" where their shots are go-ing. Of course, against these people, opponent cues are invaluable in aiding reaction time. Other players seldom make movements that tip off their shots. Of all players, probably rank beginners and ad-vanced players display the least reliable opponent cues. Beginners often do not know where their shots are going, and advanced players have learned to disguise most of their shots. If good players tip off their shots, the cues will be subtle—or will be decoys. Skilled players may intentionally display certain movements hoping that opponents read them and respond incorrectly.

In light of the above, the importance of opponent cues must be kept in perspective. Against most opponents your players are probably well advised to rely on cues sparingly. However, acknowledging their limitations, opponent cues can sometimes be instrumental in helping your players react faster.

Coaches should consider what their players should do to best utilize these cues. The first suggestion is that players become as familiar as possible with each particular opponent's game, as cues are often unique to the individual. Many competitors have idiosyncracies that tip off certain shots. The more your players compete against these players, the more adept they become at identifying those cues. Perhaps even better, have your players watch their future opponents play others. This is especially valuable because your players are free to give their undivided attention to picking up any such cues. Also, during actual play the opponents may pick up your players' cues quicker than your players learn theirs.

In observing opponents, your players should position themselves behind the end of the court opposite the person they will be playing. This perspective best displays the cues the opponent may betray. For example, recognizing that an opponent always hits down-the-line passing shots from an open position and crosscourts from a closed position can help players anticipate and intercept passing shots they might otherwise fall victim to.

Your players need to know what to look for when watching a future opponent play. What opponent movements normally indicate which shot will be forthcoming? No research has answered this question. However, there are a couple of cues that players might be able to use reliably against nearly all opponents. One occurs when they are receiving serves. Many servers will vary the speed and spin of their serves, which poses a reaction problem to receivers because they typically prepare differently to react to different serves.

The amount of spin a server puts on the ball depends primarily on where contact is made. The further back over the head the ball is contacted, the more the spin and the less the ball speed. The further out away from the body (within a reasonable range), the flatter and harder the ball will be hit. As there is nothing servers can do to disguise the location of the toss, this is an opponent cue. Your players can and should learn to use it.

The second opponent cue reliable against most players is late stroke preparation. Watching beginners play, it is all too painfully obvious when they are not getting their racket back in time to play the approaching ball. When they do manage to cleanly play the ball they will almost assuredly not hit a crosscourt return, as they cannot meet the ball out in front. Consequently, players who recognize late stroke preparation in an opponent know relatively well where the ball is coming.

Undeniably, it becomes more difficult to recognize when advanced players will be late on shots. They can sometimes be strong and quick enough with their wrists to flick the ball crosscourt. However, at times, all players, regardless of ability, are fortunate just to be able to reach a shot. It can be apparent that they do not have time to either get their racket back or position themselves to play the ball out in front. This is an important thing for players to watch for. When opponents are late in both racket preparation and positioning, they will likely have to hit the volley or ground stroke down the line. This is especially true for backhands because of the need to meet the ball further out in front to crosscourt a backhand.

Game-Situation Cues

The third type of cue that can serve as a stimulus for players originates from event probabilities and provides a means of making educated guesses. If we are aware that a particular event is more likely to occur than another, we can base our reaction on this information. For example, suppose one of your players knows that the opponent tends to hit most overheads crosscourt. When this situation arises, your player begins reacting to cover the crosscourt smash before the ball is even contacted. This is done based on the greater probability of this shot than of one being hit down the line.

Although game-situation cues might not be as reliable as the ball's trajectory or the opponent's movements, they can and often do serve as important stimuli. Ball cues appear too late in some situations; opponent cues appear early but are not always present and not always reliable. Considering the limitations of ball and opponent cues, game-situation cues must at times play a critical role in reacting quickly.

On Vic Braden's television series, "Tennis for the Future," an interesting finding was reported that illustrates the importance of game-situation cues. Braden's researchers attached a measuring device directly to the pupils of Vitas Gerulaitis' eyes. This instrument was capable of monitoring where Gerulaitis was directing his gaze while volleying. Gerulaitis, incidentally, was considered one of the fastest-reacting players in professional tennis. The researchers wanted to find out which opponent cues Gerulaitis was reading that enabled him to react so quickly and successfully.

The researchers claim to have found that Gerulaitis was not normally even looking at the groundstroker, let alone at a specific body part. At the time his opponent was executing a passing shot,

Gerulaitis was often looking into the stands or all around, which strongly suggests that he was not even trying to use opponent cues, but rather was using game-situation cues. He was reacting so fast because he was anticipating what was going to happen.

How can players learn these important game-situation cues to react as quickly as Gerulaitis? First, for situations where unusually rapid reaction is required, they must be taught to guess. Unusually rapid reaction is needed when the opponent is about to put away a high volley or a short overhead, or when a player has made a short approach shot and the opponent has an easy choice of passing shots. In such a predicament, unless the opponent is an erratic beginner who might hit the ball right at your player, your player has to guess. If your player does not guess, he or she will be left standing flat-footed as the ball passes or floats by overhead.

Granted, guessing will result in players sometimes going one way while the ball goes the other, which can be embarrassing. But suffering a little embarrassment is probably better than waiting and always being late. Your players can take consolation in the fact that the professionals guess wrong too.

What can your players do to read situations and consequently enjoy a higher rate of success? For one thing, they have to guess right more than half the time. But the most important thing is probably to learn their opponent's game. They can do this both by playing the opponent frequently and by observing the opponent playing others. Again, observing offers the most efficient learning opportunity.

Players can base game-situation cues on two things. The first is their opponents' preferences. Some players do not like to lob. Some like to hit forehand drop volleys. Some always hit second serves to the backhand side. The list could go on and on. Some opponents are very cooperative in their predictability, and your players need to take advantage of it.

Game-situation cues can and should also be based on opponent weaknesses, which effectively limit the responses your players need to anticipate. How many athletes are without an Achilles' heel? Not many. Look for your opponent's weaknesses and exploit them. A common weakness is the inability to consistently hit good backhand crosscourt passing shots. Instruct your players to generally move to take away the line and force opponents to make the more difficult shot. Much of the time opponents will choose not to attempt the crosscourt backhand and your players will be advantageously positioned for the down-the-line shot. If the opponents do attempt the crosscourt, odds might still be in your player's favor.

REDUCING SELECTION-OF-RESPONSE TIME

We previously used the "haystack" analogy to illustrate that the fewer responses a tennis player has to choose from in readiness, the more quickly one can be initiated. One of the major reasons experienced tennis players react much more quickly than inexperienced players is that they have learned the importance of preparing a limited number of responses to fast reaction-time situations. This section explains how this process applies in tennis situations.

Essentially, to reduce response-selection time players must learn to prepare the least number of responses for a particular situation. Experienced players know how they will respond to different events. For instance, they know the exact type of movement to make when a down-the-line passing shot is on its way. Similarly, they have a specific response ready for when a crosscourt pass is identified. Consider the following examples.

Suppose you are in the happy situation of having your opponent in trouble. She is at the net and you have an easy ground stroke to play from inside the baseline. The opponent must commit herself in either one direction or the other. Your task is to wait until she has committed, then to hit the ball in the other direction. To be able to wait long enough for your opponent to move, you need to program yourself. As you see the situation developing, think to yourself: Drive down the line if she does not move; topspin crosscourt if she moves. You are presenting the brain with a two-choice reaction-time menu. If you do not prethink the situation, you may not be able to wait until the opponent commits, because once she moves (or does not move) you have to select a proper response from a larger number of possibilities, which takes the brain much longer.

Take a second example. You are having difficulty reacting to a powerful serve in a doubles match. You could react faster if you decided in advance what kind of return to make. For instance, you might wish to block the shot crosscourt at the server. In essence, you have reduced a potentially complex response-selection situation to a two-response situation: a blocked forehand crosscourt or a blocked backhand crosscourt. Of course, if the net opponent is creating problems by frequently poaching, you might need to expand the size of your response-selection menu by at least one shot. It would behoove you to have a specific shot in mind in case the net person does move across to intercept your crosscourt return. It would delay your reaction time to wait to see the poach and then decide whether to lob, hit a slice shot behind, bang a topspin drive right at the net person, or try something else entirely.

These examples show how the thought process of reducing potential responses can help players react faster. You can probably think of many more reaction situations that your players can study and benefit from. Coaches can begin to improve their players' response-selection skills by working on them in practice. You can accomplish this by incorporating three concepts into practice sessions.

1. Design your drills and scrimmages to force your players to react rapidly. If an opponent (human or mechanical) projects easy, predictable shots to them, they will not need to make difficult response-selection decisions.
2. Emphasize to your players that in fast-reaction practice situations they need constantly to be telling themselves to prepare certain responses ahead of the shot. They might first try doing so on the service return, when they have ample time to plan a response. They should then begin to apply the same thought process to other phases of their game.
3. Tell your players that after each reaction-time situation they should analyze exactly what happened. They need to consider why they reacted quickly enough, or why they did not. They might ask themselves, Was I late because I had no specific response in mind to deal with that shot?

One word of caution about the response-selection process. Players should be aware that when they prepare to make some responses they will react more quickly to them only at the expense of reacting more slowly to the responses they have not prepared. There is definitely a trade-off. For instance, suppose you are in volleying position and have limited your choices to either moving to cut off the crosscourt or moving to cover the line. By having mentally placed these two responses in a state of readiness, you will be able to initiate them more quickly than you otherwise might have. However, if the opponent surprises you with a lob, your reaction to it will take significantly longer than if you had not been anticipating the two passing shots.

Let's conclude this section by reiterating that limiting response selections can play an extremely important role in reducing reaction time. This possibility is not often considered by players and instructors, yet the best players surely use it to their advantage in many situations. Admittedly, using game-situation cues is a sort of gambling process, so if players are not in a situation that requires them to react especially fast, they should not subject themselves to possible miscalculations. If someone is hitting slow serves to them, they might be better off not limiting their options with preconceived plans. They might wait to evaluate the incoming serves and select the best riposte in each case.

Be that as it may, many times reactions must be instantaneous and players do not have the luxury of weighing possibilities. In such instances they must be aggressive and take some chances. A key point is that players can take chances and still have the odds in their favor. The majority of situations in tennis demand only two or three responses. Performers are not dealing in brinkmanship when they decide to be ready for a couple of the most likely contingencies.

REDUCING REPONSE-ORGANIZATION TIME

As you recall, the third phase of processing in the brain that affects reaction time is the organizing of responses. After a stimulus is identified and a response selected, time passes while the brain organizes the neural messages that need to be sent to the muscles. The more complex the response movement, the longer it takes to complete this organization process.

The movements made in tennis are mainly those used to run after and swing at the ball. Obviously, great differences in movement complexity exist between one player and another as they perform the same running and hitting. In volleying, one player might simply step across in front of his body, barely move the racket from the original high ready position, and then slightly extend his shoulder to punch the ball. Another player might flex her knees, jump up, shuffle a step or two, gyrate the racket a bit, use some combination of wrist-elbow-shoulder joints to swing forward, and then display a fancy follow-through accompanied by an idiosyncratic head movement. Differences in movement complexity are surely present in all phases of the game—in the way people run, slide sideways, backpedal, hit ground strokes, and so on.

Instructors often attempt to simplify the movements of their students, usually because they rightly believe excessive movements increase the movement time of the players. An extra loop in the backswing is corrected because it is seen as delaying the swing. A student preparing to hit an overhead is instructed to keep the racket behind his or her head because the smashing movement can be completed most quickly from that position.

Instructions such as these that are helpful in reducing movement time may also reduce reaction time. The response-organizing time required to make a compact punching volley is far less than that of an elaborate volley. The simpler the movement, the sooner the player can initiate the shot.

Understanding that movement complexity affects reaction time as well as movement time suggests that you might wisely double your coaching efforts to eliminate excessive motions in any of your players' movement skills. You should strive to eliminate not only those extra movements that affect movement time, but also those that do not. Tennis players are usually better off without such apparently harmless movements as fancy follow-throughs, head or pelvic motions, and even facial expressions. These movements, like the rest of their swings, must be organized ahead of time and thus are included in response-organization time.

Do not construe these recommendations to mean that every player must alter his or her swing and locomotor skills to the point that everyone looks alike on the courts. Players possess different abilities and have bodies that are mechanically unique. These factors will and should result in different styles. However, it is recommended that you simplify each player's particular style. For each of them there exists a *range of correctness* outside which he or she will needlessly be taking on increased response-organizing freight. Be particularly careful not to allow players to emulate the extraneous mannerisms of their favorite tennis professionals. Incorporating these into their own styles can be more harmful than they believe.

In this chapter and others we have repeatedly criticized the stereotypic drills where players know how and where the balls are going and play the same shots over and over. Research evidence shows these types of drills fail to effectively improve many aspects of the tennis player's game. However, from a response-planning viewpoint, such drills may serve an important function by providing many repetitions in a short period of time. If players have already mastered a good moving or stroking technique, coaches might prescribe such drilling to promote antifatigue fitness and reduced reaction time.

CHAPTER 10

Reducing Mis-Hits and Misdirected Shots

Probably all coaches have players on their teams with reasonably sound stroking techniques who still make an inordinately high number of unforced errors because of mis-hit and misdirected shots. Few coaches seem to have a good solution for this serious problem. Coaches often try to get these players to relax and concentrate more, telling them, "Just watch the ball," and "Concentrate—think about what you're doing." Another approach used to improve ball contact and direction is to encourage the players to slow their swings. "Just try to meet it," coaches say. "Easy does it. Take a nice, smooth swing. Slow down."

Concentration and anxiety-level problems are significant factors in misplayed shots; this subject is addressed in the sport-psychology section of the book. This chapter examines the effect of a slower swing on directional errors and mis-hits. Motor researchers have investigated the effects different speeds of movement have on motor performance and have come up with some surprising results. Once you are aware of these discoveries, you may never again coach tennis swings in quite the same way.

Mis-hit and misdirected shots are thought to occur for two reasons. First, *timing errors* could be responsible. If players do not time their swings properly the racket will arrive either too early or too late at the hitting area. A slightly early swing produces more of a crosscourt shot than was intended; a slightly late swing produces a shot wider than intended. Also, a mistimed swing can result in the ball not hitting the racket's sweet spot, further deflecting the ball in an unintended direction.

The second reason for misplayed shots can be *racket positioning error*. Players who fail to precisely control the racket's position in the hitting area will mis-hit shots because the ball will miss the sweet spot. A higher-than-intended swing path results in the ball contacting the lower part of the racket, whereas a lower-than-intended swing path makes the ball meet the upper section of the racket.

The first section of this chapter considers some motor research regarding how changes in movement speeds affect a player's ability to time movement. The second section looks at research findings about how changes in movement speeds affect positioning errors. The third section suggests how tennis coaches can apply research findings to reduce both timing and positional errors, thus decreasing the number of mis-hit and misdirected shots.

RESEARCH ON MOVEMENT SPEED AND TIMING

Motor laboratory studies have investigated the effect different movement speeds have on timing. For example, two groups of people are asked to move a lever through a distance and cause it to arrive at a certain location at the same time as an outside stimulus. The stimulus may be a light moving across a screen or an object sliding down a track. One of the groups is asked to move the lever at moderate speed, whereas the other group is asked to move it at near maximal speed. The amount of time that the subjects' movements arrive too early or too late is precisely measured to determine the size of their timing errors. Different kinds of such studies have produced strikingly similar results. They show the faster-moving groups as better able to time their movements to coincide with the arrival of moving stimuli.

There are two reasons that people can better coordinate their movements with a stimulus when they move near maximal speed. First, with fast movements people are able to watch the moving target longer before having to start their movement. This permits a better estimate of when the target is going to arrive at the contact area. Second, the faster movements improve timing because movements can be made more consistently. That is, people moving at maximal speed are able to make each of their movements at very near the same speed over and over again. People who move at moderate speeds show more timing fluctuations from trial to trial. They do not seem able to precisely repeat the speed of movements. This inability contributes to their inaccuracy in coordinating their movements with that of the target.

If this finding surprises you, try a simple demonstration. Hold a stopwatch in your hitting hand and place your hand in the position from which you normally begin your forehand or backhand ground stroke. Start the watch just as you begin your swing, and stop it at the point where you would be contacting the ball. Try this movement several times as you attempt to make the movement in 2 seconds. Note how many fractions of a second your movement times deviate from the 2-second target.

Now try the same task while attempting to make the movement in one second. Again note by how many fractions you are missing your target time. If you do enough trials at both speeds, you will find that your movement consistency will be superior during the faster trials.

These research findings have definite implications for the timing of tennis swings. They indicate that faster tennis swings probably allow players to better time their shots. First, as in the laboratory experiments, players must accurately estimate when an approaching target (the ball) will arrive at a specified point. A fast swing allows the players to watch the approaching ball longer before they must start swinging, and the later players can wait, the better they will be able to predict the ball's exact arrival time.

Second, fast swings should enhance timing in that faster movements can be made more consistently. Tennis players must accurately judge how long their swings take. This judgment must be automatic if they are to initiate their swings at the right time. If they do not begin at the precise moment, the racket will arrive at the contact point too early or too late.

RESEARCH ON MOVEMENT SPEED AND POSITIONING ACCURACY

Another important question is whether swinging near maximal speed helps or impairs tennis players' racket-positioning accuracy. Even when swinging fast helps the timing of players' swings, if it impairs their ability to correctly position the racket, then the overall benefits of a fast swing are subject to question. If the swing results in the racket face deviating from the desired target—up and down or in and out—by as little as an inch, the ball will not hit the racket's sweet spot and an ineffectual shot will result. Before drawing conclusions about the effect of fast swings on racket positioning, let us look at the motor research that has investigated this issue.

Carefully controlled research has been carried out on subjects who made horizontal, forward arm-swinging movements. They were asked to make these movements at various speeds. Some movements were made very slowly, some at about half speed, and some very rapidly. At each swing speed the subjects were attempting to hit a stationary target. A device was attached to their arms that allowed for careful measurement of their accuracy in hitting the target.

As you might expect, when the people moved very slowly they were able to hit the target very accurately. They probably had enough time to make adjustments during their movement in order to "zero in" on the target, much like threading a needle (although somewhat faster). The accuracy found for these very slow movements is of little practical significance to the tennis player; swinging this slowly would not hit shots with nearly enough force to send the ball over the net.

When the subjects moved at about half speed, much greater inaccuracies resulted than in the slow movements. This seemed to occur because the subjects did not have time to make corrections during their movement and also were not able to control their muscles as well at this somewhat faster speed. The faster they contracted their muscles, the less likely the muscles seemed to contract with just the right amount of force. This variability in muscle contraction resulted in movement deviations up and down and in and out. These kinds of positioning deviations could have serious practical consequences for the tennis player who chooses to swing at about half speed.

Perhaps the most interesting finding was the accuracy of the subjects when they moved rapidly. They were much better at hitting the stationary target when moving fast than they were when moving at half speed. They were almost as accurate, in fact, as when they moved at very slow speeds (Figure 10.1).

Why is this true? The best explanation so far is somewhat complicated and requires close attention for comprehension. To begin with, it is true that the more forcefully the brain commands the muscles to contract, the less precisely those commands will be faithfully carried out by the muscular system. However, another factor seems to more than offset this effect when individuals move at near-maximal speed. This factor is called the *ceiling effect*. It means that

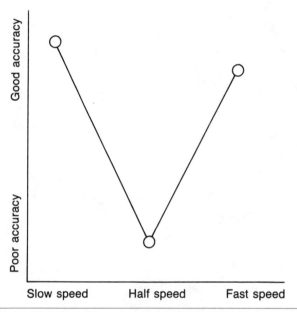

Figure 10.1   Relationship of movement speed to accuracy.

when trying to make movements at maximal speed, people reach physiological limits above which they simply cannot contract their muscles much harder. In a sense, the muscles "max out" and reach a ceiling beyond which they cannot go.

How does this "maxing out" of muscle contractions operate to improve movement accuracy? Figure 10.2 helps illustrate how the ceiling effect influences the positional accuracy of the tennis swing. Muscles A and B contract to move the arm and racket toward the ball. Besides moving the arm forward, Muscle A, because of its positioning toward the top of the shoulder, also has a direct role in lifting the arm. Being located below the shoulder, Muscle B has a direct role in causing a lowering of the arm. When swinging at half speed you realize that both Muscles A and B might not contract with just the amount of force intended. It is this imprecision in contraction that causes inaccurate placement of the arm (and thus the racket). For example, if Muscle A contracts a little more forcefully than intended while Muscle B contracts as intended, the movement path will deviate slightly upward. The same end result occurs if Muscle A contracts as intended but Muscle B contracts less forcefully than desired.

When players swing at near-maximal speed, this imbalance of opposing muscles tends to diminish. Both Muscles A and B will likely contract as expected because both are contracting at near

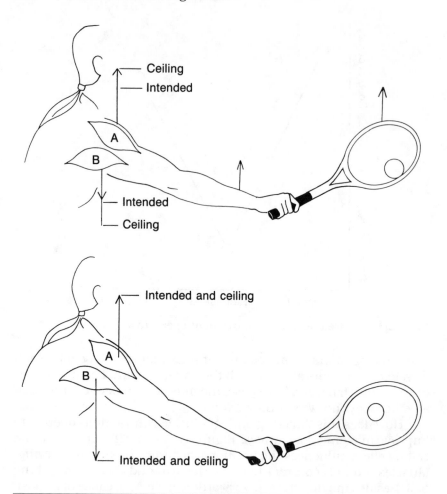

Figure 10.2 The ceiling effect results in accurate tennis strokes.

their physiological limit. It is impossible for one or the other to contract much more than intended. Some variability might still occur because one muscle fails to contract as hard as intended, but at least one dimension of variability is eliminated, reducing the potential imbalance. The disastrously low swing situation where Muscle A contracts less than desired and Muscle B contracts more than desired may occur in half-speed movements, but will virtually never occur when swinging near maximal speed. Better accuracy results from this physiological ceiling effect.

APPLICATION OF
MOVEMENT-SPEED RESEARCH TO TENNIS

As we have seen, research clearly indicates that when individuals make very rapid movements, both their timing and racket-positioning accuracy are likely to improve. Therefore, when players are mis-hitting and misdirecting shots, coaches should encourage them to contract their muscles forcefully, not to slow down or take it easy. Athletes will be much better off if they make their swings nearly as rapidly as possible rather than trying for a slow, flowing swing.

Coaches may be troubled by two practical concerns about applying this research. The first concern could be that rapid swinging may be counterproductive in that it may result in reckless play. The other concern could be that this recommendation for near-maximal contraction of muscles seems to run counter to what is being done by some of the top professional players. Their swings often appear to be flowing and effortless.

In response to the first concern, the recommendation is not that tennis coaches instruct their players to hit the ball *harder*. Two ways exist for players to engage in near-maximal muscular-contraction swings without hitting the ball any harder. One way is to shorten their backswings. A forceful swing from a short backswing will hit the ball at the same speed as a longer swing made at a less intense speed. Although both swings would result in the same ball velocity, the shorter, fast swing would be much easier to time and control.

Another way of swinging hard without overhitting is to direct the muscular energy into producing a topspin. A player can swing very hard at a ground stroke or serve without hitting it overly hard if the racket swing path is not directly at the ball. The practical advantage of how topspin helps players better keep the ball in play by allowing them to hit the ball higher over the net is clearly recognized by players and coaches. Motor research supports this practice for another reason. It allows forceful contraction of muscles and a rapid, accurate swing without hitting the ball excessively hard.

The second concern with the practice of near-maximal contraction swings is that top players seem to swing so effortlessly. Although there is no research that has monitored how forcefully professional players contract their muscles, it is likely that most of their swings are done near maximal-contraction levels. Two factors lead to the mistaken impression that professional players are not hitting the ball forcefully. The first is that much of the general population's exposure to professional tennis is by way of television. Television tends to remove the viewers from the true intensity with which shots are made. The second factor is that top players are so graceful and their timing so good that the true power of their shots is sometimes overlooked. Their big looping backswings do not mean they are gliding or decelerating into their shots. It means that they are either good enough to keep extremely hard-hit shots on the court or that they are applying a great deal of spin.

To conclude, coaches should encourage their performers to accelerate forcefully into most all of their shots. They need not try to swing so hard that it causes them to lose their balance or jerk their heads. But they should be contracting their muscles forcefully enough to elicit the muscular ceiling effect. If a player is having difficulty keeping the ball in bounds because of poor timing or inaccurate racket placement, the solution does not lie in easing up. Easing up will only increase the problem. The better route is to either shorten the backswing or impart more spin. By all means, the player should continue to swing hard.

Coaches should encourage the development of relaxed, compact, forceful swings, leading to crisper shots. This recommendation applies to all but the most delicate shots, such as drop volleys and perhaps some lobs. Be on the watch for your players falling into the habit of easing up on certain types of shots. Anyone who eases up on serves, overheads, volleys, or ground strokes is inviting trouble both in timing and racket control. Even some of your big hitters might become wishy-washy when playing a forehand volley. Perhaps you have called this "the old concrete elbow." Other players might be gently pushing or gliding into their backhands. Watch most closely their second serves. Many players take big long swings at second serves but are really swinging at about half intensity. Easing up on any of these shots allows more room for error because it aggravates accuracy and timing problems.

If you are still skeptical about the research and the recommendations that have been made, try the following experiment on yourself. Scrimmage with one of your players or a patient friend. Attempt to hit about half speed by using a normally full backswing and an easy foreswing. Do this for first serves, second serves, overheads, volleys, and for forehand and backhand ground strokes. Even though your softly hit balls leave more leeway for placement errors, you will almost certainly find that you mistime and mis-hit a disturbingly large number of shots. Let this experience substantiate for you the motor-research findings concerning the effect of rapid movements on timing and accuracy.

PART III

EXERCISE PHYSIOLOGY AND TENNIS

Ann M. Quinn, MS

CHAPTER 11

Fitness—The Road to Better Tennis

In the not-too-distant past, many tennis players conditioned for tournaments *only* by playing tennis, believing it was sufficient. It was as simple as that. But for a tennis professional to reach the top on the tough competitive circuit today, he or she must not only have the necessary tennis skills, but also be mentally tough, physically fit, and eat a well-balanced diet. From the youngest junior to the college player to the over-50 competitor, players must be prepared for maximal exertion to play an entire match and tournament.

Fit players have many advantages over less well-conditioned opponents. They can hit harder, move faster, and even think quicker than their opponents. They can recover faster between rallies, have a better chance of getting to the ball and hitting an effective return, are less fatigued, are less likely to become injured, and know they will not fade in a tough match. Clearly, conditioning can make the difference between winning and losing. Merely playing the game of tennis will not get you into top condition. Match play needs to be supplemented with a conditioning program.

Former World Champion and five-time Wimbledon winner Bjorn Borg feels that he became a great player for more reasons than just his racket skills: "Of course you have to be absolutely physically fit as well. And I am. I can play for 4 or 5 hours with no difficulty. For five-set matches, that's vital." Martina Navratilova is another example of a player whose outstanding physical condition

131

enables her to play an aggressive, all-around game and helped her become the number-one player in the world. Fitness training suited specifically for tennis helps the top players and will help your players to compete at a much higher level.

Top conditioning allows every player to attain his or her maximum performance level and consequently contributes to the enjoyment of the game. However, some coaches and players, at lower levels of competition, question the need for specific conditioning programs. After all, they argue, many champions in the past succeeded without them. Back then, training by playing was the rule, and the main form of conditioning was probably on the dance floor or doing wrist exercises at the bar. However, those that did engage in rigorous conditioning showed the results of their efforts on the tennis court. Harry Hopman's Davis Cup team is an excellent example. Hopman was adamant about the necessity of conditioning and made certain his Aussie charges were in great shape. The results speak for themselves: The Australians won the Cup 16 times under Hopman's captaincy.

Today, athletes in many sports are continuing to break records in leaps and bounds. When Roger Bannister broke the 4-minute mile in 1954, it was considered a tremendous athletic feat. And it was. Today, athletes run 12 seconds faster. The reasons for the tremendous improvement in all sports are the sport scientists' increased knowledge and understanding of the athlete and the more sophisticated and specific methods of training.

Today's top tennis players are more professional in their approach to training. In addition to the best coaches, they seek the help of nutritionists, fitness experts, psychologists, and biomechanists to help them reach their potential. Martina Navratilova, Ivan Lendl, and Pat Cash are excellent examples. With an increased emphasis on interval training, overloading, and specificity (all terms we shall investigate), players are more likely to play up to their capabilities than those who let fitness develop as a byproduct of actual play. The player who hesitates is less conditioned!

Energy production for tennis and other sports is based on physiological energy systems in our bodies. It is thus important to gain a better understanding of how these systems operate to produce energy.

THE PHYSIOLOGICAL BASIS OF ENERGY PRODUCTION FOR TENNIS

To design a training program that fits the requirements of tennis, it is necessary to understand how the human body supplies the energy used on the court. There are three sources of energy: the *phosphate system*, the *lactic acid system*, and the *oxygen system*. Phosphate and lactic energy are both *anaerobic* systems; that is, they do not require the presence of oxygen. Anaerobic energy comes from high-energy phosphate substances in the muscle (phosphate energy system), or from the conversion of sugar materials in the muscle, resulting in the production of lactic acid (the lactic energy system). Fuel sources to energize activities of longer duration require a supply of oxygen; these energy supplies are termed *aerobic*. The importance and contribution of the energy systems to tennis is best explained by describing the different provisions of each of the three energy systems.

Phosphate Energy—The Anaerobic Alactacid System

The anaerobic alactacid mechanism refers to the chemical compounds ATP (adenosine triphosphate) and CP (creatine phosphate), stores in the muscles being broken down to release energy. This energy supply will support intense activity by keeping muscles supplied with ATP for periods of between 10 and 15 seconds, such as during a short sprint to a drop shot or jumping to smash a high lob. The system replenishes rapidly during rest periods—within 30 seconds the system is back to 70% and within 3 minutes back to 100%. By correctly training the phosphate energy system, the athlete enhances the explosive ability he or she needs. This ability is vital in tennis as frequently a player's speed is the difference between winning or losing a point.

Lactic Acid System—The Anaerobic Lactacid System

When rallies extend beyond the extent of the phosphate energy system, energy comes from glycogen stored in the active muscles. The anaerobic lactacid pathway is used primarily during high-intensity activities lasting 2 to 3 minutes, such as a long rally. Physiologists estimate that this energy system is required by tennis players about 20% of the time. During the typically long rallies in the French Open, for example, players break down stored sugar (glycogen) anaerobically, and ATP is formed. Anaerobic energy released from glycogen produces lactic acid, and continued strenuous exercise results in a continual release of lactic acid into the blood. This leads to fatigue and forces the player to slow down. Unfortunately, once lactic acid is produced in large amounts, it can take more than an hour for it to be dispersed. Consequently, recovery is slow.

Oxygen System—The Aerobic System

The aerobic pathway is the predominant source of energy during prolonged work at a milder intensity (an intensity somewhat less than maximal power output). The aerobic system takes 2 to 3 minutes to operate fully because of the time required to supply extra oxygen to the muscles once exercise begins. This energy system is the predominant system used by "social" doubles players during their friendly encounters. For the more serious tennis player, this energy system is in use about 10% of the time. For all players, however, oxygen to the muscles is supplied by the respiratory and circulatory systems and is used in chemical processes to generate ATP. In these aerobic chemical processes, fat, carbohydrate, and glycogen can then be broken down to carbon dioxide and water with a much greater yield of ATP then in anaerobic processes.

There are many recovery periods in a tennis match. Game analyses during major championships of 10 professional players show that a male player has approximately 8-1/2 minutes of rest for every minute of actively playing a point. Females work harder, averaging only 5-1/2 minutes of rest. These results demonstrate the attacking, aggressive style of play by men and the longer rallying games played by many women on the tour. During the rest periods between rallies and games, the aerobic system provides the energy to replenish the phosphate stores in the muscle in preparation for the next burst of intense activity. That is, during the 30 seconds allowed between points, or the 90 seconds allowed to change ends, energy reserves are refueled. Players who adequately train the oxygen system can delay the use of the lactic acid energy system, which, in turn, delays the onset of fatigue and enables concentration, skill levels, and work rate to be maintained for longer periods.

The Energy Systems Predominant in Tennis

Most sports performers obtain their energy supply from a combination of the three energy systems (Figure 11.1). The predominant energy systems in tennis are phosphate energy (70%), lactic acid energy (20%), and oxygen (10%) (Fox, 1979). Being an activity with repeated, short-duration, explosive bursts of activity, tennis derives most of its energy from the anaerobic systems (phosphate and lactic acid), and training these energy systems is most important for tennis players. However, a solid aerboic base is essential to provide some energy during activity and to enhance recovery from each effort.

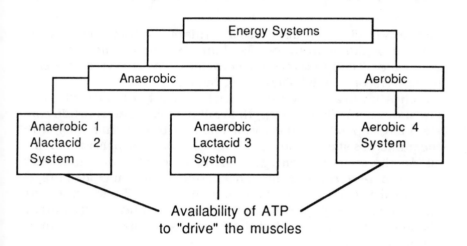

1. Without oxygen
3. Lactic acid produced

2. No lactic acid is produced
4. With oxygen

Figure 11.1 The energy systems.

Compare a tennis player with a cross-country runner who competes in the 3-mile event. The runner's energy requirements (10% phosphate, 20% lactic acid energy, and 70% oxygen or aerobic energy) are almost the reverse of the tennis player's. Unlike tennis players, cross-country runners engage in continuous activity at a submaximal workload, with no rest periods. It is during prolonged exercise (10 minutes or more) that aerobic processes play the most important role; during short exhaustive work periods (up to 1 or 2 minutes) the energy needed is derived from anaerobic processes. Consequently, if the tennis player were to follow the training regimen of this runner, maximum increases in performance would not result.

Conversely, basketball and soccer are sports that involve short, sharp bursts of activity—energy requirements similar to tennis— and thus the training in these sports would be more suited to tennis players. In fact, playing these sports is a fun way of conditioning for tennis. However, the principle of *specificity* must always be stressed; participating in other sports should only be used to provide variety in the tennis player's training program.

FITNESS AND PERFORMANCE COMPONENTS

Fitness is traditionally discussed in terms of four basic components: *cardiovascular endurance, flexibility, strength,* and *muscular endurance.* Tennis players must develop each of these components to perform optimally. They must be able to endure long, tough matches day in and day out, stretch for those hard-to-get wide and low shots, apply (force) strength to all their shots, and sustain constant force up to the end of the last point. However, in tennis, with the numerous starts, stops, and direction changes, plus the emphasis on the anaerobic energy system, there are also other very important *performance* components that must be included to specifically develop a well-conditioned tennis player. These are *agility, speed, power, response time,* and *dynamic balance. Coordination,* the ability to combine all of these factors, is essential to optimal tennis success.

Conditioning for tennis is like preparing for a tournament. Players don't practice just one stroke. They work on every shot and on all parts of their game. Likewise, it is important in the conditioning program for players to train and develop each and every one of the fitness and performance components for tennis. These components are interrelated, so training for one will also develop some of the others. For example, training for speed will also improve power and strength. Agility workouts with balls also develop speed, dynamic balance, and response time, as well as endurance if the activity is sustained for a few minutes.

These specific components of fitness and performance for tennis were determined in many ways. A study consisting of a review of the tennis literature and of questionnaires to coaches and players found that agility, speed, and power were considered the most important components on which tennis players should concentrate their training efforts. These were followed by cardiovascular and muscular endurance, flexibility, strength, response time, and dynamic balance. Physiological profiles of professional tennis players and game analyses support these findings. The necessity and importance of each of these components to tennis will now be presented and discussed. Then, more benefits of conditioning for tennis will conclude the chapter.

Agility

Agility is the ability to start and stop and to change direction quickly and effectively while moving. It is a combination of quickness, speed, and balance, making it a very important part of a game like tennis. A player must run forward, backward, diagonally, and laterally. Game analyses have shown that an average of 38 direction changes occur in each set and that some sets require more than 80 (Quinn, 1981). Agility is the key to positioning and, therefore, effective stroking. The track athlete might never be concerned with agility, but to the tennis player its importance cannot be overemphasized. It should be the cornerstone of every player's conditioning program.

Speed

The ability to accelerate and move quickly over short distances is an important asset for a tennis player. The successful player is usually the one who is quickest in getting to the ball. General factors that influence speed are strength, flexibility, power, and endurance (all of which will be separately discussed).

Speed—specific speed of body segments as well as overall body speed—can often be improved with *strength training*. The key to success lies in the principle of specificity. For example, speed of arm movement is not necessarily related to speed of leg movement. Some players may be quick with their hands, but because of lack of training, lack of skill, or excess fat, may be slow of foot.

Training should simulate on-court actions as closely as possible and be specific to the desired results. Instead of using weights only in the gym, players can gain greater benefits and increase speed if they do their running exercises on the court while carrying a weighted racket and wearing ankle weights. These exercises should include running sideways, forward, backward, and diagonally, just as is required in a match. After these tough workouts, sprinting to a drop shot or chasing a lob will seem easy.

Flexibility can also improve speed by cutting down on the resistance offered by the muscles. Athletes who engage in weight training may increase muscle bulk, which decreases their range of motion at the joints. However, this can be offset by stretching and flexibility work. Although flexible players are not *necessarily* quicker, flexibility is one factor that contributes to increased speed. It also cuts the risk of injury.

Increasing the *power* or explosive ability of a player is another key to increasing speed. Rapid acceleration and short bursts of activity around the court must be executed quickly for a player to achieve a balanced hitting position. Furthermore, a player must improve *endurance* in order to continue to repeat these short sprints through to the final game.

It is true that sprinting ability is a natural gift, but it is still possible to improve the ability with appropriate training methods. The basic principle is that the duration of the activity must be kept very short so that early fatigue will not occur. To best develop speed, 5 to 10 seconds is long enough to train at a fast running pace.

Speed is unquestionably an essential performance component, and there are many ways to help players develop it (Figure 11.2). The next chapter outlines a number of these methods.

Figure 11.2   Speed is essential for tennis players.

Strength, Power, and Muscular Endurance

Strength, power and muscular endurance are all valuable assets to a tennis player. *Strength* is the capacity of a muscle or muscle group to exert a maximal force against a resistance. It is related to *power*, which is the rate at which force is produced. In tennis, the explosive ability to apply force is very important. *Muscular endurance* is the capacity of a muscle to exert a force repeatedly over a period of time or to exert strength and sustain it (Getchell, 1979). During a tennis match it is important to be able to apply force (strength), to apply force with speed (power), and to sustain this force over a period of time (endurance).

Since strength and muscular endurance are related, emphasis on one of these components will promote improvement in the other. Strength in itself, however, is not of prime importance to a tennis player. One rarely sees on the tennis tour a player with the physique of a wrestler or bodybuilder. Nevertheless, the strength component should not be underestimated, as strength contributes to both power and speed. The ability to generate force with the racket, especially to stop and reverse the direction of a fast oncoming ball, depends on the strength of the arm, hand, wrist, trunk, and leg muscles. Strength development exercises for tennis players should be directed at these body segments. Also, the more strength players have the less energy they expend; consequently body control and timing are enhanced, which, in turn, yields better strokes and more games won.

Muscular endurance is a more important part of tennis training then strength, but a minimum strength level must be achieved before emphasis can be placed on endurance training. Unfortunately, there are no magic figures to help the coach determine that level, as it is very much an individual thing. In some sports, physiological studies have provided guidelines for optimal strength, but in tennis the topic is still to be investigated. A tennis player must be able to endure long hours on the court and to hit hundreds of strokes in a single match. The longer a muscle can contract without fatigue, the higher the muscular endurance. This type of endurance is unlike cardiovascular endurance, as the heart and circulatory system are not taxed to their fullest capacity. The limiting factor in muscular endurance is localized in the muscle group itself, so it is necessary for players to train the individual muscle groups.

Power is an essential component all tennis players must develop—even more important than strength and muscular endurance. Power is simply the product of strength and speed. Once players have developed a strength base, power can be developed through the use of light weights with quick repetitions.

The leg and trunk muscles are regions the tennis player should emphasize. Whereas most coaches agree on the legs, few understand the importance of the trunk muscles. These muscles provide an important link in the sequence of events that occur as force is transferred through the body for optimal acceleration of the racket. Electromyographical studies of the abdominal and lower back muscles during selected strokes of advanced players have shown that both muscle groups are contracting on average at 70% to 80% of their maximum intensity. That these muscles are being worked at such high intensity illustrates the necessity for coaches to include both abdominal and lower back exercises in their conditioning programs, not only to improve stroke performance, but also to aid in the prevention of injuries.

Finally, training for strength, muscular endurance, and power helps players to maintain optimal physical stamina for longer periods of time, which is especially important in tough matches (Figure 11.3). Improved quickness improves court coverage, thus allowing

Figure 11.3 Martina Navratilova demonstrates the components of strength, power, and muscular endurance.

more time for stroke preparation. Improved strength and power means strokes can be hit harder, for more pace and depth. Also stronger muscles mean improved balance and more stabilized joints, deterring injury. Playing hurt is a poor second choice to playing at peak physical condition. A player can only improve with a strength, muscular endurance, and power program.

Cardiovascular Endurance

Horse trainers call it *foundation*, runners call it a *base*, and baseball players call it *legs*. On the tennis circuit it is generally called *wind*. Whatever you call it, it is the ability to play long and hard, to recover quickly between rallies, and to be still at your peak for the last point of the day.

Aerobic or cardiovascular endurance activities are those in which large muscle groups are used in rhythmic, repetitive fashion for long periods of time, as in jogging, swimming, and bike riding. In fact, much of the time tennis players spend on a court also involves aerobic exercise, especially for recreational players. Aerobic conditioning raises the heart rate for a prolonged period of exercise at a moderate intensity. Because this type of exercise increases the efficiency of the heart, lungs, and circulation, it provides the base for the player's conditioning program.

Cardiovascular endurance is probably the most underrated component of the total physical training program. Wilmore (1977) suggested that the reason little attention has been given to endurance training for tennis is that tennis consists of repeated bouts of high-intensity work of short duration. Seldom does a run exceed 10 to 15 yards without a rest interval. From all outward appearances, tennis is an explosive type of activity; the need for endurance is not readily obvious.

Sport scientists are beginning to recognize the importance of endurance training to *all* activities, whether sprint-type, slow and skilled, or of an endurance nature. The more oxygen the body is able to take in, utilize, and supply to the working muscles, the more energy there is available, and the more work the body is capable of doing. Tennis players must repeat these explosive bursts to the ball many times throughout a match. With a good base and a high level of endurance, the quality of such activity is maintained and the athlete is still fresh at the end of the last point.

As well as facilitating athletes' performance, an increased level of cardiovascular endurance can reduce players' chances of injury and increase their concentration span. The fitter the players, the more alert they will be, the quicker their reactions will be to the ball, the quicker they will recover, and the longer they will be able to play before fatigue develops. Cardiovascular endurance is thus considered to be essential to the tennis player (Figure 11.4).

Flexibility

Until very recently pre- and postmatch stretching by tennis players was a rare occurrence. Gymnasts do it. Runners do it. Dancers do it. Numerous other athletes do it. Stretching increases flexibility, and players need flexibility to maintain a full range of motion in their body joints. A tennis player must have the ability to bend,

Figure 11.4 The Becker/McEnroe 6-1/2 hour Davis Cup match was a real test of tennis endurance

twist, and stretch the body. Good flexibility ensures this. Some players are more flexible than others as a result of their participation in other sports and different training methods. In any case, the greater the amount of time and intensity with which a player plays tennis, the greater the chances of his or her feeling tight; therefore it becomes even more important to do a regular set of stretching exercises. Flexibility is unquestionably one of the essential components of fitness for tennis (Figure 11.5). Your training program should include exercises that develop and maintain flexibility, especially in the legs, thighs, trunk, arms, and shoulders.

- Players with a high degree of flexibility have excellent range on the tennis court and are capable of reaching those hard-to-get wide and low shots.
- Stretching helps to reduce and prevent injuries to muscle tissue, ligaments, and tendons.
- Stretching aids the warm-up by loosening players up.
- Stretching helps to relax players, which is especially important before a match, when players may be a little tense and nervous and consequently tight in their muscles.
- Stretching after a workout or match increases local blood flow, reduces muscular tension, and consequently helps to minimize muscle soreness the next day.

Figure 11.5 Boris Becker stretching for a shot.

- Research shows that flexibility improvements accompany strength improvements if exercises are performed through the full range of joint movement (Miller & Allen, 1982).
- Stretching promotes circulation.
- Stretching feels good!

Response Time

The development of response time is essential in advanced tennis play, where the ball can move so fast. Response time is defined as the amount of time elapsing between the presentation of a stimulus (the opponent's shot) and the completion of the movement initiated in response to it (your return shot). In other words, it is the time a player takes to respond to and return the oncoming ball.

Response time is directly related to speed, as these two factors largely determine how fast a player can move to get into position to return a ball. The importance of these two components is further emphasized by several studies showing that outstanding athletes are superior to average athletes in both speed and response time (Hockey, 1977). Therefore, good response time and speed are vital to advanced tennis players if they want to succeed in tennis.

Once a tennis player has correctly recognized or anticipated what type of return the opponent has hit, he or she must get positioned and decide how to intercept the ball to return it effectively to the opponent's court. A course of action must be decided upon to achieve the desired outcome—that is, to win the rally.

One of numerous possible actions can be taken on each stroke. The action the player finally takes must not only correspond to the specific demands of the approaching ball, but must also be made within the framework of how the player wants to return the ball. In other words, the tennis player must decide not only the type of stroke (volley, lob, drive, etc.), but also how to execute it (flat, slice, topspin) and where in the opponent's court to direct it. All these decisions affect one's response time; consequently, movement to the ball, positioning, stroke technique, and effectiveness are also affected.

An experienced player, however, has several motor programs that he or she has previously learned and used for tennis. Thus, he or she can prepare in advance of the shot by bringing the most likely plans from long-term memory to short-term operational memory, in this way reducing the possible number of alternative plans to be searched through. This is one characteristic that distinguishes a good tennis player from a novice (Marteniuk, 1976).

Dynamic Balance

Balance is defined as the ability to maintain equilibrium of the body. There are two types of balance: static and dynamic. *Static balance* is the physical ability to hold a stationary position, just as one does in the ready position awaiting a serve. *Dynamic balance* is the ability to maintain balance and body control during vigorous movement. For tennis players, this type of balance importantly contributes to skillful performance. Tennis players must be able to remain balanced while hitting the ball. Internal forces of the body and various forces from the ground, the racket, and the ball continually cause the body to become unbalanced. As it is difficult to hit an optimal shot while unbalanced, a player needs to attain balance before impact. This will not only add power to a shot, but will aid in the timing and accuracy of the stroke.

The ability to balance easily, whether statically or dynamically, depends on the function of the mechanisms in the semicircular canals; the kinesthetic sensations in the muscles, tendons, and joints; visual perception while the body is in motion; and the ability to coordinate these three sources of stimuli. Balance can be improved through participation in sports and a variety of movement experiences. However, balance is highly specific to the activity being performed. Becoming proficient on the balance beam will not help you play better tennis. However, practicing tennis will surely be an excellent way to improve balance necessary to good tennis (Figure 11.6).

Figure 11.6   Jimmy Connors displays great balance.

And Even More Reasons to Condition for Tennis . . .

As a coach, many of your budding young champions may be mixing tennis and tournaments with homework and demanding school schedules. Thus, it is imperative that they are in top condition or the effects of overload will show up on the court. Many a match has been lost because of fatigue. In 1987, Mikael Pernfors seemed headed for an easy victory in the fourth round of Wimbledon when he led Jimmy Connors 6-1, 6-1, 4-1. But Connors won 18 of the last 25 games to stop the Swede cold. The 34-year-old Connors was in great shape, and Pernfors simply had no stamina left.

These tests of endurance occur at every level of play. As players begin to run out of energy, they lose half a step in getting to the ball. If they are out of position, their strokes will suffer and they begin to lose points. Fatigue has its mental aspects, too: When players reach the limits of their physical endurance, their competitive urge and winning instincts begin to suffer. The combination of fatigue, slowness, and discouragement spells defeat. No matter how skilled players become, if the optimal levels of physical fitness are not attained and maintained, the overall performance will be greatly affected.

Numerous benefits other than enhanced performance can be gained from a conditioning program. Being physically fit greatly reduces the chance of incurring an injury while playing tennis. Moreover, if a player should happen to sustain an injury, being physically fit will help the individual recover quickly and completely. Also, peak physical condition elevates the confidence of a player and gives him or her a great psychological boost. And, needless to say, keeping fit will increase the player's enjoyment of the game, as it improves their play.

REFERENCE

Quinn, A.M. (1981). *A physiological profile of professional level tennis players*. Unpublished manuscript, Preston Institute of Technology, School of Physical Education and Leisure Studies, Bundoora, Victoria, Australia.

RECOMMENDED READINGS

Borg, B. (1980). *Borg by Borg*. London: Octopus Books Ltd.

Fox, E.L. (1979). *Sports physiology*. Philadelphia: W.B. Saunders.

Gretchell, B. (1979). *Physical fitness: A way of life*. Philadelphia: Saunders College.

Hockey, R.V. (1977). *Physical fitness: The pathway to healthful living* (3rd ed.). St. Louis: C.V. Mosby.

Marteniuk, R.G. (1976). *Information processing in motor skills*. New York: Holt, Rinehart and Winston.

Miller, D.K., & Allen, T.E. (1982). *Fitness: A lifetime commitment* (2nd ed.). Minneapolis, MN: Burgess Publishing.

Murphy, C.W., & Murphy, W.E. (1975). *Tennis for the player, teacher and coach*. Philadelphia: Saunders College.

Navratilova, M. (1983). *Tennis my way*. Australia: Allen Lane, Penguin Books.

Pyke, F.S., & Smith, R.G. (1975). *Football—The scientific way*. Nedlands: University of Western Australia Press.

Wilmore, J.H. (1977). *Athletic training and physical fitness: Physiological principles and practices of the conditioning process* (2nd ed.). Boston: Allyn and Bacon.

Withers, R.T. (1979). Specificity and the soccer coach. *Sports Coach*, **3**(1), 16-21.

CHAPTER 12

Evaluate Your Players' Tennis Fitness

How fit are my players to play tennis? In which areas are they weak? What are their strengths? Success in tennis depends on a variety of factors, which include the fitness and physical characteristics of the players, their level of skill, their mental toughness and motivation, and the tactics they use. Many of these factors are difficult to measure objectively, leaving coaches to rely almost entirely upon their own judgment. However, some factors do lend themselves to standardized testing and can provide a useful supplement to subjective appraisals. This chapter outlines a recommended battery of tests specifically designed to evaluate tennis players.

WHY SHOULD COACHES TEST PLAYERS?

Before beginning any training program, coaches need to evaluate where their players are at present; then, at any time throughout the season, a coach must be able to identify the factors limiting their players' performances. What are their strengths and weaknesses? The more advanced the players, the more important it becomes to objectively evaluate tennis fitness and movement around the court. If a player is not very agile, or lacks stamina, opponents will quickly detect these weaknesses and concentrate their attacks accordingly.

Test results, together with coaches' subjective conclusions from watching their players perform in matches, will pinpoint each individuals' strengths and weaknesses. Implementing the recommended battery of tests will also enable refinement of the training program and valid monitoring of your athletes' progress. The tests will even aid in providing motivation for training.

Conditioning for tennis can be lots of fun and is easily within a player's reach. The results on the tennis court will speak for themselves. Stress to your players the many benefits of off-court training and the big difference it can have on their game and ranking, not to mention the psychological benefits to be gained.

WHEN SHOULD TESTS BE ADMINISTERED?

Tests should be conducted at the beginning of the year or the season, and about every 3 months, thereafter, depending on the particular player's schedule and goals. Throughout the season, the results can be used to further modify individual programs based on the player's strengths and weaknesses at that period. Also, coaches may want to test players the week before an important championship as a way of motivating them and showing them the great improvement they will surely have made during the preceding months.

WHAT DO THE TEST RESULTS MEAN?

Following the description and procedures of each test, the methods of scoring are explained and average results given. All mean scores have been determined from hundreds of tests conducted by the author over the years on advanced and professional tennis players from around the world. Advanced players are those who have achieved a very high standard of play and are nationally or sectionally ranked. Professional players are those who play on the international circuit and earn their living from the sport. The average age of tested players was approximately 18 years.

At present, no norms exist for skilled tennis players in the different age categories; thus, the averages stated with the tests may appear quite high, relative to the 13- or 14-year-old. Nevertheless, coaches can easily begin to establish their own norms and make a model of the best performer in each class. It is important, too, that individual results and improvements be closely monitored and justly rewarded. Give your players incentives and lots of encouragement to help them along the road to tennis fitness.

The following are all simple tests chosen because of their minimal use of equipment and ease of administration. There are many more sophisticated tests that yield more accurate measurements (e.g., Cybex machine, Beckman Metabolic Measurement Cart, Electronic Timing), but these all require expensive pieces of equipment and an exercise physiologist to administer the tests and interpret the results. However, if you coach near a university or hospital, you may want to consult with an exercise physiologist and have some specialized testing. This would be especially worthwhile for players recovering from injuries.

PROCEDURES FOR TESTING YOUR PLAYERS

Included in this section are all the tests you need for evaluating the fitness levels of your tennis players. In Appendix A you will find an evaluation form to facilitate maintaining records of results, so that you can chart the progress of your players.

AGILITY, DYNAMIC BALANCE, AND RESPONSE TIME

The Modified Semo Agility Test

The Semo agility test measures agility as a separate component— that is, it measures the ability of a tennis player to start and stop and to change direction quickly and effectively while moving. This test is really a measure of *planned agility*, as the performer knows his or her movements in advance. Planned agility also occurs on the tennis court when an approach to the net, for example, or other strategy is planned prior to the beginning of the point.

Purpose

To measure the general agility of the body in maneuvering forward, backward, and sideways.

Equipment

- Any smooth area 20 × 20 feet* with adequate running space around it will suffice, but a tennis court is preferable (Specificity!).
- Four cones, A, B, C, and D, placed squarely in each corner.
- Stopwatch.

*12 × 19 feet—the size of a free-throw lane of a basketball court— are the usual dimensions for this test. However, 20 × 20 feet was chosen to more closely approximate the area a player moves around on a tennis court.

Procedures

1. The subject lines up at A, in front of the cone.
2. With his or her back to the course, the subject waits for the signal, "On your mark, Get set—Go!"
3. The subject should sidestep from A to B and pass outside the corner cone.
4. The subject should then backpedal from B to D and pass to the inside of the corner cone.
5. The athlete then should sprint forward from D to A and pass outside the corner cone.
6. The athlete should then backpedal from A to C and pass to the inside of the corner cone.
7. The subject should then sprint forward from C to B and pass outside of the corner cone.
8. The subject should then sidestep from B to the finish line at A.
9. One practice trial should be given.

Scoring

The best of two trials is recorded as the score. (A recovery period of approximately 2 minutes is given between each trial.)

Average

Males: 12.8 seconds
Females: 14.2 seconds

The Quinn Agility, Dynamic Balance, and Response-Time Test

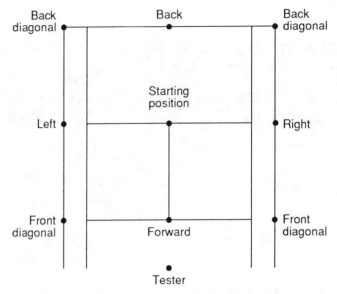

Figure 12.1 Directions for the Quinn agility, dynamic balance, and response-time test.

Purpose

This is a test designed to measure the agility, dynamic balance and response time of a tennis player—that is, the ability of a tennis player to start and stop, remain balanced, to react to her opponent (the tester in this case) and the ball, and to change direction quickly and effectively while moving. This test was designed specifically for tennis players, as the movements in this test occur so frequently in a tennis match (Figure 12.1).

Equipment

- Half a tennis court
- Stopwatch

Procedures

1. The subject begins standing in the starting position at the intersection of the service line and center line.
2. The tester stands in front of the subject (on the other side of the court) approximately 6 feet back from the net. The tester is thus simulating an opponent's position.

3. Holding a ball in his hand, the tester points to a mark and at the same time calls the direction to which he is pointing (e.g., "right"). Simultaneously, the tester starts the stopwatch, held in the other hand.

Figure 12.2 Pat Cash taking the Quinn agility, dynamic balance, and response-time test.

4. The subject must run quickly to that mark, touch it, and return to the starting position (see Figure 12.2).
5. The tester immediately calls and points to another direction.
6. The subject then runs as quickly as possible to this direction, touches the line, then returns back to the starting position.
7. The subject only has to touch the line to which she runs, not the starting position to which she returns. (This simulates running to the sideline for a shot, bending down to hit the ball, then returning to the middle of the court ready for the next shot.)
8. It is imperative that the subject watch the tester constantly. As this test simulates game situations, the subject must not take her eyes off the "ball." She must run in all directions, keeping her eyes on the tester and the ball, as though the tester were an opponent.
9. This procedure is repeated eight times (once to each direction).
10. The order of directions should change with each trial, so that it is unpredictable. A player will have to react to the tester and

the ball, just as she reacts to an opponent and the ball in a game situation.

11. The stopwatch is clicked off when the subject returns to the starting position after touching the eighth mark.

Scoring

The best of two trials is recorded as the score. A recovery period of 2 to 3 minutes is given between each trial.

Average

Males: 29.4 seconds

Females: 34.5 seconds

SPEED

20-Meter Dash

Purpose

The purpose of this test is to measure a player's speed and ability to accelerate and move quickly.

Equipment

- Stopwatch
- Two cones
- A tennis court or other suitable running area to allow the 20-meter run plus an extension for stopping

Procedures

1. Subject starts from a standing position with tennis racket in hand.

2. The tester stands at the 20-meter mark and starts the subject with the commands: "Are you ready? Get set—Go!"

3. On "go," the tester lowers his hand from overhead to his side, simultaneously starting the stopwatch.

4. The subject runs as fast as possible, and the tester stops the watch as the subject crosses the 20-meter line.

Scoring

The best elapsed time of three trials is recorded.

Average

Males: 3.16 seconds

Females: 3.58 seconds

SPEED/RESPONSE TIME

Baseline-Service Line Dash

Purpose

The baseline-service line dash is a test of one's ability to accelerate and move quickly over a short distance with a tennis racket in hand. Because the distance is so short, both speed and response time are measured in the total time of performance.

Equipment

- Stopwatch
- Tennis court

Procedures

1. Subject starts from a standing position on the baseline with a racket in hand.
2. The tester stands at the service line and starts the player with the commands: "Are you ready? Get set—Go!" and simultaneously starts the stopwatch.
3. The subject runs as fast as possible across the service line.
4. The tester stops the watch as the subject crosses the service line.

Scoring

The best elapsed time of three trials is recorded.

Average

Males: 1.23 seconds

Females: 1.37 seconds

POWER

The Vertical-Jump Test

Purpose

To measure the power of the legs in jumping vertically (and more specifically the power of the extensor muscles of the hips, knees, and ankles).

Equipment

- A smooth vertical surface of at least 4 meters high
- Chalk
- A meter rule
- For more scientific evaluation, a Lewis nomogram

Procedures

1. The subject should first rub the fingertips of the hand nearest the wall with chalk.
2. She should then stand with her side to the wall and, while reaching overhead as high as possible with her heels together and flat on the floor, press her chalked fingertips against the wall to record standing height.
3. Then, without moving her feet, the subject squats and jumps as high as possible, making another mark with her fingertips at the height of her jump (see Figure 12.3).

Scoring

The distance between the standing reach and the highest jump mark (measured in centimeters) is the score. Three to five trials are allowed, and the best trial is recorded. In this simple form, the test

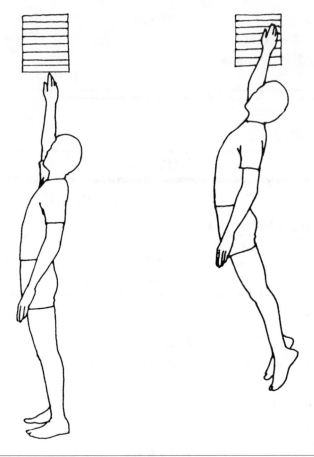

Figure 12.3 The vertical-jump test of power.

identifies those players who clearly need work to improve their vertical jump and, when periodically measured, serves as a measure of progress. However, for the test to be a true measure of power, the athlete's body weight must be taken into consideration. For example, a 60 kilogram boy who jumps vertically 60 centimeters produces less power than the 70 kilogram boy who jumps 60 centimeters.

In order to make the vertical-jump test a valid measure of leg power, the *Lewis nomogram* (Figure 12.4) can be used as follows:

Body Weight = 60 kilograms
Distance Jumped = 50 centimeters

Lay a straight-edge across the nomogram connecting the 60-kilogram (right column) and 50-centimeter (left column). Read,

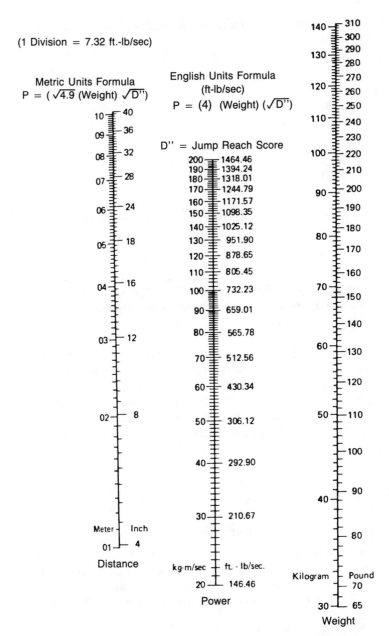

Figure 12.4 The Lewis Nomogram for measurement of leg power.
Note. From Edward L. Fox, Richard W. Bowers, and Merle L. Foss, *The Physiological Basis of Physical Education and Athletics*, 4th ed. Copyright 1988 by W.B. Saunders Company. Reprinted by permission of Wm. C. Brown Publishers, Dubuque, Iowa.

from the center column, kilogram-meters per second (kg-m/sec) as the power output.

Average

Vertical-jump test results
Males: 52.5 centimeters
Females: 39.0 centimeters

With Lewis nomogram applied
Males: 118.4 kilogram-meters per second
Females: 89.0 kilogram-meters per second

CARDIOVASCULAR ENDURANCE

Maximal oxygen uptake (VO_2max) is considered to be the best single indicator of an individual's cardiovascular endurance. In the laboratory, oxygen uptake is measured with sophisticated gas-analysis equipment while the athlete performs on an ergometer. However, for the coach, a reliable estimate of players' endurance levels may be obtained from their performance of the 12-minute-run test or the 1-1/2-mile-run test.

The 12-Minute-Run Test

Purpose

The purpose of this test is to evaluate a player's level of cardiovascular fitness. This test is based on research that demonstrates the distance one can cover in 12 minutes correlates closely with the ability of one's body to use large amounts of oxygen.

Equipment

- A stopwatch or timing device that runs for 12 minutes consecutively
- A tape measure for measuring the distance covered, or a measured running track

Procedures

1. The objective of the player is to cover as much distance as possible in the 12-minute period.
2. Start the timer and have the player run, jog, or walk for 12 minutes.

Scoring

If a measured track is used, count the number of laps completed. Otherwise, calculate the actual distance covered (generally recorded to the nearest 100 yards). The final result is tabulated in miles.

Average

Males: 1.88 miles (3308.8 yards)

Females: 1.58 miles (2780.8 yards)

The 1-1/2-Mile-Run Test

The 1-1/2-mile-run test may be preferred to the 12-minute-run test because it is easier to administer. The aim of the test is to cover the 1-1/2 miles as quickly as possible. The elapsed time is recorded in minutes and seconds.

Average

Males: 10 minutes 13 seconds (613 seconds)

Females: 11 minutes 22 seconds (682 seconds)

MUSCULAR ENDURANCE

Sit-Up Test (Bent knees)

Purpose

To determine the muscular endurance of the abdominal muscles. Contrary to what some coaches and players seem to think, tennis is not played with the upper limbs alone. It is not stronger arms that give added power to strokes, but stronger trunk muscles. In a study on advanced tennis players, Quinn (1985) found that the abdominal muscles average 67% amplitude and reach as high as 83% of their maximum intensity during play. Thus the abdominal muscles certainly must be regarded as important contributors to a tennis player's performance.

Equipment

- Mat to lie on
- Stopwatch
- An assistant to hold the player's ankles

Procedures

1. The player lies on his back on the mat, with fingers interlocked behind his head.
2. Both feet are placed flat on the floor; the knees are flexed, forming an angle of approximately 90 degrees.
3. An assistant kneels and grasps both of the player's ankles firmly. (Hold the feet down only for the purpose of testing, as doing so places the iliopsoas muscle under strain.)
4. A full sit-up is counted when the player has flexed his trunk, touched his elbows to his knees, and returned to the starting position.
5. Each time the player returns to the starting position, the fingers at the back of the head must come in contact with the floor.
6. This process is repeated as many times as possible during a one-minute period.
7. The holder counts out loud, as well as motivating the subject, especially during the last 20 seconds.

Scoring

The score is the number of sit-ups completed in the one-minute period.

Average

Males: 45

Females: 42

Note. These sit-ups are for testing only. Due to the potential strain placed on the lower back, athletes with back problems or weak trunk muscles should not perform these. Safer strength training can be done with abdominal curls.

The Push-Up Test

Purpose

To determine the muscular endurance of the triceps, pectoral, and deltoid muscles.

Equipment

• Stopwatch

Procedures

1. The subject assumes a prone position on the floor with hands directly under the shoulder joints, legs straight and together, and toes tucked under so that they are in contact with the floor.
2. The subject then pushes with the arms until they are fully extended.
3. The subject then lowers the body until the chin or chest touches the floor. At this point, the line from the head to the toes should be straight.
4. All of this movement must be performed by the arms and shoulders and not by any other body part.

Scoring

The score is the number of push-ups completed in a 1-minute period. (Modified push-ups [knees on the floor] are recommended for children, especially girls, if they are not yet strong enough to do regular push-ups.)

Average

Males: 40

Females: 25

FLEXIBILITY

The Sit-and-Reach Test

Purpose

To measure the amount of trunk flexion and the ability to stretch the back muscles and hamstring region.

Equipment

- Box, board, bench, or other flat surface
- A ruler (measured in centimeters) attached to the box

Procedures

1. The subject sits on the floor with her legs fully extended and the soles of her feet flat against the box projecting from the wall.
2. The arms and hands are stretched forward as far as possible and held there for at least 3 seconds (Figure 12.5).

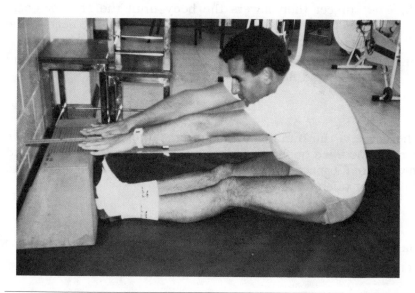

Figure 12.5 The sit-and-reach test.

3. The knees must remain fully extended throughout the reach.
4. A ruler is used to measure the distance in front of, or beyond the edge of, the box that the subject reaches.

Scoring

If players are unable to reach their toes, the distance is expressed as a negative score, whereas a measure beyond the edge of the box is expressed as a positive score. The more positive the score, the greater the flexibility. The best measure of four trials is recorded to the nearest centimeter.

Average

Males: +4.4 centimeters
Females: +11.6 centimeters

Trunk-Extension Test for Flexibility

Purpose

To measure the range of motion (flexibility) of the back.

Equipment

- A ruler with centimeter measurements
- A partner to hold the subject down

Procedures

1. The subject lies prone on the floor with a partner holding his buttocks and legs down.
2. With fingers interlocked behind his neck, the subject raises his chest and head off the floor as far as possible and holds for a count of three.

Scoring

The distance measured from floor to chin in centimeters is the score.

Average

Males: 41.17 centimeters
Females: 48.59 centimeters

STRENGTH

The Grip-Strength Test

Purpose

To test the strength of muscles of the fingers, hand, and forearm.

Equipment

- Grip dynamometer

Procedures

1. Adjust dynamometer so that it fits the subject's hand comfortably.
2. The dynamometer is gripped as tightly as possible while the hand describes a sweeping arc downward with the arm and hand free from the body.

Scoring

Record the best of three trials as read from the dial in kilograms.

Average

Males: 51.3 kilograms

Females: 35.6 kilograms

PHYSICAL CHARACTERISTICS

For a complete physical profile of each player, coaches should include in the test file measurements of height, weight, and body fat.

Height

Purpose

To measure the standing height of the subject in centimeters.

Equipment

- Stabilometer, long ruler, or a long measuring tape.
- All subjects to be suitably attired—no shoes or socks.

Procedures

1. Subject stands tall against a wall.
2. Slide the stabilometer or a ruler to make contact with the subject's head, pressing down the hair. Ensure that no downward depression occurs.

Results

Height in centimeters can now be read off the stabilometer, ruler, or tape.

Weight

Purpose

To measure the weight of the subject in kilograms.

Equipment

- Scales

Procedures

1. Subject to stand in light clothing in the center of the scales. Ensure subjects are not wearing shoes, socks, or heavy clothing.

Results

Weight in kilograms can now be read off the scales.

Body Fat-Skinfold Test

Purpose

To estimate the percentage of body fat from skinfold thickness by use of a skinfold caliper.

Measurement Sites

The sites of measurement were chosen for use with the Sloan-Weir nomograms. For males under 26 years, the best predictions were found to come from measurements at the subscapular (under the shoulder blade) and thigh. For females under 25 years, the suprailiac (above the hip bone) and triceps sites were the best predictors. There are various other assessment techniques and measurement sites for estimating body fat, many of which involve lengthy formulas and require expensive, sophisticated equipment. The test suggested here is one coaches can administer effectively and readily using the selected nomograms.

Equipment

• For optimal results, use a good pair of skinfold calipers (e.g., Harpenden or Lange) because they exert a constant pressure at varying openings of the jam. However, as good calipers are expensive, some coaches might rather use plastic skinfold calipers, which yield results accurate enough to provide important information. These are available at a minimal cost from Ross Laboratories, Columbus, Ohio.

Procedures

The general method used to measure skinfolds is as follows:

1. Measures are to be made on the right side of the body.
2. The skinfold is to be clapsed between the thumb and index finger.
3. The amount of skinfold held must be sufficient to include two thicknesses of skin and subcutaneous fat, but not muscle or fascia.
4. If there is any doubt, ask the subject to tense the muscles underlying the skinfold grasped.
5. Apply the caliper over the landmark*, 1 centimeter from the fingers clasping the skinfold.
6. Measure to the nearest .1 millimeter.
7. Repeat the procedure until two consecutive measures are within .2 millimeters.

*The *anatomical landmarks* for the skinfold sites are as follows:

Subscapula (Males)
With the subject in a relaxed standing position, the landmark is located at the lowest point of the scapula. Lift the fold at an angle of about 45 degrees to the vertical, in the natural fold of the skin.

Thigh (Males)
The thigh skinfold is located from a vertical skinfold in the anterior midline of the thigh, midway between the hip and knee joints.

Triceps (Females)
The landmark is over the midpoint of the muscle belly (on the back of the arm), midway between the elbow and shoulder joints.

Suprailiac (Females)
The landmark is 4 centimeters above the crest of the ilium. Lift the fold in line with the fibers of the external oblique muscles (the natural diagonal line).

NOTE: Measuring skinfolds with accuracy and precision is not easy. Results may vary from measurement to measurement by the same tester, let alone from tester to tester. Thus, adherence to the procedures is very important, and lots of practice is necessary to obtain consistent results. For greater reliability of results, have the same person test all subjects' skinfolds at each testing session.

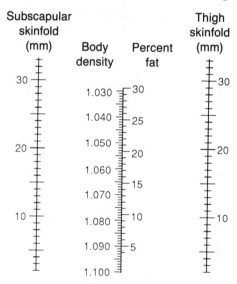

Figure 12.6 Nomogram for conversion of skinfolds to percent body fat for males. *Note.* From "Nomograms for prediction of body density and total body fat from skinfold measurements" by A. Sloan and J. Weir, 1970, *Journal of Applied Physiology,* **28**(2), pp. 221-222. Copyright 1970 by The American Physiological Society. Adapted by permission.

Nomograms for Predicting Body Fat

Body density and percentage of body fat can be quickly assessed for males and females from the graphs presented in Figures 12.6 and 12.7. Simply place a ruler joining the skinfold values and read the percentage of fat from the middle scale.

Recommendations

	Males	Females
Average:	13-17%	20-24%
Athletes:	Under 10%	Under 15%

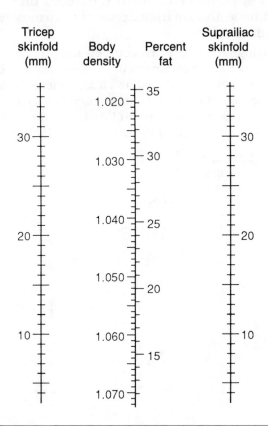

Figure 12.7 Nomogram for conversion of skinfolds to percent body fat for females. *Note.* From "Nomograms for prediction of body density and total body fat from skinfold measurements" by A. Sloan and J. Weir, 1970, *Journal of Applied Physiology,* **28**(2), pp. 221-222. Copyright 1970 by The American Physiological Society. Adapted by permission.

REFERENCE

Quinn, A.M. (1981). *A physiological profile of professional level tennis players.* Unpublished manuscript, Preston Institute of Technology, School of Physical Education and Leisure Studies, Bundoora, Victoria, Australia.

RECOMMENDED READINGS

Corbin, C.B. (1975). *Concepts in physical education* (2nd ed.). Dubuque, IA: Wm.C. Brown.

Durnin, J.V.G.A., & Rahaman, M.M. (1967). The assessment of the amount of fat in the human body from measurements of skinfold thicknesses. *British Journal of Nutrition,* **21**, 681-689.

Hockey, R. V. (1977). *Physical fitness: The pathway to healthful living* (3rd ed.). St. Louis: C.V. Mosby.

Johnson, B.L., & Nelson, J.K. (1974). *Practical measurements for evaluation in physical education* (2nd ed.). Minneapolis: Burgess.

Mathews, D.K., & Fox, E.L. (1976). *The physiological basis of physical education and athletics* (2nd ed.). Philadelphia: Saunders College Publishing.

Quinn, A.M. (1984). *A physiological profile of college level tennis players.* Unpublished manuscript, University of Kentucky, Lexington.

Quinn, A.M. (1985). *An electromyographical study of the abdominal muscles used in tennis strokes of skilled players.* Unpublished manuscript, University of Illinois, Urbana.

Telford, R.D., (1979). *Cardiorespiratory properties of trained and untrained subjects.* Unpublished doctoral dissertation, University of Melbourne, Melbourne, Australia.

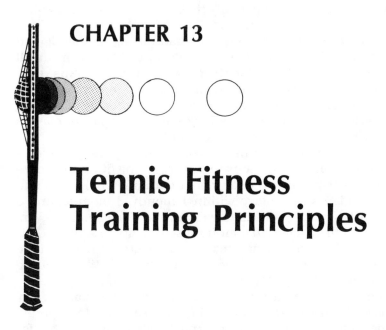

CHAPTER 13

Tennis Fitness Training Principles

A well-planned training program is based on many underlying principles to which players and coaches should always adhere. This chapter first presents these principles; afterward suggestions for the different phases of training are outlined.

TEN CARDINAL PRINCIPLES OF A TRAINING PROGRAM

There are 10 basic principles to follow when designing a training program for your tennis players. Attention to each principles is necessary if your programs are to achieve maximum effectiveness.

Define Your Goals and Make a Commitment

A player may have the best tennis coach, the best equipment, and everything that makes a good player, but these will be of no benefit unless the commitment to achieve one's potential comes from within. It cannot come from mothers, fathers, or coaches. The performers themselves must want to be the very best they can be, and this means working to improve not only their strokes, but also their fitness, mental game, and diet.

There is so much more to tennis than hitting forehands and backhands. Ivan Lendl, Martina Navratilova, and Pat Cash can all testify to that. As part of their rigorous training programs, they spend hours every day improving their fitness and movement. They adhere to special sport diets and do everything possible to achieve optimal performance. They are all excellent examples of players completely committed to becoming Number One.

Making this total commitment means defining *specific* goals—short-term and long-term. For example, regarding fitness, coaches should test their players to determine their individual levels and then set standards to achieve within 1 month, 3 months, and 6 months. Goals should be difficult, realistic, and challenging. Players should stretch themselves to their utmost capacity to achieve their goals. Any goal the athlete can reach without stretching is set too low and is no achievement or accomplishment at all. When setting goals, always be positive. Players should set themselves up for success. Set performance rather than outcome goals; for example, try to complete the all-direction line sprint in 58 seconds. Incorporate some goal-achievement strategies and identify target dates for attaining them. Record the goals in writing and place them where they can be seen every day. "Ink it, don't just think it!" Finally, don't forget to check your players' progress regularly to see if they are moving positively toward the accomplishment of their personal goals.

Coaches should reward players every time they reach one of their goals. After all, their goals set the limits of their potential and allow their dreams to become a reality.

Overload

When deciding on the kind of conditioning you will conduct for your tennis players, you must understand and apply the principle of progressive overload. To gain fitness, it is necessary to undertake a training load exceeding that to which the body is normally accustomed. Obviously, if the training load is too light, performance will not improve significantly. However, if the load is too heavy, the player will become fatigued and fail to show the expected improvements. Coaches must find a happy medium where exercise resistance for each individual is at its highest in the beginning and then is gradually increased as the player's fitness capacity improves through the course of the training program. The muscles will respond with increased capacity and efficiency.

Specificity

Specificity is very important to a fitness program. Similarity must exist between training and tennis, both in terms of the muscle groups involved and the energy systems used. Running 10 miles a day is of little training value for tennis, as players never run 10 miles on a court. Tennis players constantly start, stop, and change direction, giving their hearts the opportunity to recover between points. The majority of training should therefore be focused on short, sharp, explosive movements with plenty of stops, starts, twists, and turns. Obviously, there is no better place to train than on a tennis court.

Intensity

When conditioning players for tennis, coaches must exercise them at a level greater than that of their usual activity. This level is called the threshold for a training effect. Workouts must include activities with levels of intensity exceeding that of a match so as to ensure a well-stocked energy reserve. For a college player, professional, or aspiring champion, the level of intensity needs to be very high—not only to be able to play a few matches a day, but also to have plenty of reserve for the rigorous demands of traveling and the numerous other commitments players incur. On the other hand, social players will not need to train with great intensity for playing just a few sets each week, but certainly a fitness training program makes all players feel like winners—and not just on the tennis court.

Quality

"Quality is more important than quantity" is a well-coined phrase that also applies to a training program. For example, the player who jogs 30 minutes a day is not going to benefit as much as one who spends 30 minutes interspersing the jog with short, intense sprints. Don't forget specificity! Likewise, a fartlek run (see speed program—chapter 14) through a tree-shaded path in the mountains or along the beach with the rolling waves splashing against the sand is an experience to be savored and remembered. You probably wouldn't enjoy the same workout on the crowded track of an indoor gym. Within the topographical limits of the immediate area, coaches should do what they can to make training more enjoyable.

Here are some guidelines to help improve the quality of training sessions:

- *Plan ahead.* Plan the time, the place, whom you will train with, and what you will do.
- *Add variety.* Don't do the same session all the time. Add variety with different routines, different people, different places, and different times.
- *Set realistic goals.* Don't expect to play tennis for 5 hours on a hot, humid day, because if you can't do it you will feel you have failed when you really haven't. You just set an unrealistic goal. Remember goals are flexible. They are not cast in stone and can be adjusted according to circumstances.
- *Be prepared.* Get adequate sleep, eat sensibly, drink water frequently to replenish lost fluids, and keep a change of clothes in your bag.
- *Learn to relax.* See "Psychology" section in this book for guidelines.

Finally, remember it is up to you as the coach to enhance the quality of training.

Frequency

How many times a week should tennis players exercise for optimal results? The answer to this question will vary for each person who asks it. For weekly social players and eager youngsters, two or three conditioning sessions a week will be sufficient to maintain an appropriate fitness level. As many players are still developing their skills on the court, this must be the top priority during the learning stages. However, as your players become more skilled and their tennis training progresses in intensity and duration, it must also increase in frequency. For intermediate players, the time spent training will be well invested; tremendous strides can be made in their games with just 20 minutes of fitness training a day. For the up-and-coming juniors striving to do well in their sections and gain rankings, conditioning about 45 minutes a day, 6 days a week will make them fitter, faster, and stronger.

Many top athletes train twice daily to approach their potential, but they are wise enough to incorporate rest and recovery periods during and between sessions. You as a coach need to make sure that those athletes training a few times a day take one day off a week, or that they alternatively enjoy a relaxing day playing golf or some other sport.

Knowledge of Results

Players improve more quickly when they know the results of their performance, especially when they can see the results for themselves. It is therefore important to organize training in which improvement is measured and communicated to the performers. For example, show players their improved total time in a circuit training session (chapter 14) or an increase in speed as shown by a stopwatch. Improved times provide their own reward and satisfaction to players and give them greater motivation to train even harder. This in turn helps coaches and trainers, whom for many players are the main sources of motivation.

Individuality

As each player is an individual, it is necessary for the coach to develop individualized programs, concentrating on areas of fitness that help the player improve weaknesses and meet specific needs. Some players need work on speed and agility, others on cardiovascular endurance and power. Test results will determine the various needs of each player and ascertain his or her strengths and weaknesses.

Coaches must also realize that individuals respond differently to the *same* training. Such differences could be influenced by any number of factors—one's stage of growth, heredity, level of fitness, past experiences, eating habits, attitude toward training, motivation, habits of rest and sleep, environmental conditions, or the effect of an injury.

Variety

We have discussed variety already under quality of training, but the concept is so important that it deserves space here as well. The saying "Variety is the spice of life" certainly applies to a conditioning program. This book introduces coaches to many different methods of conditioning, encouraging them to incorporate consider-able variety into their training programs. Doing so will not only pre-vent boredom and staleness, but make for greater enjoyment and interest.

Fun

Strive to make the training sessions fun. Fitness is frequently an area of training players either dread or neglect altogether—primarily because it is not presented with variety, individuality, and fun. The fact is that with a bit of creativity, training sessions can be fun. Coaches should be challenged to make their sessions motivational and interesting. Doing the same workout day in and day out rapidly becomes boring. Aim to do something different. Use various train-ing methods and different drills, work on different components of fitness, vary the duration and intensity of your sessions, and set goals for individuals to achieve. Be sure to include competitions that are fun and to reward improvement as well as motivation. Need-less to say, with such a variety of workouts, coaches will have more fun too.

Training for and playing tennis, like life, is to be enjoyed—so have FUN!

In summary, there are 10 cardinal principles of an effective training program:

1. Define your goals and make a commitment.
2. Follow the overload principle.
3. Be specific at all times.
4. Gradually increase the intensity of workouts.
5. Strive for quality workouts.
6. Train regularly and frequently.
7. Provide a knowledge of results.
8. Tailor training to individuals.
9. Add variety in every possible way.
10. Have fun.

PHASES OF TRAINING

Tennis is played year-round all over the world; for most recreational and competitive players there are no distinct seasons as there are in football and basketball. Coaches and players therefore have some latitude in planning and should organize tournament and playing schedules that devote the necessary time to conditioning and improving strengths and weaknesses. For all players, the schedule for conditioning and skill training should be related to the importance of upcoming matches and tournaments. No matter what the competitive level of players, they need time set aside to prepare their physical, mental, and playing skills. *Preparation is the key to success.*

Off-Season

This time should be devoted to remaining active without necessarily playing tennis. Many players choose to play basketball or soccer or to engage in the latest craze, such as ultimate frisbee. Be sure to insist that your players stay healthy and keep in shape. The off-season can also be a time for more serious players to work on improving strengths and weaknesses or to engage in weight-training and conditioning programs.

Preseason

Preseason training for tennis can last a few weeks or for as long as 2 or 3 months. Time invested in preseason training could well pay big dividends to a player's game. During this time, training should involve developing the anaerobic energy system and improving on-court techniques and strokes.

Prior to Tournaments

The week or two before a tournament is not a time for athletes to be learning a new skill. It is a time for consolidation and for working on strengths. All forms of conditioning should be done on the court surface of the upcoming tournament (Specificity!). The line drills and agility activities suggested are all excellent to do during this time as they replicate the movements and energy systems used in matches. Also, the reaction drills are great to sharpen reflexes. Players should not be doing endurance activities or weight training. This is the stage of toning down the conditioning program so that players will be at their physical peak. The hard work and preparation has already been completed.

In-Season

The in-season period may continue for months on end. Emphasis should therefore be placed on learning skills and strategies; at the same time athletes need to work on maintaining the fitness and energy systems developed during the preseason. Agility, speed, and power are the most important fitness components necessary for constant improvement. Coaches should also re-administer the physiological tests to objectively determine individual strengths and weaknesses. From these results, specific programs can be developed to supplement skill sessions where necessary.

At Tournaments

For many players, participating in a tournament means being miles away from home, often without their coach and practice partners. During this time, conditioning is ill-advised. Emphasis should be placed on match preparation. There is no point in players' running 5 or 10 miles and tiring themselves out before a big match the next morning. Coaches should stress that players thoroughly stretch out, fine-tune their skills, work on match strategies, and concentrate on some movement drills on court. Then, after a cool-down, it's time for R and R—rest and relaxation.

Warm-Up

The time to get onto the court has finally arrived! The fun is about to begin. Players will be anxious to get started, but coaches must insist that the first thing players do is *warm up*. A 15- to 20-minute warm-up should be done every time players walk onto a tennis court or begin training. Warming up will improve the efficiency of the muscles, reduce the likelihood of injury, and prepare the body for the upcoming activity. Before beginning to stretch, players should increase the temperature of their muscles through some other activity. These activities should be selected taking into account the age and ability of the players. They might include the following:

- tag games (great for agility too)
- relay races
- hand-eye coordination activities, such as running, bouncing the ball with the racket, controlling the ball on the racket face, and so forth.

- basic movements specific to the game, such as side-stepping, crossovers, running forward and backward, and so forth.
- minor games
- shadow strokes
- aerobics—exercising to music, a great way to get groups motivated.

When players have warmed-up their muscles, they should then spend some time stretching out. A very thorough stretching program, plus stretching tips and benefits, is described in the flexibility section of chapter 14.

Cool-Down

At the conclusion of any tennis or training session, it is important to spend 5 or 10 minutes cooling down. A slow, easy jog and the stretching exercises described later in the flexibility section are just the thing for players and coaches alike. Cooling down allows body temperature to gradually return to normal and enhances the removal of lactic acid and the restoration of the body to its starting condition. Cooling down also helps prevent some of the soreness and tightness that often follow a tough workout.

OVERTRAINING: HOW MUCH IS TOO MUCH?

There is a very fine line between optimal or *peak* training and overtraining. Athletes at all levels seem prone to overtrain. They grow up believing the old adage, "No pain, no gain." Yet the risks of overtraining are many, including illness, injury, and lost time. Muscles get stiff and sore. Players may experience sluggishness, fatigue, and sometimes lymph node swelling or gastrointestinal disorders. Physical performance typically declines; players may even lose interest in the game or suffer a decline in school or other work.

Coaches can help athletes prevent overstress by emphasizing these basic fitness principles:

- Attempt to equalize stress by alternating training sessions of high intensity with low-intensity work.

- Gradually increase overload so that the stress of training loads is progressively manageable for each player.

• Have athletes check their pulse each morning before rising. Average the daily rates; if they vary by more than five beats, suspect illness or overtraining. The level of tiredness upon rising in the morning is also a measure of overstress.

• Keep a close watch on body weight. A rapid weight loss could indicate impending problems due to poor eating habits, dehydration, nervousness, or excessive fatigue.

• Encourage players to watch for other useful indicators such as weakness, pain in joints, abnormal color or cloudiness of urine, or abnormal skin color (pasty or pale).

• Avert overtraining by adding variety to workouts. Repetitious practices result in staleness.

When it comes to overtraining, *prevention* is the key, not correction after the fact.

CHAPTER 14

Total Fitness Training for Tennis

Tennis demands a great deal of physical effort in addition to expert skill with the racket. To nurture success, coaches must assume a responsibility greater than that of merely improving fundamental stroking ability during practice. They must prepare their players for rigorous competition, which involves a lot of practice on the tennis court. However, tennis is a *slow* developer of such components as cardiovascular endurance, flexibility, muscular endurance, strength, and power. Thus, the training program should include activities to develop these necessary components more quickly. This chapter is filled with such drills! Improved fitness for your players will be the key to better positioning and movement around the court, better stroke production and performance, and increased confidence. Clearly, an effective physical conditioning program based on exercise physiology principles is essential if a peak performance level is to be attained.

DRILLS TO IMPROVE AGILITY

Drills are good to use in improving agility. Try to make them as much fun and as game-like as possible for best results.

GENERAL ON-COURT SPRINTS

The aim of the following drills is to enhance footwork, speed, agility, and balance on the court. All sprints must be done on a tennis court, preferably on the same surface as that of upcoming tournaments. These drills involve forward and backward running, sidestepping, and diagonal runs, thus simulating all the movements a player makes on the court. As some sprints are repeated several times, they will also aid to increase endurance. Most importantly, however, they are specific to tennis and the movements made while playing. It is this specificity that is essential to any conditioning program for tennis.

The first few drills should be a regular part of everyday training for advanced players. Coaches who administer these drills should chart each player's performance and monitor improvement not only in the times but also in the agility players exhibit as they move around the court. It might be a good idea to make a competition out of these drills. Give a reward (anything from a free lesson to a granola bar) to the best performer, or, just as importantly, to the player who improves the most over the season. At the Nick Bollettieri Tennis Academy, for example, conditioning competition was very intense. Some players issued challenges over the dinner table!

All-Direction Line Sprint

Starting Position

The center mark on the baseline. Return to this position after each sprint, reversing the direction in which you run. Note: You must touch each line you run to and also the starting position each time you pass through it.

1. Sprint to the "T" intersection (service line and center line), then sidestep along the service line to the right singles sideline, and touch. Return in the same pattern to the starting position.
2. Repeat 1, but to the left singles sideline.
3. Run on the diagonal to the service line and singles sideline (right), touch, then backpedal diagonally back to the start.

4. Sidestep across the baseline to touch the right singles sideline.

5. Repeat 3, but to the left diagonal (singles sideline and service line).

6. Repeat 4, but sidestep across to the left singles sideline.

7. Run on the diagonal to the net and (right) doubles sideline, touch, then backpedal diagonally to the start.

8. Sidestep across the baseline to touch the right doubles sideline.

9. Repeat 7, but to the left diagonal (doubles sideline and net).

10. Repeat 8, but sidestep across to touch the left doubles sideline.

11. To complete the routine, sprint forward to touch the net, then backpedal to the starting position.

Variations

- Have competitions for the record.
- Run against a partner at the opposite end of the court.
- Make this a "killer" line sprint and have athletes complete it two or three times consecutively. This will really test their fitness and endurance!

Average Time

Males: 53.37 seconds

Females: 60.90 seconds

Test yourself against the pros. The times in these drills are the averages obtained from over 30 touring professionals and are included to give you some guidelines for your top players to work toward. Coaches should establish realistic goals for each class or team according to age and ability levels.

Cues to Call Out

1. Service line—singles sideline right
2. Service line—singles sideline left
3. Short diagonal—right
4. Singles sideline right
5. Short diagonal—left
6. Singles sideline—left
7. Long diagonal—right
8. Doubles sideline—right
9. Long diagonal—left

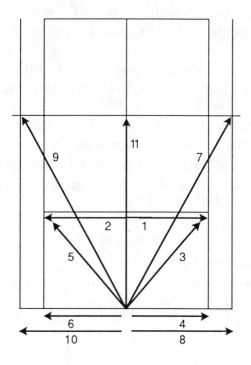

Figure 14.1 All-direction line sprint.

10. Doubles sideline—left
11. Net—baseline (finish)

Forward/Backward Line Sprint

Starting Position

Against the backstop.

Aim

To improve forward and backward movement on the court.

1. Sprint backstop to service line.
2. Backpedal service line to baseline.
3. Sprint baseline to net.
4. Backpedal net to service line.
5. Sprint service line to net.
6. Backpedal from the net all the way to the backstop.

7. Sprint backstop to baseline.
8. Backpedal again to the backstop (finish).

Average Time

Males: 18.82 seconds
Females: 20.90 seconds

Cues to Call Out

1. Standing; touching backstop—Ready, set, go!
2. Service line
3. Baseline
4. Net
5. Service line
6. Net

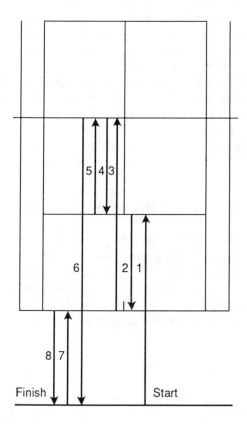

Figure 14.2 Forward/backward line sprint.

7. Backstop

8. Baseline

9. Backstop (finish)

Your players might require a few lessons to learn these routines, but once learned they can be administered quickly and efficiently. If you have a group lesson with four players per court, have two players go against each other at opposite ends of the court; then while these two catch their breath, the other two players can perform. You may occasionally want to participate in a drill yourself so that you can better judge the intensity of the workouts. Kids always love to play against their coach—and if they win it makes their day!

Remember the ninth cardinal principle—variety, the spice of life! Don't do the same old drills day in and day out. Your players will become stale and bored, which is just what you want to avoid. The following section presents many ideas for agility drills. If you want to change some of them to suit your players' needs, that's great. With a bit of imagination, the sky's the limit.

In observing a match, a coach may notice a player is slow running in a particular direction (e.g., running forward to a short ball, or backward for a lob). Maybe the player is weaker in his or her takeoff leg and a little slower getting to the right. Whatever the player's weakness, the following drills will be sure to improve it. To make training even more specific, have your players do these drills with their rackets in hand. Because all players have specific areas that need work, a variety of drills are presented under separate headings.

Forward Killer for Explosive Starts and Stops

This is a tough one, designed to improve forward speed, starting, stopping, balance, and endurance. Begin at the baseline and sprint forward to the service line and back. Then sprint to the net and back. Then, to the service line of the other side and back to the baseline. Then all the way to the opposite baseline and back. Then begin again, reversing the order of the sprints. Remember—have fun!

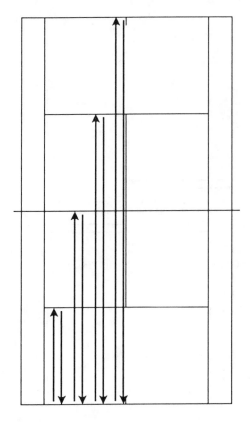

Figure 14.3   Forward killer for explosive starts and stops.

Across-the-Court Runs for Explosive Starts and Stops

Repeat the above sprints, but run forward and backward across the court (or sideways if lateral movements are what you need). Running this way, large groups can effectively train against each other. Have relays, two per team. Use three or four courts, if available.

If it's work on backpedaling you need most, run the entire drill backward. Running sideways across the court will serve to improve

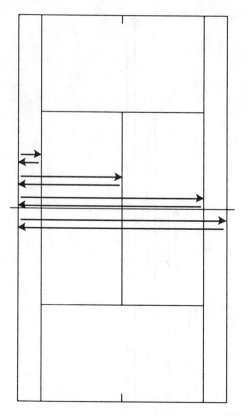

Figure 14.4 Across-the-court runs for explosive stops and starts.

lateral court movement. Adapt the drills to your needs. The possibilities are endless.

SIDEWAYS SPRINT DRILLS

The following drills simulate lateral movements across the court.

Sideways All-Line Drill

This drill involves touching each line and returning to the left doubles sideline as you sidestep across the tennis court. Repeat two times without stopping.

Variations

- Do this drill using two courts, if available. The player continues touching each line and returning to the far doubles sideline after each line is touched.

- Sidestep and touch each line you pass over. Continue down the courts if there are a row of courts. Then return to the start and repeat with the opposite leg as the lead leg.

- Emphasize keeping low, bending the knees more. This will make the drill tougher and will strengthen the quadricep muscles. Remember to hold the racket in the ready position.

- This drill is also effective for forward running, pivoting as you reach each line (likewise for backpedaling—see "Across-the-Court Runs").

- Run the drill with large groups. Have relays, two per team—make it competitive fun.

Volley Drill

As the name implies, this drill requires the performer to simulate playing volleys while moving from side to side. With racket in hand (to increase wrist strength put the racket cover on your racket as well) play a forehand volley on the singles sideline, then a backhand volley on the center line. A player must move sideways and position his or her feet correctly to play each volley (for a right-handed player, left foot in front for a forehand and right foot for a backhand volley; reverse for a left-handed player). This drill is so quick that players hardly have time to put their heels on the ground. They are always on their toes. Begin by doing this drill 20 times and gradually increase. Pros will usually do 75 to 100. To make the drill more enjoyable, do it to music.

Variation

This is the same as the drill above, except the players, instead of volleying, must bend their knees to play a low forehand and backhand respectively. This is an excellent drill to force players to bend, especially if your students are often lazy and just drop their racket heads.

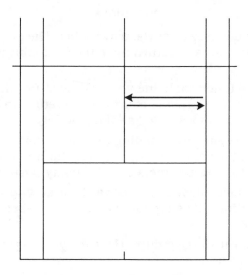

Figure 14.5   Volley drill.

Figure 14.6   Yannick Noah demonstrating how to get down to play low balls.

DIAGONAL SPRINT DRILLS

The 'W' Drill

Simply follow the arrows, beginning at the left net post, backpedaling to the singles sideline, then running forward to the center and service lines, backpedaling again to the singles sideline, then running a sprint for match point to your opponent's angled dropshot (near the right net post).

Note: As players' fitness improves, the coach should increase the quantity of these drills, allowing only a 30-second rest between each one.

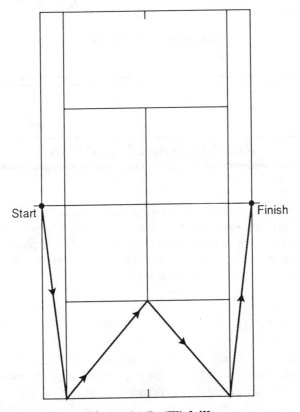

Figure 14.7 'W' drill.

The Bow-Tie Drill

Again, just follow the arrows, alternating forward sprints with back-pedaling. Don't forget to bend and touch each line you run to and to get your correct foot into position.

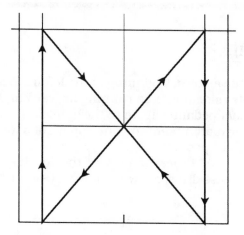

Figure 14.8 The bow-tie drill.

ROLLING-BALL ROUTINE

Rolling-ball drills are excellent for agility and help players develop hand-eye coordination, learn to watch the ball, and judge ball speed and direction. These routines also require that a player bends to get to a ball which, of course, is a good habit to acquire. It is best to do these drills on a tennis court.

Center-Up Drill

The coach stands at the "T" intersection with six balls. The player begins in the ready position at the center mark on the baseline. The coach rolls a ball along the ground within the singles court. The player must run to the ball, roll it back, then return to the center again. As the player returns to the center, the coach rolls the next ball.

The coach begins by alternating rolling the balls side to side. Once the player understands the drill, the balls can be rolled in any direction. Force the player to constantly change direction and do a lot of stopping and starting. Fifteen balls in a row is good to start. Gradually increase the number as players improve their fitness.

Variations

* Use only the service box area.
* Vary depth, speed, and spin of balls.
* Bounce and throw balls to players along with rolling them.

The following ball recovery exercises are yet more excellent agility drills.

Figure 14.9   Rolling-ball routines.

BALL-RECOVERY DRILLS

The objective in these drills is to pick up all the balls, put them in a basket as quickly as possible, then put them back in their places on the court.

Timed Recovery Drill

Begin at the baseline. Sprint to pick up the first ball. Backpedal to the baseline and place the ball in the basket. Follow this procedure with all other balls. It does not matter in what order they are picked up. Once all the balls are in the basket, begin putting them back in their places on the court one at a time. The coach times the player from start to finish (i.e., after all the balls are back in their original positions). This drill can be repeated as players become more fit.

Variations

- Compete against others. Have two people per team, one picking up the balls, the other putting them back. This adds competition and motivation, which are important aspects of any conditioning program. Alternatively, the teams can compete against each other at opposite ends of the court.
- Set balls up on a diagonal if you require movement to a particular side.

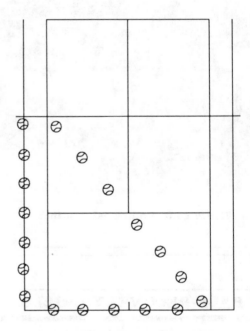

Figure 14.10   Ball-recovery drill.

- Instead of running forward and backward, sidestep.
- Increase the number of balls.
- Take down the net and increase the distance between balls to make players run the length of the court.

Although agility is one of the most important fitness components for tennis, many coaches and players still fail to include agility drills as part of their training program. Coaches need to get their juniors off on the right foot. After all, footwork is the name of the game: "Footwork is one of the most important, yet most overlooked aspects of championship tennis. . . . In fact, when a player misses a crucial shot the fault usually lies, not in the stroke itself, but in the footwork" (Groppel, 1984, p. 36).

Many of the agility drills just described have the added benefit of developing players' balance, coordination, speed, cardiovascular endurance, and speed endurance. The specificity involved is also helpful. Use the offered variations to spice up your program and to help your players enjoy getting in shape.

DRILLS TO IMPROVE SPEED

Speed training goes by a number of names. Physiologists call it *anaerobic conditioning*, coaches sometimes refer to it as *interval training*, and many players just call it *running windsprints*. Whatever you call it, speed training adds up to hard work. With variety, however, coaches can make speed training fun. There are certainly plenty of activities to choose from. Motivate your players by setting up challenges. Tell them, also, that speed is absolutely essential for tennis players.

Before beginning any sprint training, players should jog and stretch so that the muscles are warm, joints are loose, and the heart is prepared to work harder. Once started, increase speed gradually. A player should not go all out for the record on the first sprint. Also, when a sprint is completed, be sure players slow down gradually and don't try to stop abruptly. Finally, don't forget to have your players cool down and stretch out at the end of a workout.

PRESEASON

Speed training should be implemented in the off-season or pre-season and should emphasize (a) running with high knees, (b) correct technique, (c) acceleration runs, (d) down-hill runs, and (e) hopping about 50 meters (to increase power and strength in the quadriceps). Studies show that increased speed in sprint running often requires improved technique, achieved by altering body position, stride length, and/or stride rate.

Speed-Resisted Training

Speed-resisted training is also best done during the preseason. The player can use either isokinetic strength-training equipment (see strength section), or weighted clothing or equipment—for example, running uphill through sand, or practicing strokes and movements on court with the cover on the racket. The latter is great for improving speed and agility and will also aid in developing arm strength, making the racket feel lighter during play. It should be noted that although speed-resisted training is helpful and useful, there is no substitute for actual on-court sprints.

YEAR-ROUND DRILLS

Line sprints, rolling-ball routines, and ball-recovery drills can be done throughout the year to improve speed. These drills are excellent in increasing a player's speed around the court because they are so specific to tennis. Please refer to the agility section for detailed descriptions.

Remember that as well as practicing drills, one of the easiest ways of increasing speed to the ball is through good court positioning. Where a player stands while awaiting an opponent's serve or next shot in a rally can mean added seconds in getting to the ball. When possible, a player should take position in the middle of the angle of possible returns. Then he or she can adjust according to the oncoming shot. He or she can also move closer toward the net (without straying outside the angle), thus giving the opponent less court in which to hit. The angle stays the same but the arc gets smaller the closer the player moves in.

Interval Sprinting

Using the interval training format, the guidelines for developing a short-sprint program are as follows:

- duration of work period 0 to 15 seconds
- intensity of work 100% maximum
- duration of recovery period 1 to 2 minutes
- work/recovery ratio 1:5 to 1:10
- repetitions of work/recovery sequence 5 to 15

An example of a typical 15-minute session of short-sprint training would be 10 repetitions of 50 meters run in 7 seconds every 80 seconds. The duration of sprint repetitions must be kept very short (5 to 10 seconds) so that athletes can reach maximum speed without incurring early fatigue.

Acceleration Sprints

These sprints are run in less than 5 seconds each, with the players in a variety of starting positions as happens in a match. The aim is to accelerate as quickly as possible, as time is very short. For variety, try starting these sprints from lying, sitting, or kneeling positions.

Longer Sprints

Because acceleration work does not allow sufficient time for maximum sprinting speed to be reached, it is necessary to extend the length of the sprint. Gradually increase running speed from jogging to striding and finally to sprinting. The jogging, striding, and sprinting intervals may consist of 30-meter to 100-meter segments. The recovery period should consist of walking or a light jog. Thus, players jog 50 meters, stride 50 meters, sprint 50 meters, walk 50 meters, and then repeat. Because recovery between repetitions is nearly complete, this type of training develops speed and strength.

Wind Sprints

This method of training consists of alternating jogging with short sprints. A player could jog 30 meters, sprint 10 meters, then repeat 10 times. Players increase jogging and sprinting distances as they improve. For example: Jog 40 meters, sprint 15 meters, 10 repetitions; or jog 60 meters, sprint 20 meters, 10 repetitions; or jog 80 meters, sprint 25 meters, 10 repetitions.

Fartlek Training

Yes, you did read the word correctly! *Fartlek* is actually a Swedish word meaning *speed play*. It involves alternating fast and slow running over natural terrain. It is really like an informal interval training in that neither the work nor relief intervals are precisely timed. Such a program will develop both speed and endurance. An example of a training schedule for a workout using the fartlek method is as follows:

1. Warm up by running easily for 5 to 10 minutes.
2. Run at a fast, steady speed over a distance of 1 to 1.5 kilometers.
3. Walk rapidly for 5 minutes.
4. Practice easy running, broken by sprints of 60 to 70 meters, repeating until fatigue sets in.
5. Run easily, injecting 3 to 4 swift steps occasionally.
6. Run at full speed for 175 to 200 meters.
7. Run at a fast pace for 1 minute.
8. Finish the routine by running a few laps around the track.

Spot Running

Run in place, sometimes slowly with the knees raised to waist height, other times as fast as possible, with feet scarcely leaving the ground. Always keep on the toes. To begin, do this exercise in sets of 50 counts (one count each time the foot touches the ground), followed by 15 seconds rest. As fitness develops, increase the number of counts and sets and reduce the recovery periods. This exercise is excellent for quickness, leg strength, and endurance.

Stair Running

Stair running is an excellent way to keep your legs moving. Many pro players run the steps of their local stadiums as part of their training. Alternate workouts by running up every step, then returning at a slower pace to the start. Or alternate steps. This drill also develops strength and builds up endurance.

Keep Alert!

Last, but certainly not least—keep alert! Focus your eyes, ears, and energy on the ball. Think only, *The ball.* As the great player Rod Laver once said: "Nothing but the ball. Glue your eyes on it. Marry it. Don't let it get out of your sight." If you are totally alert to the ball at all times, you'll get to it sooner. Jimmy Connors is a perfect example of a player who focuses all his senses on the ball. Doing so has become habit for him. Any player can make it a habit if he or she practices. *Practice intensely to play intensely.*

As fitness improves, coaches can apply the overload principle to increase the intensity of workouts by

- increasing the number of sprints,
- increasing the distance of the sprints,
- shortening the time between work intervals,
- increasing the level of activity during the relief intervals, and
- increasing the frequency of training per week.

However, keep in mind that your athletes are training for tennis not the track team. Concentrate on short sprints specific to tennis and give players the same chance to recover their breath that they have between points and games in a match. I suggest you limit the speed workouts to two sessions per week. And if players are very tired, sick, or injured, don't do sprints. They should always listen to their bodies and obey its signs.

Implementing speed-improvement drills into your program will soon make your players quicker in getting to the ball, in charging the net to put away a volley, and in sprinting back to the baseline to retrieve a lob. In tennis, quicker players are always more successful.

A STRENGTH, POWER, AND MUSCULAR-ENDURANCE PROGRAM FOR TENNIS

Weight training is an effective means of developing strength, power and muscular endurance. However, like all the programs suggested, if it is to be helpful to tennis players, it must be specific to tennis, exercising the muscle groups that are used in the game. Players should work on weight training year-round, with greatest emphasis during the off-season, a gradual decrease during the preseason, and another reduction during the playing season, when emphasis should be concentrated on agility, speed, and tennis skills.

The type of weight training you use in your program depends on what equipment is available. Different equipment requires different muscular contractions. There are four basic types of muscular contraction. An *isotonic contraction* (also called *dynamic* or *moving)* is a muscular contraction with concurrent shortening of the muscle such that the joint angle changes. An *isometric* or *static contraction* occurs when a player exerts a maximal force against an immovable object, such as a cable tension device. Here, strength training is specific to the angle at which it is directed, as opposed to developing strength throughout the range of motion. Isometric exercises are beneficial during injury rehabilitation in which joint motion may be harmful but strength should be improved. An *eccentric muscle contraction* occurs when a muscle lengthens while contracting, such as in lowering a weight. Eccentric contractions are used in resisting gravity, such as when running down a hill. During an *isokinetic contraction*, an athlete exercises at a constant angular velocity and the tension developed by the muscle is similar at all joint angles over the full range of motion (Figure 14.11).

Figure 14.11   Chip Hooper on a Nautilus machine.

General Guidelines for Strength, Power, and Muscular-Endurance Training

Just as there are four types of muscular contractions, there are four types of programs structured around them. As exercise depends on the equipment available, the assessment of specific needs, time constraints, and individual goals, this section, rather than outlining specific tasks, will concentrate on the basic principles of weight training and how they might apply to your conditioning program. For safety reasons and optimal results, it is crucial that players have good hands-on instruction when using weights to ensure they use proper techniques. Improper techniques result in injuries.

Isotonic Exercises

The ideal training program using the isotonic technique is as follows:

Set 1 = 10 repetitions at a load of half with 10 repetition maximum (RM)

Set 2 = 10 repetitions at a load of three quarters with 10 RM

Set 3 = 10 repetitions at a full load with 10 RM

A set is the number of repetitions done consecutively without resting (in this case, 1 set = 10 repetitions). Once the learner can do more than 10 repetitions, the load is increased to a new 10-RM load. A repetition maximum is the maximum load a muscle or muscle group can lift over a given number of repetitions before becoming fatigued. For instance, if a player can press 100 pounds 10 times without undue strain, a half 10-RM load is 50 pounds.

Because isotonic exercises involve the full range of motion of the muscle in one contraction and develop greater muscular endurance than isometrics, they are recommended as a sound means of developing strength and muscular endurance (USPTA, 1988). Isotonic exercises can also enhance flexibility and, because players are able to see work being accomplished, might offer a psychological advantage that isometric exercises cannot provide.

Isometric Exercises

Like isotonic exercises, isometric exercises have been shown to produce significant gains in strength in short periods of time. However, several isometric contractions are required at different angles to produce the same results as isotonic contractions. Many studies have compared the two methods, and isotonic programs have emerged as the most favorable means of developing muscular strength and endurance. However, as previously mentioned, isometric exercises are recommended for players recovering from injury.

Eccentric Contractions

Weight-training programs based on eccentric contractions are rarely adopted by coaches. The little information available on such programs indicates that they can increase strength, but not as effectively as other programs. Like isometric contractions, eccentric contractions are recommended mainly for therapy and rehabilitation.

Isokinetic Programs

Isokinetic program are the newest to weight training. They require the use of expensive equipment, which is a drawback for many coaches. Unlike isotonic exercise, isokinetic exercise ensures that the muscles involves are overloaded at all stages of the movement. The rate of strength gain has been shown to be faster and greater with this method than with isotonic or isometric training programs, which is to be expected, as a greater number of motor units are activated. Consequently, greater demands (greater overload) than previously possible can be placed on the muscles being exercised. Isokinetic programs are *strongly recommended* for tennis players (Figure 14.12).

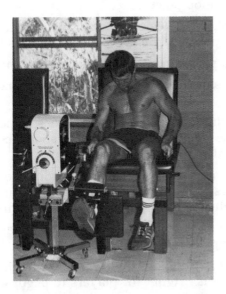

Figure 14.12   Player working out on Cybex equipment.

General Considerations in Strength, Power, and Muscular-Endurance Programs

There are several general concepts to consider when planning strength, power, and muscular-endurance programs for tennis players.

• To develop muscular strength a program should consist of a low number of repetitions (for example, a set of 6 to 10 repetitions), at a high level of resistance.

• Developing muscular endurance requires several repetitions at a low level of resistance. (Weights less than 66% of your maximum effort for that muscle group, with as many repetitions as possible.)

• To develop power, athletes should exercise at a medium level of resistance (relative to the drill) at a fast rate. (Weights should be in the range of 30% to 60% of maximal strength, with 15 to 25 quick repetitions.)

• Any of the exercises for strength done with a relative increase in speed will develop power.

• If a player shows a weakness in a specific area, specific weight training for the muscles involved should be prescribed.

• Ease into a program with lighter weights and fewer sets.

• Performers should exhale during a lift and inhale as they lower the weights.

• Nautilus training specifications and fitness experts recommend that large muscle groups (back, legs, chest) should be exercised first, followed by smaller muscle groups (arms).

• Leave 48 hours between weight-training workouts to allow time for muscles to recover; do no more than three sessions per week, except when training under a knowledgeable coach.

• There is no need to distinguish between males and females when prescribing exercises.

• At this time, physiologists do not have predictors regarding what specific age is "right" for players to begin weight training. As each player's physiological development occurs at a different stage, it is recommended you seek a physician's advice before starting an athlete on a weight program. One 14-year-old may be only 11 years in terms of physical growth, whereas another 14-year-old might have the physical attributes of a 16- or 17-year-old. In any case, I encourage younger players to concentrate mainly on practicing the fundamentals of the game. Weight training can wait a while. For conditioning, I recommend participation in several other sports and activities offered in school physical education programs.

• Because they lack the male hormone, testosterone, responsible for muscular hypertrophy, females will generally not develop muscle bulk with weight training. Coaches should stress this point, as many people do not understand the physiological basis for muscular development. Some women still believe that weight training will make them look masculine. They need to understand that besides the added benefits of increased strength, power, and muscular endurance, increased muscle tone will firm them up and improve their appearance. Coaches should tell the women they teach that they have everything to gain through weight training and only fat to lose!

• Conversely, male players, because they have testosterone, will increase muscle bulk through weight training. Coaches must emphasize that the objective of weight training is improved athletic ability for tennis, not bodybuilding. Excessive focus on building muscle bulk may have diminishing returns in terms of quickness and agility.

• For tennis players, weight-training emphasis should be placed on the legs, groin, back, trunk, abdomen, shoulder, forearms, and wrists.

• Coaches should maintain a log or record of a player's progress, keeping account of weights, repetitions, and sets. Such a record will help motivate and encourage your players as they keep track of their improvement.

Circuit Training

Circuit training is another excellent way of developing not only power, strength, and muscular endurance, but also all the other components of fitness for tennis. It consists of performing three times a series of exercises that the player must complete as quickly as possible at stations.

Figure 14.13 shows a circuit designed specifically for tennis players. Set up on a tennis court, it requires no equipment but a few balls and a racket. Utilization of space is effective, as 20 or more people can be readily accommodated. The activities are arranged so that different muscle groups are exercised in turn. The circuit is completed three times and takes approximately 30 minutes; thus, it is a fast and efficient mode of training. If the training group is small and if time permits, individual loadings can be prescribed by testing each player for one minute on each item. The number of repetitions completed in this time is then halved to establish the number that must be completed in the circuit. Thus, every player is working to a maximum against the clock! Improvement is apparent by decreases in the time required to complete the circuit.

The circuit presented here is just an example, which an easily be modified. Select exercises according to the conditioning effects needed. Remember the principle of specificity and have the exercises resemble movement in play or train the muscle groups used in tennis.

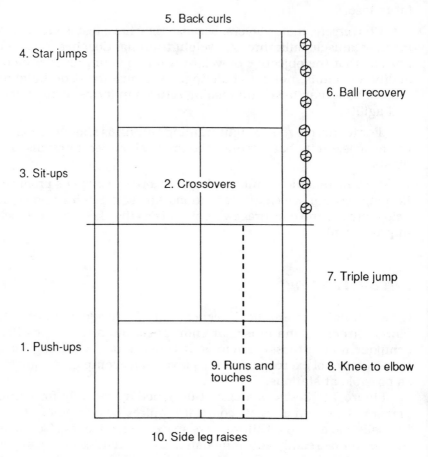

Figure 14.13 The tennis circuit.

Other Ways to Develop Strength, Power, and Muscular Endurance

Besides weight training and circuit training numerous other ways exist to develop the components of fitness. The following exercises are suggested:

- Sit-ups, trunk twists, and other forms of abdominal exercises
- Push-ups
- Chin-ups
- Leg exercises, such as leg raises, knee to chest, scissors, bicycles, etc.
- Arm exercises, such as sky punches, arm pushes back and forward, arm twists, windmills, arm circles, and so forth
- Ball squeezes for building up the wrist and fingers
- Playing tennis with a racket cover on, for developing strength in the grip, wrist, and forearm
- Aerobics and calisthenics
- For junior players not ready to begin weight training, the use of one-pound plastic weights

Clearly, there are so many ways to improve power, strength, and muscular endurance that there is no reason not to introduce variety into your training program. Make it fun for everyone.

ACTIVITIES TO IMPROVE CARDIOVASCULAR ENDURANCE

As running undoubtedly develops cardiovascular endurance, it should be an integral part of conditioning programs for all players before the season approaches. Because I stress the principle of specificity, I will rarely have players do a 5- or 10-mile run, simply because they never have to run this far on a tennis court. However, if players are out of shape or have had a long break, since regular activity, continuous running will develop their aerobic fitness and get them back on the road to winning tennis.

Continuous Running

A continuous training effort usually lasts between 15 minutes and an hour. This type of running is sometimes referred to as LSD (i.e., long, slow distance) or, more commonly, jogging. After training for about 10 minutes, the player can stop and count his pulse for 6 seconds. This count is them multiplied by 10 to determine the heart rate in beats per minute. The jogging pace will vary from player to player but should be fast enough to bring the heart rate to 150 beats per minute. Studies have shown that distance alone without some minimum level of intensity does not guarantee improvement in circulorespiratory endurance. At the same time, the purpose of continuous running is not achieving an intense pace. The "talk test" is a useful guide to the intensity of training. Players should be able to converse freely during a continuous routine. Through continuous running, players form a foundation for training that involves a greater intensity or speed of effort.

Fartlek Training

Long runs can be blended with Fartlek training by interspersing short bursts of faster work throughout a continuous running session. This type of training develops both speed and endurance (see Speed section).

Specific Tennis Runs

Players may gain still greater benefits from a running program if they incorporate into it the kinds of quick stops, starts, and changes of directions that occur in match play. The lunging, leaping, twisting, turning, and stretching a player must do on the court can also be part of the run. For that matter, what better place than a tennis court to train? Players can run around the circumference of the courts doing short sprints, crossover steps (used in reaching for wide volleys), backpedaling, diagonal sprints—whatever their imagination comes up with. For best results, repeat these drills well beyond the first signs of fatigue, giving short recovery periods, as between points in a game.

Interval Training

Interval training has probably produced more successful athletes than any other system of conditioning. As the name implies, interval training is a series of repeated bouts of exercise alternated with periods of relief. Light or mild exercise usually constitutes the relief period. This process results in more intensive work completed without the accompaniment of higher levels of fatigue. For example, by breaking up a 60-second sprint into six 10-second sprints with a 30-second recovery period between each (walking, for example), the same amount of work can be accomplished with less fatigue. The advantage is that the athlete is able to work harder during the shorter work periods. All of the 10-second sprints can be completed faster without causing the level of fatigue a 60-second sprint causes.

The overload principle as applied to interval training is accomplished through the manipulation of five variables:

- The distance and intensity of the work period
- Number of repetitions during each workout
- Duration of the recovery period
- Type of activity during the recovery period
- Frequency of training per week

A simple interval training program for tennis players is presented in Table 14.1. A good place to begin is on the tennis court. Just take the net down and you're ready to start. Beginning from the base line each time, have your players do eight sprints to the service line, six sprints to the net, four sprints to the service line at the opposite end, and two sprints to the opposite baseline. Then work backwards. If you wish, do this drill to replicate court movements—running sideways, backward, on the diagonal, or doing crossovers.

Individual differences make it unwise to develop "cookbook" programs to meet all possibilities. Instead, by applying the basic guidelines and manipulating the variables, you can design individual training programs to match the present fitness level and recovery capacities of your players.

Table 14.1   Tennis Interval Training Program

Set	Repetitions	Distance	Time	Dispatch time
1	8	Baseline (Bl) to service line	3 sec	12 sec
2	6	Bl to net	5 sec	20 sec
3	4	Bl to service line (other end)	8 sec	30 sec
4	2	Bl to baseline (other end)	10 sec	40 sec
5	4	Bl to service line (other end)	8 sec	30 sec
6	6	Bl to net	5 sec	20 sec
7	8	Bl to service line	3 sec	12 sec

Note. Heart rate must decline to 150 beats per minute between repetitions. Heart rate must decline to 120 beats per minute between sets. During recovery periods the player should be encouraged to continue light activity, which promotes faster removal of lactic acid. Work-relief ratio = 1:3.

Advantages of Interval Training

- In addition to developing cardiovascular endurance, interval training offers other advantages as well. It is excellent for improving speed.
- It enables a more rapid improvement in energy potential than any other method of conditioning.
- The athlete can work at very intense anaerobic rates for brief periods of time.
- It rests on the sound physiological fact that an athlete can produce a much greater total workload in a training session if bouts of exercise are spaced.
- Recovery, especially from lactic-acid accumulation, is hastened by mild activity during recovery periods.
- It enables a precise control of stress.
- Progress is easily observed.
- The flexibility of the program helps reduce the boredom that occurs in prolonged continuous exercise.
- It is a program that can be performed almost anywhere and requires no special equipment.

Interval Skill Drills

Interval drills that enable players to practice skills while developing their aerobic and anaerobic systems are valuable in training. An example of such a drill is hitting 20 forehands at the singles sideline (balls fed by a coach) and returning to the center mark between each shot. Alternating down-the-line and crosscourt shots with another player is another example. The coach should supplement these drills with interval training that does not involve skill development. Because the commitment to skill often inhibits a player from running at top speed, his or her energy systems do not get fully taxed during interval skill drills.

On-Court Agility Sprints. Many of the drills outlined in the agility section are also excellent ways to improve endurance. Try them and you'll soon realize!

Aerobic Dancing. This latest fitness craze is also excellent for developing many of the components of fitness for tennis, especially endurance. Exercising to music is lots of fun. Just be sure the leader is qualified so that players do not risk injury or do useless or harmful exercise.

Circuit Training. This method of training is excellent for developing all the components of fitness for tennis. A description of circuit training and a sample circuit are provided in the strength, power, and muscular endurance section.

Stair Running. See speed section.

Spot Running. See speed section.

Jumping Rope. See agility section.

All of these methods are good ways to build up your endurance and add variety to your program.

Other Ways to Improve Endurance

Participating in any sport or activity that requires at least 30 minutes of sustained and moderately vigorous activity will develop cardiovascular endurance. It is a good idea to get out and do something besides tennis every now and then. Try bike riding, swimming, skiing, aerobic dancing, basketball, soccer—whatever you like to do. While working at Bollettieri's, I often organized soccer or basketball games on Saturday afternoons. The young players thought it was great fun getting to play along with the pros.

The methods just described should provide a progressive increase in the amount of work accomplished. Players should continually try to increase the length of the work periods, the speed at which the work is done, and the distance over which it is done. The activity should be continued beyond the point of initial fatigue and sustained until players are thoroughly tired. The heart rate is a good guide to pace. Good aerobic workouts three or four times per week will soon have your players feeling fresh at the start of the final game.

A FLEXIBILITY PROGRAM FOR TENNIS

This program is designed specifically for tennis players as both a prematch warm-up and a postmatch cool-down. Because flexibility is specific to each joint, a player might have an extensive range of movement in some areas of the body and below average flexibility in other areas. Consequently, each joint must be stretched individually and measured individually. Factors limiting range of movement in the various joints are bone structure, connective tissue, muscle bulk, and skin.

The following program employs the methods of static stretching and PNF (proprioceptive neuromuscular facilitation) stretches. No ballistic stretches (a bouncing motion) are included. Although ballistics have been used extensively for many years, it is now known that such exercises strain the muscles and activate the stretch reflex. This causes pain as well as physical damage from microscopic tearing of muscle fibers. This tearing leads to the formation of scar tissue in the muscles and results in a gradual loss of elasticity. The muscles become tight and sore. The methods of static and PNF stretching are strongly recommended because they do not activate the stretch reflex and do not cause pain.

Static stretches consist of a slow, steady movement to place the muscles on stretch, then a holding time of about 15 seconds at the end of the range. It is important that there is no bounce or jerk in the movement.

PNF stretches have proved to be very effective in improving flexibility. The muscle group involved is contracted isometrically for 6 seconds against the immovable resistance provided by a partner. The exercises thus provide a means of promoting muscular strength and flexibility simultaneously.

As stretching for tennis includes stretching the entire body, I will proceed anatomically from area to area. Because doing the same stretches every day can be monotonous, I will describe many different ones for you to choose from. Before beginning, be sure to take special note of the following stretching tips!

Stretching Tips

These tips will make stretching more effective.

• A warm-up should be completed before the stretching exercises are begun (see warm-up section).

• Stretch at least 15 minutes prior to your match or practice session to warm up and loosen the muscles, to avoid muscle pulls and tears, and to prepare the body for the forthcoming activity. The 15 minutes or so it takes to stretch is well invested. Martina Navratilova sums it up: "I have found that I play much better tennis when I am thoroughly limber." You will find the same is true for you.

• Don't bounce. Stretch and hold for at least 20 seconds. Bouncing and jerking induces the stretch reflex, causing the muscle fibers to contract and increasing the chances of a muscle tear.

• Slow, steady, and easy are the cardinal principles of all stretching.

• Don't be fooled. When done correctly stretching is *not* painful. Learn to pay attention to your body; pain is an indication that something is wrong. Stretching should be done slowly, to the point of tightness, but not *too far*. If it hurts, you've gone too far.

• Stretch your tight side first. We all have a tendency to stretch our "good" side first, that is, the more flexible side. Consequently, we spend more time developing that side and less on the side that needs more work. To even out the difference in flexibility in your body, stretch your tight side first. This will help considerably in limbering up.

• Stretching is not a contest. Proper stretching means stretching within your own limits, relaxed and without comparisons to what others can do. Stretch properly and in time your flexibility will improve. Don't expect overnight results. Stretching, like learning a new tennis skill, takes time and practice.

• Stretch after workouts to increase local blood flow, reduce muscular tension, improve circulation, and wind down. This will also help reduce any muscle soreness the next day.

• Stretch at night too. Many players find that stretching at night before bed or while watching television is a relaxing way to wind down and relieve tensions.

• For best results, stretch daily. Improvements in flexibility are quickly lost if a player neglects to do the exercises.

• Flexibility in the *legs, thighs, trunk, arms,* and *shoulders* is especially important for tennis.

• Don't lock (hyperextend) your joints. This places stress on the ligaments, which cannot lengthen and shorten the way muscles do. It also creates excess pressure in the joints.

• Don't arch the lower back or neck. Experts believe that arching the back can cause some of the fluid in the discs to seep out and cause harmful damage to the discs. Activities involving forceful or weight-bearing arching of the back should be discontinued.

• Don't swing or do fast exercises. Swinging occurs from momentum and has the most effect on the ligaments in the joint. Little or no muscle action occurs. Abrupt swings and fast exercises that require a sudden change of direction can tear muscle fibers. Such exercises will not correctly strengthen muscles.

• Don't overbend a joint. The knees, elbows, and neck are the most vulnerable joints. Ligaments, cartilages, and tendons will be strained and may tear if these joints are exercised beyond the point where muscles are in control.

Stretching Specific Anatomical Areas

Specific areas of the body need particular attention when stretching for tennis.

Neck

Begin your flexibility routine by stretching the muscles of the neck.

Neck Stretches

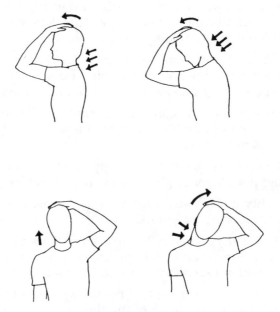

Figure 14.14   Neck stretches.

Flex your head forward very slowly. With one hand gently pull head over, back, and down. Hold at each position for 20 to 30 seconds. Repeat to the right and left. *Do not* make a circular motion or drop the head backward, as this can aggravate the atlas and occipital bone and cause injury to the discs in the neck.

Shoulder, Upper Back, and Arms

Figure 14.15   Shoulder, upper back, and arm stretch.

These stretches are excellent for the shoulders, upper back, and arms. With arms overhead, hold the elbow of one arm with the hand of the other arm. Gently pull the elbow behind your head as you bend from your hips to the side. Do this slowly on both sides, holding the stretch for 15 seconds. This exercise is great for loosening up your arms and shoulders. Also, leaning to the side will stretch the large muscles of the upper back, the latissimus dorsi, and the quadratus lumborum.

Arms, Shoulders, and Back

Figure 14.16   Arm, shoulder, and back stretch.

To stretch arms, shoulders, and back,

• Interlock fingers above the head. With palms facing upward, push your arms slightly back and up. Hold this stretch for 15 seconds. You should feel the tightening in your arms, shoulders, and upper back.

• Again, with fingers interlocked overhead, bend forward from the waist with arms outstretched in front of you. Hold.

• A variation of this stretch is to interlock hands behind you and push arms up behind your back as high as possible as you slowly bend forward at the hips. Hold for 15 seconds. Feel the stretch in your shoulders and upper arms. You are also stretching the lower back, upper back, and neck. Keep your back straight and your head level. Don't lock your knees.

• Keeping legs extended and knees unlocked, one leg in front of the other, repeat the stretch just described. This will stretch your hamstrings as well as the other

Arm and Shoulder PNF Stretch

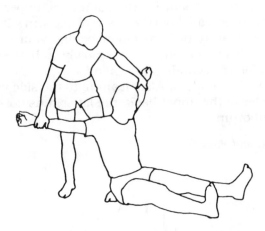

Figure 14.17   Arm and shoulder PNF stretch.

Your partner stands behind you holding your outstretched hands (palms facing outward). He or she gently pulls your hands inward while you attempt to push outward. Hold for 6 seconds; repeat three times.

Sides

A PNF stretch is best for improving flexibility of the muscles in the sides.

Side PNF Stretch

Figure 14.18   Side PNF stretch.

Leaning to the right side with the left arm overhead and the right arm extended by your side, push against your partner and try to stand up. By pushing on your upper arm to provide resistance, your partner is strengthening and increasing flexibility in the muscles along the side of your body. As with all PNF stretches, hold for 6 seconds and repeat three times. Then do the same to the opposite side.

Abdominals

There are several exercises that are beneficial in increasing flexibility of the abdominal muscles.

Abdominal Curl-Downs

Sit with knees bent (to relieve lower back strain), feet flat on the floor, chin tucked toward your chest, and hands across your chest.

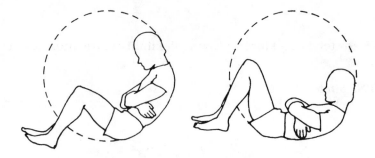

Figure 14.19   Abdominal curl-downs.

Slowly roll backward toward the floor, one vertebra at a time, to about the middle of your rib cage. Without uncurling the spine completely (to lie flat on the floor), slowly return to your starting position by curling up. Repeat slowly and smoothly.

Elbow-Knee Abdominal Stretch

Figure 14.20   Elbow-knee abdominal stretch.

Begin lying on your back with knees bent, but this time interlock your feet slightly off the floor. Also interlock your fingers behind your head. Slowly sit up to touch your elbow to the outside of your opposite knee. Uncurl and repeat to the other side.

Trunk Twister

Figure 14.21   Trunk twister.

Lying on the floor with knees bent, sit up very slowly, twisting the body to the right and reaching to touch the floor with both hands as far back as possible. Hold the stretch. Return to the start and repeat to the left side. This will loosen and stretch muscles in the abdomen, side, back, and shoulder regions.

Lower Back

These exercises are especially important, as the most common injury to tennis players involves the lower back. Take your time when stretching your back. Concentrate on the exercise and relax.

Knee-to-Chest Back Stretch

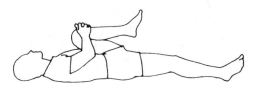

Figure 14.22   Knee-to-chest back stretch.

• Lie on your back outstretched with the back of your head on the floor. Slowly bend your right leg toward your chest and hold for 15 seconds. Be sure to keep your lower back flat. Repeat to the other side. This may seem a slight stretch, but it is very good for the legs and back.

• Modify the exercise just described by pulling your right knee across your body toward your opposite shoulder to create a stretch on the outside of your right hip. Hold this stretch for 15 seconds and repeat to the opposite side.

• As another variation, pull both legs to your chest at the same time and curl your head up toward your knees.

Stretch for the Lower Back and Side of Hip

Figure 14.23   Stretch for the lower back and side of hip.

Lie on your right side with knees slightly bent toward your chest. Slide your left knee up to your chest and then drop it to the floor. Using the right hand, push your left leg toward the floor until you feel the stretch in your lower back and side of hip. Turn your head to look toward your left hand, extended to the side. Hold for 20 seconds. Relax and return the leg to the starting position. Turn on your left side and repeat.

The Spinal Twist

Figure 14.24 Spinal twist.

• This is an excellent stretch not only for the lower back, but also for the upper back, the sides of the hips, the waist, and the rib cage. Sit with right leg outstretched as shown. Bend your left leg and cross it over to the outside of your right knee. Now twist at the waist and bring your bent right elbow to rest pushing on the outside of your knee. Your left hand should be resting behind you, your head turned to look over your left shoulder. Maintain this position for 15 seconds. Then switch sides.

• To make this stretch more difficult, sit with right leg turned inward and repeat.

The Beach-Ball Stretch

Hold your abdominal muscles in as if they could touch your backbone. Flex your knees and let your arms come forward as if you have a very big beach ball pushed into your stomach. Keep your ribs and hips vertical and your knees and shoulders forward. If you feel no stretch, round your head over a little, push your knees forward more, tuck under, and tighten your buttocks.

Figure 14.25   Beach-ball stretch.

Groin

Use the following stretches to increase flexibility in the groin area.

Groin Stretch

Figure 14.26   Groin stretch.

• From a sitting position, push the soles of your feet together and gently lean forward, bending from the hips until you feel the stretch in your groin. Hold this position for 20 seconds. Pushing down with the elbows on your legs will increase stability and balance and make it easier to stretch.

• With legs outstretched, bend forward to grasp your toes and pull the upper body down toward your feet. You will feel the stretch along the entire length of your inner thigh and along your back. Hold for 30 seconds.

Side Lunges

Figure 14.27 Side lunges.

In a lunging position with one leg extended and the other bent, lean to one side and feel the stretch in your groin. Place hands in front of bent leg for support. The further you lean to the side the more you will feel the stretch.

Stride Stretch

Figure 14.28 Stride stretch.

This is a variation of the stretch just described. Simply turn forward to lean on your hands, keeping your right leg flexed under your chest and your left leg stretched out behind. Keep your weight up on the toes and balls of your back foot and your forward heel on the floor. Lower your hip down toward the court. Hold this stretch for 30 seconds. Likewise for the other leg. Make sure when doing this exercise that you do *not* have your knee forward of the ankle, as this will hinder the proper stretching of the hip and legs. This is an excellent stretch for the groin, hamstrings, and hip.

Hamstrings

To improve flexibility in the hamstring area, the following stretches are beneficial.

PNF Hamstring Stretch

Figure 14.29 PNF hamstring stretch.

Lie outstretched on your back with your arms relaxed by your side. Raise your right leg as far as possible, keeping it straight. Your partner kneels at your side and slowly and gently provides resistance by pushing your leg forward toward your head. You resist your partner and try to push your leg down. Hold this position for 6 seconds and repeat three times. Try to go a little bit further each time. Make sure your opposite leg is kept flat on the ground at all times. If you're strong, your partner will also get a great workout!

Hamstring Crossover Stretch

Stand and cross one leg in front of the other with the feet close together. (Keep the toes of your front leg on the floor, with your heel up.) Slowly bend forward, keeping your back leg slightly bent (heel on the floor) until you feel the stretch. Hold this position for 15 seconds, then slowly return to the starting position. Repeat to the other side.

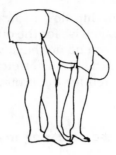

Figure 14.30　Hamstring crossover stretch.

Ballet Stretch

Figure 14.31　Ballet stretch.

Sit with the left leg outstretched, the other leg flexed with the foot resting on the left thigh. Slowly lean forward with your upper body and reach for your left foot with both hands. Feel the stretch in your hamstrings of the extended leg and in your back. Hold this position for 15 seconds and then repeat with the other leg.

Quadriceps

To stretch the quadriceps, use the following exercises.

PNF Quadriceps Stretch

Lying on your chest with one leg outstretched and the other bent, attempt to lift your thigh as high as possible. Your partner assists by placing a hand under your thigh and slowly lifting against your resistance. Follow the same procedures as for all PNF stretches, holding for 6 seconds and repeating three times.

Figure 14.32   PNF quadriceps stretch.

Kneel Stretch

Figure 14.33   Kneel stretch.

From a kneeling position, slowly lean backward to find a comfortable position you can hold for 20 seconds. If you are tight, do not overstretch. If necessary, place your hands on the outside of your legs for support as you balance yourself lightly forward. As you will feel, this is also a good stretch for the ankles.

Correct Hurdler's Stretch

Sit on the ground with one leg slightly flexed in front of you. (This will protect the lumbar spine from strain.) The other leg is diagonally flexed behind you with the inner part of the thigh on the ground. The foot should be pointing down along the line of the lower leg and should be relaxed. *It is very important that you do not let your foot flare out to the sides when doing this stretch, as this may cause overstretching of the medial collateral, ligaments of the knee.* Slowly and carefully lean diagonally back onto the forearm and elbow opposite the bent leg. Keep the unused shoulder up and reach that arm forward. Hold this stretch for 30 seconds. To increase

Figure 14.34   Correct hurdler's stretch.

the thigh stretch, lift the hip of your bent leg a little and hold for 20 seconds. You should not feel any strain in your knee. Repeat this stretch to the other side.

Standing Quadriceps Stretch

Figure 14.35   Standing quadriceps stretch.

Stand on your left foot with your leg unlocked. Bend your right leg and lift it up, knee forward and high, and grasp your ankle. Carefully swing your bent right leg down and back, pointing your knee straight down to the floor. Push your right foot back against your hand while your right hand pulls your bent leg back. Push your foot away from your buttocks while making almost a right angle with your bent leg. Hold the stretch for at least 30 seconds. The stretch should be felt along the front of your thigh. Do *not* squeeze your knee by pushing your heel toward your buttocks! Repeat with other leg.

Calf and Achilles Tendon

To increase flexibility and prevent injuries to the calves and Achilles tendons, use the following stretches.

The Achilles Stretcher

Figure 14.36 Achilles stretcher.

• Stand with your torso leaning forward against a fence or wall, the upper body, head, chest, and abdominal muscles all in line. Stand with one leg in front of the other, the front leg bent and the back leg extended. Both heels should be flat on the ground and feet pointing forward. Slowly move your hips forward, keeping your lower back flat. Hold for 20 seconds. Do not bounce. Repeat with the other leg.

• As a variation to the exercise just described, position your back foot at different angles.

• To stretch the soleus muscle and lower part of the calf muscle, lower your hips downward and bend your knees slightly. Your back should still be flat and heels down. Hold for 20 seconds.

Stair Stretch

Figure 14.37   Stair stretch.

If a stair is nearby, you can use it to stretch your calves. Place the ball of your foot on the edge of the stair and slowly allow your heel to drop below the stair level. Hold onto the railing for balance and drop the heel very slowly.

Ankles

The last specific area of the body you need to stretch are the ankles.

The Alphabet

Figure 14.38   Alphabet.

Sitting on the ground, lift your right leg and keep it elevated off the ground throughout the exercise. By moving your ankle joint, perform the alphabet, making the letters A to Z (capital letters) with your foot. Performing the alphabet ensures complete range of motion about the joint. This exercise strengthens the ankle and surrounding muscles, as well as the quadriceps muscles. Repeat with the other leg.

Concluding Your Stretch Routine

A whole body stretch is good for concluding your stretching routine.

Whole-Body Stretch

Figure 14.39   Whole-body stretch.

• Lie on your back outstretched on the ground with your legs extended, toes pointed, and arms extended overhead. Stretch and hold for 20 seconds, then relax. This is a good exercise for the muscles of the rib cage, stomach, spine, shoulders, arms, ankles, and feet. Repeat three times.

• A variation of this stretch is to flex the ankles and pull in with the abdominal muscles as you stretch.

• These exercises are excellent ways to complete a stretching routine, warm-up, or cool-down as they decrease tension and tightness to relax your entire body.

Now that you are all stretched out and thoroughly warmed up, it's time to hit the court. Good luck!

IMPROVING RESPONSE TIME

"Any significant improvement in reaction time is achieved by a greater awareness of appropriate stimuli and by repetition of appropriate responses, which reduce central nervous system processing time" (Sharkey, 1984, p. 61). This can be achieved by

- sharpening reflexes,
- developing anticipation skills through match practice,
- learning the type of game an opponent likes to play,
- anticipating an opponent's next shot, and
- sharpening reflexes through repetitive practice.

SERVE DRILL

In this drill either the coach or a good player serves a variety of balls of different speeds and spins from the service line. This will force your player to focus on the ball from the toss and react without hesitation. The key in this drill is to see the ball early, react to it quickly, and execute a return effectively.

VOLLEY DRILL

As a variation to practicing reaction volleys, have your player stand in front of the net to hit balls you feed him or her for winners. Make a game out of this drill by having markers on either side of the player to indicate the area that must be defended. Any ball the player misses is then a point to the coach and every ball the player hits for a winner is a point to him or her. Reverse roles and play against your pupil. Difficulty may be increased by spreading the markers farther apart and feeding balls faster. This drill is great for improving reaction and also is tremendous for developing anticipation, sharpening reflexes, and practicing covering the net area (Figure 14.40).

Figure 14.40   Volley drill.

BASELINE DRILL

The volley just described can also be applied to a player at the baseline, with the coach standing in front of the net firing the balls.

Finally, it should be emphasized that response time is a component of speed. These two factors largely determine how fast a player can get into position to return a ball. Thus, all activities practiced to increase speed will also aid response time.

Dynamic Balance

Dynamic balance can be improved through participation in sports and a variety of movement experiences. However, as balance is highly specific to the activity being performed, practicing tennis is the best way to improve balance that will enhance tennis performance. The tennis player's ability to get into a balanced hitting position to hit the ball is most important.

In between shots and points, players should always return to the ready position: the feet parallel and shoulder-width apart, weight evenly distributed on the balls of the feet, and the body leaning slightly forward to enable quick movement in any direction. Knees should be flexed to provide the quick spring needed; eyes should be on the ball and/or the opponent.

It has been my experience coaching in the United States that many American juniors, as a result of years of fed-ball drills, time their bodies to the position of ball contact and not to their stroke, which causes a hurried, cramped swing and a poor result. The problem essentially boils down to laziness. Rather than preparing early and getting to the position where the ball will be hit *before* the ball gets there, players take their time and try to arrive as the ball arrives. Players must avoid hitting difficult shots on the run when there is no need to. Players can never prepare too early for a stroke. They should always get into position and be ready for the oncoming ball. Beat the ball there. By doing so, players will be in a more balanced position to hit the shot, as well as aiding the timing and accuracy of their stroke.

Players are usually caught off balance because (a) they were not quick enough in getting to the ball, (b) they were forced to stretch wide for a shot, or (c) they did not anticipate an opponent's return. Therefore, the best way of improving balance is included in all activities that involve agility, speed, response time, footwork, and flexibility. And when playing tennis, make *sure* to return to the ready position between shots and points.

Now your players are specifically trained for tennis, so keep up the hard work. If they, in turn, are willing to work hard, you can improve their games immensely. As Victor Hugo once said, "People do not fail because they lack strength but more often because they lack will." Remember—your body is like a machine. It must be maintained well to give maximum performance. Needless to say, keeping fit will increase your enjoyment as it improves your play. Discover that fitness *is* one of the keys to better tennis.

REFERENCES

Groppel, J.L. (1984). *Tennis for advanced players: And those who would like to be.* Champaign, IL: Human Kinetics.

United States Professional Tennis Association (USPTA). (1988). *The USPTA sport science and sports medicine guide.* Wesley Chapel, FL: Author.

CHAPTER 15

Eating Like a Champion

Part of coaching players for championship caliber play means supplying them with sound nutrition information and encouraging them to develop healthy dietary habits. Coaches should stress the importance of weight control and good nutrition. It is difficult to control everything your players eat, but you can teach them what a nutritionally balanced diet is. Although you cannot be expected to be current on all the latest nutrition research or to have read the countless articles in magazines, books, and newspapers, there are some facts and fallacies you need to be aware of. You should also know the nutritional values of various foods and be able to advise your players what to eat before and during a match or what to do to lose a few pounds. You should have an understanding of some of the nutritional problems that athletes face, such as low iron, anorexia nervosa, or the problems of the many fad diets.

WHAT IS GOOD NUTRITION?

Nutrition is the study of the food we eat and how the body uses it. Foods provide us with a variety of nutrients essential for building and repairing body tissue and for providing the energy needed for efficient functioning. For optimal performance, the athlete's diet

235

must contain all the nutrients necessary for general well-being and also those that will help them cope with the extra stresses of training. These essential nutrients include protein, carbohydrates, fat, vitamins, minerals, and water.

Protein

Protein is needed to build, repair, and regulate the function of the body's tissues and is thus essential in a tennis player's diet. Protein is found mainly in meat, fish, poultry, cheese, eggs, milk, nuts, and bread. Protein should constitute about 12% to 15% of the athlete's diet. Greater quantities will deprive exercising muscles of vital water and may inhibit the elimination of waste products produced by the muscles during exercise.

Carbohydrates

Carbohydrates are the major sources of energy for the body during rallies on the court, as tennis players use muscle glycogen, glucose, and fat for fuel. Carbohydrates are much more efficient in utilizing oxygen than fats or protein. Foods that contain a large proportion of carbohydrate include breads, pastries, cereals, pastas, rice, fruits, potatoes, and vegetables. These foods make up approximately 55% to 60% of an athlete's diet and should be increased during successive days of strenuous training and on competition days.

Fat

Common foods rich in fat include butter, margarine, oils, meat, milk, chocolate, and ice cream. Fat is a secondary source of energy and should make up about 25% of a player's diet. Moderate deposits of fat in the body tissues serve as a reserve fuel supply; some deposits are necessary for the support and protection of certain vital organs. Fats are also necessary as a source of essential fatty acids and as carriers of the fat-soluble vitamins.

Diets high in saturated or animal fats (all possible sites for hydrogen molecules, are filled with hydrogen molecules) are thought to lead to increased incidences of artherosclerosis and cardiovascular disease. The American Heart Association strongly recommends that the amount of saturated fat in the average diet be reduced. Coaches should emphasize that vegetable oils and plant sources are the best, as these fats are unsaturated, which means that some of the hydrogen sites are unfilled.

Too high a fat content in a player's diet slows the emptying of the stomach and delays digestion. The maximal oxygen capacity of the blood is also reduced, thus decreasing aerobic power and peak performance. Nevertheless, fats enhance flavor and increase satiety, so we can't expect athletes to give them up entirely.

Vitamins

Vitamins are essential for your health and to the growth of tissues. They do not supply energy themselves but help in releasing the energy from the food we eat. Because the water-soluble vitamins (B complex and C) cannot be stored and are excreted as waste products daily, they must be included in one's daily food intake. The fat-soluble vitamins (A, D, E, and K) are stored in the liver and fat tissue. These vitamins can be toxic if present in excessive amounts. Scientific evidence suggests that a varied and well-balanced diet should provide all the vitamins a tennis player will need (Table 15.1). Additional vitamins have not shown to improve athletic performance.

Minerals

Minerals such as calcium, sodium, potassium, iron, and iodine are essential in the proper functioning of nerves and muscles and are a major component of body structures such as bone, muscle, and skin. Ample supplies exist in a balanced diet, but iron intake should be monitored carefully, especially for females. (Red meat, deep green vegetables, raisins, and enriched or fortified breads and cereals are the best dietary sources of iron.)

Water

About two thirds of the human body is water and water is second only to oxygen in importance. Water provides the important functions of transporting nutrients and hormones throughout the body and removing wastes from the body. Water also plays a vital role in regulating body temperature. Water is obtained not only by drinking it, but also from the foods we eat. The necessity for water before, during, and after matches will be discussed in more detail later.

Table 15.1 Vitamin Summary

Vitamin A	Promotes vision and healthy skin
Sources	Liver; eggs; milk; butter; cheese; yogurt; carrots and other yellow vegetables; green leafy vegetables
Vitamin B	Promotes healthy skin, especially around the mouth, nose, and eyes; promotes a well-functioning nervous system
Sources	Milk; whole-grain cereals and breads (wheat-germ bread); meat; poultry; fish; vegetables (beans, peas)
Vitamin C	Promotes the healing of wounds and strong teeth and bones
Sources	Citrus fruits and juices; tomatoes; bean sprouts; green leafy vegetables; strawberries; cantaloupe
Vitamin D	Promotes strong bones and teeth
Sources	Milk; eggs; meat; cheese; butter; the sun; fish-liver oils; canned tuna; sardines
Vitamin E	Assists vitamins A and C, certain fats, and the red blood cells in performing their specified roles in the body
Sources	Whole grains and cereals; wheat germ; vegetable oils; eggs; liver; fruit; vegetables; seeds; nuts; navy beans
Vitamin K	Necessary for proper blood clotting
Sources	Green plants such as spinach; cabbage, and kale; also produced by the bacteria normally inhabiting the intestines

FOOD REQUIREMENTS—MEETING EVERYDAY NUTRITION NEEDS

A balanced diet provides us with the daily essential nutrients, vitamins, and minerals (Table 15.2).

When we refer to a balanced diet, we mean one that contains a variety of foods from the main food groups: fruits and vegetables; dairy products; whole-grain breads and cereals; and protein foods such as lean meat, fish, poultry, eggs, and/or alternate vegetable protein such as peas, beans, or nuts. A deficiency in any one of these can mean trouble on the court.

Table 15.2   Menu Suggestions for Players in Tournaments

Note: These suggestions are not for those desiring to lose or gain weight.

BREAKFAST

1 glass of orange juice (not orange drink) or an orange
Any fresh fruit (will vary from season to season)
1 glass of raw skim milk
2 slices of whole-wheat bread
1 whole-wheat or bran muffin
Natural yogurt (nonfat)
Bran or muesli or organic rolled oats whole grain, preferably with
    low-fat milk
Pancakes—no butter or syrup

LUNCH

Fresh juice or water
Serving of brown rice with raw vegetables
Steamed vegetables
Sandwich (whole-grain bread, lettuce, cheese, tomato, honey, etc.)
Salad
Natural yogurt
Fresh fruits

DINNER

Whole-grain pasta or spaghetti
Steamed vegetables
Salad
Cabbage, lettuce, beets, greens, spinach (valuable fiber foods), potatoes
    (steamed or boiled), sweet potatoes, pumpkin, carrots, string beans,
    bean sprouts, broccoli, celery, and avocado (foods rich in unrefined
    starch)
Note: Red meats have been exluded from these suggestions because of
their high fat and protein content. Also, steaks and the like require
vital energy for the long digestion process, detracting from on-court
energy.

SNACKS

Fresh fruit (e.g., apples, oranges, bananas)
Dried fruit, sugar free (apricots, dates, raisins, currants, sultanas, etc.)
Nuts and seeds, unsalted
Cookies—whole grain with nuts, seeds, or dried fruit
Whole-grain bread and muffins
Low-fat, natural yogurt with fresh fruit added
Granola (unprocessed and natural)
Water (as desired)

What if a Player Is a Vegetarian?

Vegetarianism is a complex topic that will be touched on only briefly in this text. There are various classes of vegetarianism. A strict vegetarian, a *vegan*, eats only foods of plant origin, whereas other classes of vegetarians may eat such animal products as milk, cheese, and eggs, which help meet nutritional requirements. The nutritional requirements of the vegetarian are no different from those of anyone else, of course. Because some essential nutrients are eliminated from their diet, vegetarians need to be more knowledgeable concerning food selection so that deficiencies in calories, vitamins, minerals, and protein do not occur. Foods rich in iron (nuts, beans, dried fruits), calcium (green leafy vegetables, dairy products), zinc (beans, grains, whole-wheat bread), and riboflavin (green leafy vegetables) should be included in the vegetarian's daily diet. For the vegan, vitamin B_{12} supplements may be necessary, as B_{12} is not found in plant foods. For other vegetarians, eggs, fish, and dairy products will prevent a deficiency state.

A vegetarian diet is more healthy than a diet containing a lot of red meat, as red meat contains a large amount of cholesterol and saturated fat. Red meat is also high in protein, but the vegetarian can obtain sufficient protein from grains and vegetables to develop muscles and maintain strength. Players who eat eggs and dairy products in addition to plant foods will easily meet their needs. Sometimes the vegetarian athlete will not get enough iron or zinc because these minerals are best found in meats. However, vegetables, dried beans, and grains will provide fair amounts of these minerals.

Health-related benefits of a vegetarian diet include low levels of saturated fat, the absence of cholesterol in plant foods, a high fiber content, and the low calorie content of many vegetable products. Of most importance to the coach and athlete is that a vegetarian diet does not appear to affect physical performance capacity either positively or negatively.

Does an Athlete
Need to Take Vitamin Supplements?

A varied diet sufficient in supplying the energy needs of an active athlete will provide adequate vitamins and minerals. Taking pills for each vitamin is simply not conducive to good nutritional conditioning. Nevertheless, today's advertising continues to warn us that we are not receiving an ample supply of vitamins from the foods we normally eat and are therefore risking vitamin deficiency. Moreover, some companies have used subtle advertisements to suggest that vitamin supplements will help you run faster, become stronger, and increase physical performance. However, there is no substantial scientific evidence to support the use of vitamin supplements by well-nourished athletes or highly active individuals. Consuming vitamins and nutrients naturally available in foods is the best way of meeting the body's needs and preventing vitamin overdoses.

What About Iron?

Players of all ages should be aware of the iron content in their diet and their iron level, which can be quickly determined by a simple blood test. Iron is critical to oxygen use. Without sufficient iron, performance capacity is diminished, and the body's ability to transport and use oxygen is decreased. The body loses iron through such routes as the skin, hair, and sweat. Females lose additional iron during menstruation. The recommended daily allowance (RDA) is 10 milligrams for men and 18 milligrams for women and teenagers of both sexes.

A ferratin test (for iron) is strongly recommended for players who lack energy (assuming the absence of obvious causes such as lack of sleep or no breakfast). Make sure players are aware of the foods rich in iron: liver, meats, eggs, dried beans and peas, whole-grain products, green leafy vegetables, and dried fruits (apricots, dates, figs, and raisins). Iron supplementation by commercial products might be recommended for anemic individuals, women with heavy menstrual blood flow, and those players on a restricted caloric intake. The majority of players simply need to follow a balanced diet with iron-rich foods included.

KNOW YOUR ACTIVITY NEEDS

The most important function of food is to supply energy for our bodies. Without energy, cells cease to perform their functions and soon die. Energy is typically measured as heat and expressed in calories. Calories exist in abundance in favorite desserts and in all the foods people like most. Scientifically speaking, a calorie is the amount of heat required to raise the temperature of one kilogram of water one degree centigrade. Lists of caloric values for common foods have been published extensively and are thus not included here.

How caloric needs are determined varies with each individual, depending on the amount of physical activity, basal metabolism, sleep, growth, and maintenance of body temperature. To determine caloric output, every activity of the day must be accounted for, from sleeping to eating to working out. Once caloric output is calculated, it must then be balanced by food intake of similar caloric value. Coaches should refer to nutrition books to learn how to determine the energy input and output of various foods and activities.

As an example, a serious adolescent practicing intensely will burn up between 400 and 600 calories per hour on the tennis court. On the other hand, the lazy member of the team may burn only about 200 calories per hour. Amounts will vary according to the intensity of the practice session and the individual's build and metabolism. Players undergoing intense practices and weight training will need to increase their caloric intake to match their energy demands during periods of heavy training; likewise, during periods of rest and relaxation, their intake should be reduced.

PREMATCH NUTRITION

The best prematch meal is high in unrefined complex carbohydrates, low in fat and protein, and includes plenty of liquids.

Carbohydrates provide the fuel to energize a player before a match or workout. Because they are much more efficient in utilizing oxygen than are fats and proteins, carbohydrates provide ready energy.

Some examples of appropriate foods for a pregame meal are listed in Table 15.3.

Foods high in fat and protein should be avoided on the day of competition. This means no fatty or fried foods. Fat slows the emptying of the stomach and delays digestion. Protein (including

Table 15.3 Suitable Foods for Prematch Meals

Steamed vegetables, potatoes	Fruit juice or water
Bread, cereals (whole grain)	Fresh fruit
Sandwiches (whole-grain bread)	Salads
Spaghetti	Pizza (no oil or meat)
Pasta or noodles	Brown rice

the traditional pregame steak) can inhibit the elimination of the waste products produced by the muscles during exercise and should be limited.

Candy bars do not provide quick energy. Chocolate is essentially a fat and is slow to digest (4 to 6 hours). Also, the sugar contained in candy draws fluid from the body into the gastrointestinal tract, causing premature dehydration and diminished performance.

To prevent discomfort and allow for adequate digestion, prematch meals should be eaten 3 to 4 hours before the match. Overeating should definitely be avoided. The food should be non-irritating and appetizing. It should be fresh and simple. The athlete should drink several glasses of water along with the meal. A high-carbohydrate snack is recommended 2 hours before the match.

DURING THE MATCH

As tennis matches or practice sessions can go on for hours, serious tennis players must know how to deal with heat and humidity. Fluid intake is very important to ensure maximum performance. Tennis players should begin taking in extra fluids the day before a match. As noted, it's wise to also drink a lot of water with the prematch meal. Research indicates that a fluid loss equal to as little as one percent of body weight reduces physical work capacity. Where fluid loss equals about 4% to 5% of the body weight, the athlete can expect a 20% to 30% reduction in capacity for heavy work. In other words, the 100-pound teenager who loses 4 or 5 pounds during a match will be struggling to perform to anywhere near his or her capabilities. The fluid loss could well mean the difference between winning and losing a match.

The American College of Sports Medicine has given low marks to popular commercial sports drinks for fluid replacement during physical activity. Numerous research studies have shown these drinks contain too much sugar, salt, and/or electrolyte concentration and consequently delay the absorption of water from the stomach to the water-deficient parts of the exercising body that need it the most. Water, water, and more water is the best thing to drink during matches.

It is, however, possible to drink too much water during a match. Remember, the object is to replace the water the body loses, not to overload the supply. Your motto should be "little and often." Tennis players are fortunate in that the break allowed at the changes of ends is ideal for regular and frequent replacement of lost water.

AFTER THE MATCH

Several general rules apply to postmatch nutrition.

- Most players do not feel like eating soon after a match because it takes some time for the body to revert to its readiness to digest food after vigorous activity. Rest and relaxation after a match will restore the appetite.
- Be sure to replace lost fluids, but not too hastily.
- The postmatch meal can be any palatable, good-sized, balanced meal, preferably low in fats and high in carbohydrates to replenish one's reserves.

WEIGHT CONTROL

Observers of the tennis players on the circuit can readily see that many players are overweight, especially among the females and lower rankings. Overweight players have reduced speed, agility, endurance, and, consequently, reduced resistance to injury.

Crash Diets

Maintenance of appropriate body weight is important for optimal performance. However, a crash diet is not the answer. Many such diets recommend daily caloric intake as low as 600 calories. This amount may be sufficient for a sedentary person, but not for a tennis player training hard and participating in tournaments. Those 600 calories will be burned in just over an hour of tough practice, leaving the player with no energy. Also, the player is as likely to gain the pounds back as quickly as he or she lost them. Moreover, there is often considerable risk associated with crash diets. We are told in the magazines and press about all the success stories, but there is another side of the coin. For example, many players at the Nick Bollettierri Tennis Academy tried such diets and some ended up in the hospital. Many others complained of low energy and weakness. One of your duties as a coach is to not let this kind of thing happen. Following fad or crash diets will not educate players in eating nutritionally and they will be no better off than when they began. Be especially careful of some of the diet-conscious girls, many of whom do not need to lose weight at all.

Determining Ideal Weight

Height/weight charts that enable people to compare themselves with the average male or female are not especially accurate and are often inadequate guides to "ideal" weight. Many athletes who are low in body fat but are very muscular will be overweight according to these charts. Unmistakably, it is the proportion of fat tissue in the body that determines one's proper weight. This proportion can be estimated by the use of skinfold calipers. Refer to the testing section of chapter 12 for the procedure and to Table 15.4 for percentages.

Table 15.4   Recommended Body-Fat Percentages

Sex	Average	Obese	Athletes
Male	13 to 17%	20%	Under 10%
Female	20 to 24%	27%	Under 15%

Being overweight results from a caloric intake greater than the number of calories burned for exercise and basal metabolism. Excess calories are stored as fat and result in weight gain. Five hundred unburned calories each day will result in one pound of weight gain in a week. (One pound of fat = 3,500 calories.)

Calorie intake should *never* drop below 1,200 calories a day for females or 1,500 a day for males. Of course, this minimum will be much greater for athletes in training. A balanced, nutritious diet is essential to retain health and energy, *even when trimming excess weight.*

Dieting should be a gradual process. Losing more than 2 or 3 pounds per week (7,000 to 15,000 caloric differential) is not recommended and may result in burning off water and lean muscle mass, not fat.

Forget the idea of spot reducing. Despite the many health clubs that advertise such programs, spot reducing is impossible. Weight is lost first in the area of greatest fat concentration. Excess pounds can be easily lost by decreasing food intake and increasing physical activity. It is important to stress here that three meals should be eaten daily, as skipping meals usually only results in overeating at the next one. Foods such as donuts, pastries, cookies, snack machine goodies, desserts, soft drinks, and the like should be eliminated altogether. Also, no second helpings.

Regular exercise is recommended for losing weight because it firms the muscles and increases the calories used per day, thus assuring weight loss from fat, not lean muscle mass. Vigorous exercise also decreases the appetite and raises the body's metabolism for 6 to 8 hours afterward.

Getting in the habit of eating sensibly and exercising regularly will prevent the "roller-coaster syndrome" of gaining, dieting, losing, and regaining.

Hints for Losing Weight

Here are some other hints for losing weight sensibly.

- Eat a light meal in the evenings.
- Eat slowly and chew thoroughly.
- Don't have second helpings.
- Eat low-calorie nutritious snacks (e.g., celery, carrots, fresh fruit).
- Drink two glasses of water before meals.
- Don't eat between meals.
- Keep a diet diary of everything you eat. Plot your progress and reward success.
- Always count your calories. Know and avoid those foods high in calories.

Gaining Weight

Although many people long to be slim, being so is a problem for some. No matter how much these people eat, they cannot put on weight. I remember rising every morning at six to make shakes with all kinds of fruit to help a group of players gain weight. They had additional high-calorie shakes for lunch and dinner. But helping these players gain was not the easy task I had envisaged! If you have some players who you think need to gain weight, the following guidelines will promote desirable increases in muscle weight as opposed to fat weight.

- Calorie intake should be equal to or slightly greater than the body's caloric need. This can be achieved by eating an extra helping of each food or by eating snacks. Some people prefer to eat five to seven small meals a day rather than three big meals, to avoid feeling bloated.

- Engage in weight training. This will promote muscular growth for added body weight.
- Conserve energy. Living at a rapid pace with little time for relaxation prevents the efficient utilization of the diet. Slow your tempo of living, get more rest and sleep, and reduce unnecessary physical activity.
- Consume a wide variety of foods. High-calorie blender drinks can help provide extra calories to equalize calorie output. Equalizing calorie output is important during intensive training and is also conducive to gaining weight. Such foods as ice cream, milk, fruits, honey, and peanut butter are easily blended to make tasty milk shakes that can be consumed several times a day in addition to the regular meals.

THE IMPORTANCE OF BREAKFAST

Breakfast is commonly skipped because a person does not feel hungry in the morning or because he or she is running late. However, tennis players who skip this meal will hamper their performance. Before breakfast, the body's blood sugar is low, which decreases muscular efficiency. Without breakfast, this hypoglycemia presents its symptoms as fatigue, headache, nervousness, irritability, depression, and dizzy spells. Also, skipping this meal deprives the body of the essential nutrients that have been depleted during the evening and sleeping hours.

THE IMPORTANCE OF SLEEP

Adequate sleep and rest are essential to maximal performance. The tissue building-and-repair processes so vital to athletes—especially at the time of intense training or important tournaments—occur principally during sleep and rest. Adequate sleep during periods of heavy training and competition enhances full physical and mental restoration of the player's body.

The quantities or prematch meals will vary for each player and situation. For example, the meal prior to a five-advantage-set Davis Cup match that could last for hours will be much greater in quantity than that prior to a best-of-three tiebreaker-set doubles match. Also, as juniors are still growing, they will eat varying quantities, so it is not practical to fix arbitrarily the amount a player should eat. It is best to let the individual judge. Players usually know how much is too much and how much is not enough.

Eating like a champion requires that one eat a balanced diet providing the right number of calories and all the essential nutrients: protein, carbohydrates, fats, vitamins, minerals, and water. Vegetarians and players on weight-loss diets must ensure that they are getting all the essential nutrients. These principles apply to *all* players, no matter what age or ability. A deficiency in any one of these nutrients will mean a deficiency on the court. The foundation of successful players depends on their developing correct nutritional habits. Unfortunately, there are no magic or miracle foods designed specifically for athletes. The main difference between the diet of the athlete and the nonathlete should be the number of calories consumed. Finally, a special competition diet and plenty of liquids will ensure optimal performance. Good luck to all your champions!

RECOMMENDED READINGS

Bailey, C. (1977). *Fit or fat.* Boston: Houghton Mifflin.

Ballentine, R. (1978). *Diet and nutrition: A holistic approach.* Honesdale, PA: The Himalayan International Institute.

Clark, N. (1983). *The athlete's kitchen.* New York: Bantam Books.

Darden, E. (1976). *Nutrition and athletic performance.* Pasadena, CA: The Athletic Press.

Eisenman, P., & Johnson, D.A. (1982). *Coaches guide to nutrition and weight control.* Champaign, IL: Human Kinetics.

Robertson, L., Flinders, C., & Godfrey, B. (1978). *Laurel's kitchen.* Petaluma, CA: Nilgeri Press.

Williams, M.H. (1983). *Nutrition for fitness and sport.* Dubuque, IA: Wm. C. Brown.

PART IV

PSYCHOLOGICAL SKILLS TRAINING FOR COMPETITION

James E. Loehr, EdD

CHAPTER 16

Mental Training for Tennis

I often refer to the area of mental training as the last frontier of sport research. We have become very sophisticated in most areas of sport science over the last 20 years, and in many ways the advances have been remarkable. Our knowledge and understanding of exercise physiology, biomechanics, motor learning, and nutrition as they relate to athletics have greatly helped coaches improve training strategies. Unfortunately, the area of psychological training has lagged far behind most of these sport-related sciences. This is not due to lack of interest or commitment to its importance. To the contrary, sport scientists, as well as coaches and athletes, generally feel that the psychological aspect of athletic performance is extremely important. The fact that we have not made commensurate advances in this area of study is a reflection of the enormity of the challenge facing the general study of psychology. Advances in sport psychology are being made daily, but we have a long way to go.

Our confusion as players and coaches in the psychological area is reflected in the way we train. Most coaches have very clearly defined approaches to training athletes in biomechanics, fitness, injury prevention, and nutrition. Although coaches know intuitively how important the mental area is, they are often at a loss as to how to approach it systematically. Study of the practices of our most successful coaches often reveals that a significant part of their genius is the ability to provide effective learning opportunities in the psychological area. When these coaches are asked what they do to systematically train their athletes psychologically, many say they do very little, if anything. Many say they feel that this area of training must be left to the individual.

Despite what they say, however, we often find upon closer examination that they are practicing sound psychological training principles throughout all aspects of their coaching. The reason more coaches do not systematically provide mental training opportunities for players is that they literally do not know what to do. Accordingly, they spend most of their time on things they are comfortable with—working with stroke production, conditioning, and so on. They feel comfortable dealing with backhands, forehands, serves, and volleys. They usually know how to handle problems related to agility and speed or concerning injury rehabilitation and prevention. They have a well-defined system for correcting problems and organizing the learning environment. Most coaches operate from some kind of training system in these areas.

However, when someone comes to these same coaches with problems concerning self-confidence, temper, concentration, choking—problems clearly psychological in origin—how do they respond? Some, even after identifying a problem as primarily psychological, turn to physical training strategies that have little relevance to the problem at hand. An example is to stress working on mechanics in the hope of eventually bolstering the player's confidence through improved skill levels.

Another reason coaches shy away from psychological training strategies is that some athletes are skeptical or feel uncomfortable with learning in this area. Unfortunately, there is a certain stigma associated with psychological weakness that is not associated with physical weakness. It is quite all right to have a biomechanically unsound backhand—this is no reflection on one's character. But if one has a decent backhand and cannot execute it under pressure—if there is something psychological preventing proper execution—the problem becomes much more personal. It is one thing to miss a forehand, but quite another to "choke" one.

THE IMPORTANCE OF THE MENTAL FACTOR

Players and coaches are generally surprised to learn that as much as 80% of a match is spent doing things other than playing points. The vast majority of time is spent changing ends, waiting to serve and return serve, and *thinking*. The interesting thing is that, traditionally, nearly all training in tennis has been directed at the 20% to 30% of time spent hitting balls. Players rarely if ever train for the other 70% to 80% of match time that deals essentially with the psychological dimension.

Talent, Skills, and Mental Toughness

The role of psychological factors in athletic performance can be conceptualized in a variety of ways. One of these can be referred to as the one-third, one-third, one-third formula. The first third of competitive success is the athlete's God-given talent—his or her genetic potential. We frequently hear coaches talk of the naturally gifted athlete. This is an aspect that the athlete theoretically cannot change and is the one dimension in the formula that will never be objectively known.

The second third of the formula has to do with acquired physical skill. To become a great tennis player, one must possess exceptional physical skills. Form, technique, and footwork must be precise and efficient. Environmental stimulation is the major contributing factor here. Early tennis experiences, coaching experiences, and competitive opportunities constantly shape the kinds of learning that take place. This area is generally where coaches and players spend most of their training time. Coaches train to improve mechanics, speed, reflexes, and so forth in an effort to move the athlete to higher levels of competitive play.

The last third of the formula deals with the psychological or mental component of competition. Mental toughness, competitive strength, and the ability to hold up under pressure represent acquired skills that are clearly tied to environmental factors. These diverse factors include such things as parental influence, success/failure experiences in school, the nature of coaching the athlete has had, the interaction of siblings, competitive successes and failures, and the list goes on and on. Coaches tend to feel less comfortable with this area of training because it seems almost too complex, indefinable, and varied from individual to individual to be dealt with systematically.

Try this exercise: Take the top 20 men or women in tennis today and rank them according to the talent/physical skill/mental skill formula. Make three columns and rank all the players in these three areas. In the second column consider stroke precision and efficiency, and, in the third, such things as attitude, intensity, and control under pressure.

Now contrast the three column rankings with each player's actual ATP ranking. You are likely to see some surprising differences. Players today must have the full three-part formula to be great. As previously noted, coaches can do nothing about the talent third of the formula. They must focus their efforts 100% on impacting those areas of training that they *can* directly influence. They can certainly teach players better stroke production, court positioning, and fitness. They can also most assuredly help players develop substantial mental toughness. To leave the psychological learning third to chance or to trial and error learning is a serious mistake. The psychological aspect of tennis is simply too important an element of the success formula to leave unguided.

Coaches' Psychological Skills

Intensive study of what separates outstanding coaches from the pack invariably reveals that they are intuitively able to provide consistent learning opportunities for mastery of the psychological aspects of the sport. Our best coaches are good psychologists. When one examines just how much of coaching involves psychology, the result is startling. It is estimated that as much as 70% to 80% of what coaches do relates to psychological issues. Decisions about discipline, tournament schedules, rule enforcement, diet, doubles teams, captains, parental involvement, travel schedules, and challenge matches clearly affect players psychologically. And then there are all the issues that are strictly psychological: concentration, confidence, choking, temper control, attitude, motivation, intensity control, mistake management, and so on.

To simply teach a player a forehand or a serve is one thing, but when we speak of coaching, we are talking about a much more comprehensive learning interaction. Coaches attempt to help athletes coordinate all aspects of their lives so that they have the best possible chance of realizing their competitive goals. Truly effective coaches need to have well-defined approaches to learning in both the physical and psychological realms. In coaching we are working with the spirit of the player; accordingly, coaches must have precise systems for training their players in the psychological aspects. Regardless of how complex the area of psychological training may appear, coaches must develop an effective system for coaching their players in mental skills. They must strive to develop a workable model consistent with their coaching convictions and values, a model that reflects the most current and responsible technology extant in the area of psychological training.

Champions Master Mental Skills

How have players like Becker, Connors, Lendl, Evert, Navratilova, and Graf become such great, mentally strong competitors? They were not born with exceptional powers of concentration, fight, confidence, and drive. They did not seek the services of sport psychologists. Nor did their coaches have any specialized psychological training. They simply *learned* these mental skills. We must ask why and how they learned them.

Mastery of the mental skills required for competitive success is similar to mastery of physical skills. Vast individual differences exist in the learning of physical skills, and the mental area is no different. Some learn mental skills with relative ease, others with considerable difficulty. Much of the learning in the mental area, as in the physical, is trial and error. If one hits enough balls, he or she eventually learns the strokes. Trial and error will eventually work, but a good teaching pro using sound methods will significantly reduce the time it will take to acquire sound strokes.

The same is true for the emotional area. If one plays enough matches without burning out from all the frustrations, he or she will eventually learn the necessary competitive skills—with or without coaching. However, the time, frustration, and risk of burnout are substantially greater than with a well-defined learning system. Most of the great players of the past were fast learners who also had great coaching in both the mental and physical areas. Rather than working from any systematic model, however, these coaches simply drew from their intuitions and instincts when it came to the mental area.

Developing Consistency

The bottom-line test of mental toughness in an athlete is consistency. Consistency is the trademark of our most enduring champions in tennis. Day in and day out, they rise to the occasion. Regardless of how they feel physically, of court conditions, wind, cheating opponents, extreme pressure, and travel problems, they consistently perform near the upper range of their talent and skills. Over and over they find a way to play their best when they want it most. They do not ride the same performance roller coaster as so many of their less successful opponents.

How do they do it? Part of the answer, of course, is physical. Consistency is clearly tied to sound biomechanics, fitness, and proper diet. Even when all such physical factors are in place, however, we often see inconsistency, and it is here that we look to the psychological area for answers. What, then, must happen psychologically for a player to consistently perform toward the upper range of his or her talent and skill? Another way of asking the question is, "What makes consistent *peak performance* possible from a psychological perspective?"

The Emotion-Performance Link

My research and experience in response to these questions have led to the following understandings:

• Performance consistency is the result of emotional consistency. Players on an emotional roller coaster during play will typically find that they are on a performance roller coaster as well. The more ups and downs in emotional state players experience during play, the less likely that their performance levels will stabilize in the upper range of their capabilities.

• There is a very real connection between the athlete's performance and his or her emotional state at the time. Some emotional states clearly facilitate high-level consistency, whereas others have precisely the opposite effect.

• Peak performance is directly linked to a specific kind of emotional state. This emotional state might best be referred to as the *ideal performance state.*

• Emotional states lead to different states of physiological arousal. Changes in feeling states correspond to measurable biochemical changes that affect critical performance variables such as blood pressure, heart rate, muscle tension, body temperature, and others. Players change biochemically as they experience shifts in feeling state and mood; these changes either facilitate or undermine their ability to achieve peak performance.

• An ideal performance state (IPS) exists for every athlete and for all teams. This IPS is essentially a constellation of feelings that stimulates constructive physiological changes.

• From all that is known, the IPS is similar for all athletes across all sports, and the ideal emotional climate for competition is remarkably constant from sport to sport. There are subtle differences experienced from one individual to another and from gross motor skill sports to fine motor skill sports, but the overall feeling component of the IPS is very similar.

• Controlling the IPS during noncompetitive play is considerably easier than in competitive play. The real difference between social tennis and competitive tennis is obviously the issue of pressure. The challenge in competitive play is to create the ideal balance of emotions in spite of escalating pressure.

• Our best competitors have achieved substantial control over their IPS during competition. They have learned to trigger this delicate balance of feeling across a wide variety of performance situations. They have learned to control how they feel in response to such adverse circumstances as poor courts, bad draws, and obnoxious or cheating opponents.

• Controlling one's IPS is clearly related to a constellation of acquired mental skills. The primary purpose of mental training is to help players acquire these mental skills.

• Competitive success and mental toughness require a high degree of control of the IPS. The more athletes practice and rehearse mental skills associated with competition, the more quickly they will acquire control over this delicate emotional balance.

THE IDEAL PERFORMANCE STATE

From all that researchers have been able to determine thus far, the ideal emotional climate for competition is characterized by a combination of feelings: physical relaxation, mental calmness, low anxiety, energy intensity, and optimism. It is important to note that these are ideal feelings and that they need to be experienced *during* play, not prior to or following play.

Physical Relaxation

When athletes are performing at their highest levels, they consistently report that their muscles feel relaxed and free. When players report that their muscles feel tight or tense, either between points or during points, their performance typically suffers. Relaxation to an athlete has a very specific meaning: It relates to relaxation of the muscles, not the mind. Athletes frequently confuse muscle relaxation with mental relaxation. As we shall see, the ideal combination for high-level performance is a rather unusual feeling combination of relaxation of the muscles with high mental alertness and intensity. Anything a player can do prior to or during a match that helps sustain the feeling of muscle relaxation will generally contribute to more consistent play.

Mental Calmness

Players consistently report that during their finest hour they experience a very real sense of mental calmness. There is a stillness characteristic to high-level play and intense concentration. Athletes frequently report that they experience a sense of slow motion perceptually. Balls seem to slow down, targets get bigger; they never seem rushed. As players lose this sense of calmness, as they begin to feel as though their inner VCR has been turned to fast-forward, performance levels consistently drop. A fast, accelerated psychological state generally contributes to more errors and compounds the player's task of being a good problem solver during play. Mental toughness in sport seems to be tied directly to the athlete's ability to sustain the feeling of calmness during crisis and adversity.

Low Anxiety

I have always felt that the greatness of players like McEnroe, Laver, Connors, Evert, and Navratilova is in large measure due to their ability to perform so well under pressure. As players report that they are feeling increasingly more pressure and anxiety during match play, performance levels consistently drop. From all that we know, the reality is that *no one* performs well under pressure. The genius of our greatest players is that they are able to go into pressurized, difficult, and potentially threatening situations and *eliminate* the pressure. They are able to somehow create relatively pressure-free climates within themselves. An essential skill for competitive success, then, is the ability to create such an internal pressure-free climate.

Energy Intensity

The feeling element that consistently surfaces as being number one in importance among athletes is the feeling that they are positively energized during performance. The word that coaches use is *intensity*. In fact, coaches often describe successes and failures on the part of players and teams by using the word intensity. "We won today because we played with great intensity." Players have their own terminology for describing this special state of energy. They use words like *pumped, psyched, jazzed,* and *wired.* This is the emotional element in the formula that serves to raise athletes' arousal level to an optimal point.

Interestingly, what we have thus far established is an apparent paradox. The combination of physically relaxed, mentally calm, and feeling no pressure combined with a heightened sense of energy, power, and activation seems implausible, if not impossible. But time after time, this is precisely what occurs when athletes are performing at their peak. As we shall see, any strategy that enables an athlete to increase his or her control of this positive energy feeling will be extremely important.

The energy experience itself is very specific. We can become energized from both positive and negative emotion. As a source of energy, positive emotion has clearly different performance consequences than negative emotion. When athletes become energized in the form of challenge, inspiration, excitement, and joy, they are much more likely to achieve high-level consistency than if they are activated essentially from their negative emotions. Negative emotions include feelings of anger, frustration, resentment, and fear. Intensity levels can be equally high with either positive or negative activators. But the ideal climate for competition time and again is reflected in the context of high energy stemming nearly exclusively from the positive emotions.

Optimism

It comes as no great surprise in our research that an ideal emotional climate is characterized by a sense of positivism and optimism. What is surprising is the consistency with which an optimistic, positive attitude proves to be part of the IPS. Not a single peak performance occurred when athletes were feeling pessimistic or negative about themselves or the situation. Positive, optimistic thinking is critical to competitive success and is fundamentally linked to establishing the right emotional climate during competition. When athletes begin acting and feeling negative or pessimistic about themselves and their situation for whatever reason—mistakes, cheating opponents, weather, bad calls—the likelihood of peak performance is nearly nonexistent. Again, it is easy for players to feel optimistic and positive when things are going their way. The real test of competitive strength is to maintain a sense of optimism and positivism in one's attitude and feelings when things start going badly.

Enjoyment

Plain and simple. When we can enjoy, we can perform. It is easy to enjoy winning. Our most successful competitors have learned to go well beyond simply loving to win. The critical difference here is the ability to love the battle, to love the struggle. Clearly, the ideal emotional climate for performing at one's peak is characterized by a real sense of enjoyment. Those who literally love competition make great competitors. Many athletes have it all backward. They will have fun if they perform well and if everything goes the way they would like it to go. What the IPS research demonstrates is that creating a state of enjoyment, a state of fun, is a prerequisite to establishing the right balance physiologically and psychologically, and is therefore indispensable to competitive success.

Sense of Effortlessness

When athletes are performing near the upper range of their capabilities, when they are in their IPS, they have a sense of effortlessness regarding their play. Although they are giving 100% commitment in energy, they have the feeling it is all coming very naturally and easily. Many athletes are guilty of trying to force a great performance—of trying too hard. Invariably, this results in excessive muscle tension and overarousal. The ideal climate for performing at one's peak is characterized by the sense of letting things happen quite naturally, while simultaneously giving 100% effort to the task. This is a very unusual balance, but it is exactly what is experienced by an athlete performing at a peak level. Peak performance cannot be forced; it occurs quite naturally or it does not occur at all. What players must essentially do is create the conditions emotionally and psychologically that allow it to occur. It is most likely to occur when the athlete gives 100% effort to the task of letting it happen naturally and spontaneously.

Automaticity

The ideal climate for high-level performance is consistently described by athletes as occurring within the context of feeling very automatic and instinctive. The more athletes report that they have to think about and analyze their mechanics in order to hold the performance together, the less likely they are to achieve high levels of performance output. Instinct is always swifter and truer than conscious, deliberate thought. Analyzers make notoriously poor performers. Players frequently describe the sensation of automaticity in this way: "It is almost as though someone else were hitting the shot."

Alertness

Alertness can best be described as a heightened state of awareness. When athletes are performing in an ideal emotional climate, they invariably report a very keen sense of alertness and personal awareness. Players report that during a match they are very aware of the direction of the wind, of which ball persons have the balls, of where their opponents are making most of their errors; they are aware that their opponents are starting to show fatigue or nervousness, and that the sun has shifted more directly in line with their serve. But they are not distracted by any of this. The heightened sense of awareness and alertness serves to make athletes very intelligent problem solvers. It seems to be one of the critical variables that enable players to self-regulate well. Players are able to read their own nervousness and maintain a sense of pace, intensity, and focus largely because they are so keenly aware of how their bodies are working.

Mental Focus

When athletes are performing exceptionally well, they invariably describe a state of intense mental focus or concentration. They are able to focus their attention on whatever is relevant. They are able to resist being distracted from the appropriate target. And the interesting thing is that the concentration seems to occur quite naturally. In the IPS, players are not telling themselves to concentrate on trying to find ways to improve their overall focusing. They are able to focus their attention on the task at hand quite spontaneously and naturally.

Self-Confidence

When athletes perform at the upper range of their talent and skill, they consistently report a feeling of high self-confidence during the performance. The confidence is not so much that they will win, but that they can perform well and can control their levels of performance during play. The feeling of self-confidence is a critical feeling component to the IPS. When athletes feel confident they tend to be more relaxed, to feel less pressure, to remain calmer, and to solve problems more intelligently. Confidence is nothing more than a feeling and, as such, is highly controllable. I shall outline strategies that coaches can use to help athletes sustain a feeling of confidence, particularly in the midst of crisis. The more athletes acquire control over the feeling of confidence, the tougher mentally they are likely to be, and the greater competitive success they are likely to enjoy.

Control

Time and again players reported a feeling of being *in control* when they were performing at their highest levels. The sense of control was most directly that of being *emotionally* in control. Players sensed that they were truly in charge of their own emotions. They did not feel victimized by the circumstances of play and, in fact, had the feeling of actually dictating their emotional responses to the events taking place. They felt in emotional harmony with themselves and the world around them regardless of how crazy things may have become. The feeling of emotional control persisted throughout the match regardless of crisis or adversity.

There are many things that take place during a match over which the athlete has little or no actual control. What seems to separate our best competitors from the also-rans is that they are able to control *all* events essentially by controlling their emotional response to events. This enables them to always remain in control. An ideal emotional climate for competition is one where athletes sustain the feeling that they are in complete control and, most important, in emotional control.

THE TYPICAL MATCH REQUIRES PROBLEM SOLVING

When you analyze a typical tennis match from the perspective of crisis or adversity, you begin to get the feeling that competitive success is associated in a direct way to the player's problem-solving skills. As suggested earlier, the true test of competitive strength is the way an athlete responds to crisis. Triggering one's IPS when everything is going right requires little in the way of mental skills.

Most match situations, however, present a continuum of problems. Every time momentum switches, it is a crisis. Every time a player senses that he or she is beginning to get tight, it is a crisis. Every time a player misses an easy sitter or a break point, it is a crisis. Consider the example of breaking down a match into a series of problems:

Problem # 1: John has been sick with the flu and has had very little practice.

Problem # 2: John is feeling very weak and a little dizzy before match time.

Problem # 3: John is feeling irritated and somewhat negative prior to the match.

Problem # 4: John arrives 15 minutes before match time only to learn that the match has been delayed for an hour and a half.

Problem # 5: John's first-round match is against a player who is noted for getting everything back. John knows that in order to win, he is going to have to stay out on the court and hit lots of balls. Having just gotten over the flu, he's not sure he can last.

Problem # 6: John gets a slow start in the match. He elects to serve and loses serve the first game.

Problem # 7: John has an opportunity to break back in the second game but misses an easy pass.

Problem # 8: Weather begins to change; winds pick up and become gusty.

Problem # 9: John loses the first set 6-3 after double-faulting on set point.

Problem # 10: John gets a very bad call on break point in the first game of the second set and loses the game.

Problem # 11: John gets another bad call after breaking back and getting the score to 3-all. John asks for a line judge.

Problem # 12: John double-faults twice in a second set tie-breaker, but manages to win the set 9-7 in the tiebreaker.

Problem # 13: John's opponent starts drop-shotting and lobbing in the first game of the third set and John feels humiliated and angered.

Problem #14: John gets down two breaks in the third as a result of his opponent's lob/drop shot tactics.

Problem #15: John fights back to 3-all and then quickly proceeds to lose serve and go down 4-3.

Problem #16: John's opponent gets into a prolonged argument over a line call with the umpire. John stands around what seems to be an eternity before the dispute is finally resolved.

Problem #17: John misses an easy break point at 5-all.

Problem #18: John double-faults on his first match point.

John wins the match in a tiebreaker in the third set.

After reading the above progression of problems, your initial reaction may be that this is an unusually problematic example. Actually, if you chart a match in terms of problems, you will likely find that many more problems present themselves in a typical match than in the example just described. Competitive success is really tied to an athlete's ability to solve or overcome problems. So many tennis players go into match conditions expecting things to be just perfect. They are, in fact, quite surprised when presented with problems with courts, balls, strings, rackets, line calling, and so on. It has been my experience that when athletes are taken by surprise, they are in trouble.

In order to achieve emotional control and emotional consistency, athletes must perceive problems in a unique way. Our best competitors have learned to actually thrive on problems. Jimmy Connors is at his best when conditions are at their worst. He feels that the crazier things get, the better it is for him. He uses problems to intensify his feelings of energy, of fight and determination, and he knows that most of his opponents will do precisely the opposite. To be competitively strong, athletes must realize that problems are part and parcel of athletic performance and, in fact, it will be their emotional reaction to those problems that will determine how far they go. Training athletes to develop correct emotional responses to problems is a key element in successful coaching.

CHAPTER 17

Mental Strategies for Selected Problems

This chapter offers concrete mental training strategies for five common areas of difficulty for coaches: tanking problems, temper problems, choking problems, prematch preparation problems, and parental problems.

TANKING PROBLEMS

Tanking means withdrawing energy and commitment. In the tennis vernacular, it means throwing in the towel before the match is over. It is one of the most common psychological problems competitors face. We all have a strong tendency to withdraw from situations that are unpleasant or threatening, and competition can be extremely threatening. As pressures mount, as athletes become more and more frustrated, as their performance levels create serious discrepancies between how well they are actually performing and how well they think they should be performing, there is a natural tendency to resolve the psychological crisis as quickly as possible. One of the most common ways players resolve such problems is simply to tank. They withdraw energy, commitment, and effort, and this helps remove their sense of ego involvement in the activity. The more psychological distance from the activity, the less pain, the less anguish, the less threat to the player's self-esteem. It is almost as if someone else were involved—certainly not *me*.

The tanking response can occur in major, obvious ways or in subtle ways that are difficult for an observer to detect. A major tank is generally reflected in the athlete's giving up on winning and just going through the motions. This is evidenced by a total lack of intensity, effort, and energy expenditure and a lifeless, nonmotivated, apathetic appearance. More subtle forms of emotional tanking include partial decreases in commitment, energy, or overall intensity levels. Players may tank a point, a game, or an entire match. The likelihood of the tanking response depends on how stressful or threatening the situation is to the player's self-esteem and on the nature of the player's coping skills.

Tanking is actually a variation of the psychological defense mechanism called *withdrawal*. For most athletes, withdrawal is initially one of the most common strategies for resolving psychological conflict and is actually the most disruptive to overall performance levels. Initially, the tanking response occurs unknowingly. Players do not consciously decide to withdraw energy and commitment to prevent damage to their self-esteem. They simply discover that when they do withdraw energy, commitment, and effort, they hurt less inside. Players often explain their losses by saying, "I just wasn't in it today," or, "If I had really put out today, I could have won."

It is very threatening for players to give 100% effort and still be defeated by someone they know should not have come close. If you give less than 100% and lose, you have a way out psychologically. You lost not because the other player was better, but because you "couldn't get into it." Players who allow themselves to tank when things get psychologically risky have tremendous difficulty stabilizing performance levels. Because they withdraw when things get tough, they never learn how to break through problems of choking, temper, and managing pressure and crisis.

Competitive success demands that players *close* the option of tanking. Regardless of the outcome of their efforts, they must refuse to withdraw energy and effort. This is actually the first step in elevating the mental skills of developing players. They must confront and eliminate the tanking response from their stress-coping arsenal. Once this psychological response tendency has been effectively shut down, a variety of new, exciting learning possibilities become available in the psychological area.

Coaches need to deal strongly and firmly with the tanking response because it is a psychological coping tendency over which athletes can exercise considerable voluntary control, particularly once it is brought to their attention. Once players are confronted with the information and become more aware of the problem, voluntary control is quite possible. Players may not be able to avoid getting nervous or choking, but they can always avoid the tanking response once they know about it. Coaches should make effort and commitment the number one performance demand they make of their players and accept few, if any, excuses for players resorting to the tanking response.

Coaches must take considerable care not to jump to conclusions and interpret a player's behavior as a tanking response. I have repeatedly seen coaches make an incorrect analysis of a player in this regard during competition. Upon closer examination, and through postmatch discussions with players, it was learned that during those times when players appeared to be tanking they were actually under so much stress and pressure that their feet simply would not move. They appeared lifeless and uncaring but, in effect, were really paralyzed by the stress. This is not an uncommon scenario.

It is also common for players to appear to be tanking when they are simply trying to relax and calm themselves during the heat of battle. Parents and coaches can become extremely upset when they witness some of these behaviors because they interpret them to mean that players are not trying. Coaches must come to understand players' psychological make-ups and be very clear in their interpretations of what is really happening. To accuse players of giving up or of not being tough competitors because they appear to be throwing in the towel, when in reality that is not the case, simply piles more pressure, frustration, and confusion on the player.

Steps for eliminating the tanking response include the following:

1. Raise your players' levels of self-awareness. Help them become fully cognizant that in pressure situations they have a tendency to withdraw energy and effort as a way of protecting their self-esteem.

2. Explain thoroughly to the players why tanking occurs and the effect that the tanking response will likely have on their development as competitors. The most important point to have them understand is that as long as they tank under pressure they will probably never learn how to handle match pressures constructively and become mentally tough.

3. Communicate to players directly and firmly that as their coach you will no longer accept the tanking response. You realize that tanking is normal and in many respects a logical response to stress, but, as coach, you do not accept it as a viable alternative. Let your

players know that they have the ability to control the tanking response and that they must begin to do so. They may well not be able to control the choking response, or how well they play overall. At times they may even be unable to control their anger response. But there is no situation, outside of illness, in which they cannot control their expenditure of effort.

4. Set specific match or practice goals regarding the expenditure of energy and have players rate how well they have done on a daily basis. To be great competitors, athletes must first eliminate the tanking response and then gradually move to the point where they can skillfully regulate *positive* intensity levels.

5. Carefully monitor each athlete's progress and be very tough on lapses. Make certain, however, that what appears to be a tank really is a tank before you take action.

6. Prior to every match make sure players are committed to give 100% effort regardless of the outcome. Help them understand that they will have achieved success as far as you are concerned as long as they enter and exit from crisis without reducing their commitment of energy and effort. If players live up to their commitment but still lose, you as coach must respond to them as you promised. Always reward effort over outcome.

TEMPER PROBLEMS

Just as with tanking, every player who has ever achieved any real competitive success has had to conquer the tendency to handle pressure, disappointment, and stress by losing his or her temper. When you examine the junior years of many of today's great players, you find that as youngsters they were noted for their un-controllable tempers; Bjorn Borg is an excellent example. At some point in their careers nearly all players have faced this issue; either they have found satisfactory answers to it and moved forward or they have become, in a sense, stalemated by their inability to control their temper. Actually, there is considerable similarity between tanking and temper. In a sense, the temper response *is* a tank. We might refer to the withdrawal of energy as a withdrawal tank and allowing energy to turn negative (as in anger and rage) as a temper tank. To fully understand the role anger and temper play within the stressful conditions of competition, we must again look to the issue of stress for answers.

In many respects, the temper response helps to preserve the delicate internal balance of self-esteem. As crisis mounts and players begin to make more and more mistakes, feelings of hopelessness and frustration increase. Players often find that anger and rage help to break their nervousness and discomfort over what appears to be an irreconcilable conflict. *The heart of the psychological conflict is the discrepancy between how well players are actually playing and how well they think they should be playing (based on their self-concept).* One way of resolving the conflict is to simply "lose it" in temper or anger. "I played lousy and not because I'm really that lousy, but because I got upset and lost my temper." Players who explain away losses by saying they became enraged and lost control are shielding themselves psychologically from the uncomfortable reality of what really happened.

Another justification for the temper response has been expressed by many players as they introspectively search for answers. Players often cannot stand the thought of opponents or spectators believing they are really as bad as they are playing. They use temper to communicate to their opponents and to the crowd that this is not the real level of their skill. "If I just continue playing without making any fuss," they reason, "people will think I'm really this bad." This strategy rarely works and, in fact, typically builds the confidence of the opponent who perceives that the player has lost it mentally.

On the positive side, those with serious temper or anger problems are generally fierce competitors. They hate to lose. They are very strong motivationally and can play with great intensity. Unfortunately, as soon as crisis strikes or their play falls below their expectations, they submarine their efforts and become their own worst enemies.

Players often feel they have little or no control over their temper. They feel helpless. "All of a sudden something triggers inside my head and I just lose it," they explain. It is true that once the powerful negative emotions start flowing, players often have little control. The most important point in all of this, however, is that when coaches get tough with temper and anger problems, when they refuse to tolerate even minor bursts of such negative emotion, players get in line very quickly.

As long as temper is an allowable option, players will take it. It is a perfectly natural and predictable response to the inevitable frustrations encountered in competitive tennis. Coaches who allow the temper response are doing a real disservice to their players. They are simply prolonging the time it will take for players to acquire the mental skills essential to success. As long as players can resort to either the temper or the withdrawal response, their psychological development as competitors will be delayed.

Strategies for dealing with the temper response include the following:

• Set very clear consequences for loss of temper.

• Be strict and persistent in your enforcement of breakdowns in this area.

• Reduce pressure to win. Keep pressures to be perfect, to excel, to win during matches at an absolute minimum.

• Put all of your coaching pressure on your players to keep their energy positive and optimistic and to maintain a good attitude. This is something you know they can accomplish if they really put themselves on the line. Pressures to win will simply complicate the issue.

• Insist that players adhere to your code of behavior in practice as well as in matches. Make no exceptions.

• Help players understand the dynamics involved in the temper response. Many players find themselves becoming extremely angry and losing their tempers at precisely those times when they are feeling the most anxious and nervous. Help players understand, if this is the case, how their anger is tied to pressure. Athletes often feel more comfortable being angry and upset than they do feeling nervous and tight. Unfortunately, as long as they allow themselves the option of getting angry and upset, they never learn how to work through the problems of nervousness.

• Outline a specific set of procedures that players are to follow in response to mistakes. For example, players might try turning and walking away, showing no emotion. If players feel themselves becoming angry, they should take time to focus their thoughts on things that will help defuse the anger immediately. Another strategy is to have players trigger deep diaphragmatic breathing immediately following a mistake.

• Have players mentally rehearse through visualization how they intend to manage mistakes and crises during the upcoming match or practice. Insist that they do their homework before showing up for play. This will substantially help them exercise more direct control over their negative emotional states.

• Make a special effort to determine if players' moodiness is in any way attributable to changes in sleep patterns, diet (particularly sugar intake), or overall stress levels in their lives. Such factors often contribute significantly to emotional control problems and must be included in any successful solution.

• Require that athletes with temper problems keep a daily diary of their successes and failures and that they evaluate their performance every time they leave the court.

THE CHOKING RESPONSE

Players constantly refer to lapses in performance in conjunction with choking. Athletes frame this response in colorful vocabulary: the gag, the iron elbow, the clutch. The most accurate explanation for choking defines the phenomenon in physiological terms. Choking is simply a natural biological response tendency. It is nature's instinctive "fight or flight" alarm. Our ancestors found the tendency to choke not only useful, but necessary for preservation of the species. When a predator suddenly appeared on the scene, a biological alarm was sounded that prepared them to either fight for their lives or flee from the danger as fast as possible. A number of very predictable physiological reactions were involved: dilation of the pupils, rapid, shallow breathing, elevated blood pressure, increased heart rate, decreased blood flow to the extremities, and increased muscle tension. The entire body became mobilized for life-preserving action.

There are few saber-toothed tigers or other predatory beasts waiting for a tasty meal on the tennis court; unfortunately, however, our physiologies continue to respond as though there were. When players step up to serve at 4-all in a tiebreaker, the life-preserving physiological response is triggered. Unlike their ancestors, however, players can neither fight nor flee. They must delicately coordinate their fine motor skills, balance, agility, and speed so as to perfectly execute a series of complex biomechanical movements.

In effect, what mentally tough competitors are able to do is insulate themselves against their bodies' natural biological alarm system. One way they do this is to work to perceive crises and problems within the competitive arena in such a way that they no longer produce the fight-or-flight response mechanisms. This is no easy task, as the psychological risks and pressures of match play can be formidable. What the player really faces is transforming the event from one that is perceived as threatening and upsetting to one that is challenging and inspiring. That, we have learned, is what our greatest competitors are able to do time after time.

In an important sense, choking is an indication of something very positive. The choking response is actually two steps ahead of the tanking response and one step ahead of the temper response in terms of mental skill development. Choking indicates that a person is very ego-involved in what he or she is doing. They are out there risking something of themselves; they are putting themselves on the line. When athletes choke, it also indicates that they are very strong motivationally. Elimination of the tanking response often brings forth the temper response, and eliminating the temper response often leads to the choking response. In this sense, players who begin choking may actually be showing psychological progress. The more opportunities athletes have to learn to deal constructively with pressures and crises, the more quickly they will break through. As long as they are allowed the tanking and temper options, mastery of choking is delayed.

It is a mistake to expect your players never to choke. The fact is, everyone chokes. We do so because the result of the contest is uncertain. There is much on the line in competitive tennis—a great deal of self-esteem, pride, perhaps the team's welfare, and often money. Things can get very threatening very fast. When this happens, the choking response appears. No one is immune. The difference between the top 50 players in the world and the rest of us is that the top 50 choke less often and overcome it more quickly. For them, choking may last for a point or two; rarely does it last for games or sets at a time.

The choking response is not under direct voluntary control. A coach should never put pressure on a player not to choke; that is like putting ice on something you intend to thaw out—what you get is more of the same. As long as a player is feeling considerable pressure, the biological alarm will likely be triggered and the choking response will be there. In many respects, choking is on the same par as not being able to get to sleep at night. Though we rarely discuss our insomnia within the context of choking, we often have no more control over falling asleep than we do over choking. So often I hear parents and even coaches berate players because they consistently choke on big points. This is a tragic mistake. When players choke they probably wanted the point badly. It was not that they did not try hard; if anything, they were guilty of trying too hard.

Suggestions for dealing with chronic choking problems include the following:

• Remember that choking is normal and is tied to the way players perceive a situation as threatening. Help players understand the relationship between the way in which they choose to perceive adversity and the tendency to choke.

• Coaches should try to obtain as much information as possible about the past history of the player and those situations that have typically produced choking problems. When does the athlete typically choke? Where and how does it typically happen? Try to understand how the individual player's psychology contributes to the build-up of pressure during match play.

• Whenever possible, deemphasize the importance of winning. Your task as a coach is clearly to decrease whatever pressures exist on players who repeatedly choke. Help them see things in a less threatening context.

• Help players increase their self-awareness so that they can quickly tell when they are entering a biological alarm state. Help them to read when their muscles start becoming tight, when they begin to feel overly anxious, or when they start to experience a sense of pressure.

• Do not have players set out *not to* choke. The more players dwell on not choking, the greater the likelihood they will. Players need to be setting goals in positive areas, goals that they can pursue aggressively. If you set them a goal not to choke, you are actually setting a negative goal that reduces the athlete's feeling of control and aggressiveness.

• For players who tend to exaggerate the importance of a particular event, spend some time discussing with the athlete the worst possible scenario that could occur. For a player who can envision handling the worst thing that could ever happen, anything is manageable. Have athletes imagine what would happen if they were to lose in the worst possible way. Have them project what their world would be like the morning after. Then have them imagine that years have passed and that they are looking back at this one event in the context of their entire playing career. In nearly all cases, this puts the particular match in perspective. For all practical purposes, the match in this context is nearly always meaningless. The only real value it may legitimately have is that it represents another opportunity for the player to learn to execute strokes more efficiently and effectively, to fine-tune emotionally, and to learn to become a better competitor.

• Help players learn to play one point at a time. Help them learn to focus on the present and to play each point as if it were the only point in the match. The choking response is always tied to fear of what may happen in the future. To perform well, one must ignore the future and the past to focus on the present. The more players practice playing each point as though it were the single most important point of the match, the more they will begin to perceive all points to be equal in value. If all points deserve deserve 100% effort and have equal value, then there really are no big points. Once players begin playing all points as though they have equal value, the pressure dynamics change.

• Most players have the tendency to push, to get very conservative, and to play it safe as the pressure mounts. They start playing *not to lose* as opposed to playing *to win*. Players should have a very clear-cut set of guidelines to follow regarding the style of their play when they are nervous. That style for most players should be to become more aggressive while at the same time resisting the temptation to go after first-ball winners. The goal should be to get more aggressive, but to also "work the points."

• If a player has a stroke that consistently breaks down under pressure, you should carefully examine the biomechanics of that stroke. In all likelihood it is the stroke that needs fixing, not the player's head. Strokes should allow the competitor to continue to play aggressively and to keep balls in play despite being slightly nervous or tight. If a stroke does not allow for that, it should be reconstructed.

• Have your players become more ritualistic under pressure. Whenever players start to get tight or nervous, they should adhere to a predetermined pattern of movements, gestures, and thoughts, such as blowing on their hand, bouncing the ball a set number of times, swaying back and forth, or taking a deep breath and thinking *aggressive*. The more ritualistic players become, the greater the likelihood of their dealing with choking.

• A general rule is to take more time, not less time, as the pressure mounts. Most players tend to start racing, to speed up as the pressure increases. Constantly give players feedback as to how well they maintain their pace under pressure. As they find themselves struggling to deal constructively with pressure, recommend that they intentionally slow down.

• Have players practice breath control both off the court and on the court. It is very possible to short-circuit nature's biological alarm response with something as simple as executing a few deep diaphragmatic breaths. Breath-control training can be a great help to athletes as a strategy for preventing choking. Taking deep breaths prior to serves and serve returns when in trouble is always worthwhile.

• Athletes who often get a slow start in matches due to nervousness should try working into a full sweat just before going on the court. Have them get a good solid workout as close to the time of play as possible, perhaps in rigorous stretching, rope jumping, calisthenics, or jogging. This helps reduce muscle tension and clears the psychological effects of pressure.

• Constantly emphasize the importance of having fun and enjoying oneself in the competitive arena. Help your players train to create a state of enjoyment and fun during competition. The more athletes really enjoy competition, the less likely they are to trigger the choking response or to experience interfering fear, stress, and anxiety.

• Help your players train to begin perceiving crisis and adversity as challenges. This takes time and is a long educational process. Use every opportunity to help players learn new, more constructive emotional responses. In the long run, it is here that you will make your greatest impact on their success in coping with choking problems.

• Prepare a precise plan of action that athletes are to employ as soon as they become aware that their biological alarm has been triggered. Take the guesswork out of managing stress and crisis for them. Have your players become very specific in how they plan to react when faced with a situation that ushers in the choking response.

PREMATCH PREPARATION PROBLEMS

Many psychological problems related to match play can be traced directly to poor preparation. Many players have never trained to develop a systematic prematch preparation routine. Over and over again, players just show up for matches and find themselves unready to perform their best. Prematch preparation routines are sometimes referred to as prematch rituals. They serve to help players achieve an optimal state of readiness prior to the start of a match or point. All players should be given the assignment to discover their own best prematch rituals. Rituals can be discussed in three categories: the week before the match, the day before the match, and the day of the match.

Rituals the Week Before the Match

Players should formulate a regular pattern of eating, dieting, exercising, drill work, and visualizing that optimizes their chances of performing well in competition. They should begin following this pattern of activity, which should extend to their sleep habits as well, the week prior to competition, as its routine will help prepare them for the demands of the upcoming match or tournament. As for exercising, the last 2 days prior to a tournament, players should be tapering off. Workouts should be less intense to allow the body to regenerate itself and be 100% ready to perform. Players should develop visualization routines to use during the week before the tournament; these should emphasize themes of success, solutions to past problematic situations, and match goals.

Practice routines during the week before a major tournament should be designed to build confidence and get players feeling good about themselves. In fact, anything you can do to strengthen players' belief in themselves will probably help them achieve a high performance level. In most instances, the final week should involve progressively more match play and progressively less drill. The intent is to simulate actual conditions of competition as closely as possible in terms of court, wind, balls, and pressure. Most players find that the week prior to the tournament is a time when it is especially important to remain disciplined and focused. This helps athletes feel they deserve to win, that they are in control and emotionally strong.

Rituals the Day Before a Match

Most players find that following a clearly defined ritual the night before a match is very important. The ritual includes how much sleep they get, what time they go to bed, and what time they get up. There is no question that sleep plays a major role in helping people to handle stress and in preparing the body for a difficult workout.

Another important aspect of the ritual is goal setting (see later section on this subject). The night before a match, players should be clear as to what they intend to do and achieve in the next day's match. One way to help players establish match goals is to have them write out precisely those things they intend to accomplish. Have them spell out their goals in clear detail and, most importantly, make a strong commitment to control those things over which they have control. Committing the whole process to writing can be helpful. Also potentially useful is to have athletes talk into a tape recorder about everything they intend to do, then listen to their commitments prior to the match.

The third method for reinforcing prematch goals is to have players spend time vividly visualizing the accomplishment of those match goals. Most importantly, players should visualize to prepare for adversity. If players do their homework by writing, talking, or visualizing about match goals and potential problems, they are much more likely to respond psychologically and physically in positive ways. They have prepared constructive solutions to disruptions that might occur during competition.

Rituals on the Day of the Match

Rituals on match day should include when to get up, what and when to eat, and the nature and timing of the prematch workout. Players should also include a dressing ritual—when to dress and what to wear. Experience has shown that what we wear can often have a powerful influence on the way we feel. Some clothes seem to help us feel strong, fast, or attractive, whereas other clothes have precisely the opposite effect. It is important that athletes select the clothes for competition that stimulate confidence and positive feelings.

Most athletes find that a 30-minute quiet time prior to match play is very helpful. During this time, athletes are involved in a final rehearsal of what they intend to do in the match. It is now that they should read what they prepared in writing the night before, or listen to the tape they may have made concerning match goals and play. This is also an excellent time for players to visualize and imagine what they intend to accomplish during their match. Most players find they prefer to keep to themselves right before a match, rather than watching matches or socializing. What is important is that players determine what ritual works best for them, and then that they follow it as much of the time as possible.

Setting Match Goals

Listed below are examples of unrealistic versus realistic prematch goals. Players must focus their efforts to successfully meet match goals over which they have control. Placing pressure on players to meet goals over which they have little control simply adds more conflict, frustration, and guilt.

REALISTIC PREMATCH GOALS	UNREALISTIC PREMATCH GOALS
(factors players can control)	*(factors players cannot control)*
1. To give 100% effort regardless of the outcome. To be able to say at the end of the match, "I did not tank at any point during the course of the match. I gave my best effort throughout the entire match—point by point."	1. To win the match.
2. To maintain a predominantly positive and optimistic attitude during the course of the match. "Positive emotions are what energize me during play."	2. Not to choke.
3. To project a strong physical presence during the course of the match, regardless of how I feel. "Even if I have to fake it, I'll try to project the image of a champion."	3. Not to get tight or nervous.
4. To be totally responsible for myself, so I can say, "I played with both feet on the court. I did not look for an easy excuse, and I did not blame my performance on anything external. I never used a problem as an excuse."	4. To win the big points.

PROBLEMS WITH PARENTS OF YOUTHFUL PLAYERS

Parents play a pivotal role in the development of successful competitors. Without their support, encouragement, and caring, young athletes will often not persevere through all the difficulties and hard knocks. Over the last several years, we have learned a great deal about the effects of certain parental practices on the development of young tennis players. Because parents of developing athletes have few, if any, real guidelines to help them define their roles, it is very easy for them to make mistakes. Following natural parental instincts often proves to have disastrous consequences.

I am a firm believer that parents need to be trained to be effective and that training should most appropriately be done by coaches. Coaches can see more clearly than almost anyone else in young athletes' lives the effect of certain parental practices. Most parents become involved in a competitive sport very innocently. Children start lessons and parents get involved in transportation and paying the bills. Suddenly they find themselves thrust into the middle of the highly pressurized, complex, and confusing world of competitive junior tennis. They realize that if they do not play an active role, their sons or daughters could quickly fall behind.

Tips for Dealing With Parents

The following tips may prepare coaches to help parents more accurately define their roles.

• Help parents understand that they should not be putting pressure on their children to win. Parents often make the mistake of thinking that if their children would only try harder, they would win more. Parental pressure to win is often the most difficult kind of pressure young players have to face. Parents must understand that if they contribute at all to increased pressure, they simply add more problems to impede their children's progress and performance. It is most important that they understand that kids, just like adults, perform best in a pressure-free environment. The more parents can emphasize fun, enjoyment, and the intrinsic value of playing the game, the more likely they are to see their children achieve competitive success.

• Help parents understand that they should not be viewing their son's or daughter's tennis as a business investment. There is no question that junior tennis at the national or regional level can be terribly costly. When parents begin to think that someday they will get a financial return on their investment, invariably the youngster starts feeling increased pressure. Help parents think of the money spent as investment in *the person*. Help them to perceive the expense as akin to that of education or musical instrument lessons. Playing competitive tennis is a life experience that should prove invaluable to the young athlete as a developing, maturing person. If parents feel that competitive tennis is not a healthy and worthwhile personal experience, they should clearly reconsider if they want their child involved. The more tennis becomes a financial investment with an expected return, the greater the likelihood it will get completely off track.

• Help parents understand that they should get neither too excited when their children win, nor too upset if they lose. Most importantly, they should never tie special privileges or rewards to winning. One of the most damaging practices of parents is to withdraw attention, love, or affection when their children lose. This kind of pressure can have significant short-term and long-term negative consequences for the athletes. They quickly realize they are no longer competing to win the match, but rather to win the love and approval of their parents.

• Help parents not to confuse their own egos with those of their children. We see it all the time: When the child double faults, the parent double faults; when the child makes a stupid play, the parent feels stupid. It is easy for parents to become overly ego-involved. If ever you hear parents talk in terms of "we"—"We're playing at three," "We lost today,"—take the time to correct them. Parents need a lot of help in this regard; without assistance from an objective party, they quickly get in way over their heads.

• Help parents not to show negative emotions or nervousness as they are watching their children play. Help them to learn ways to project positive feelings from the sidelines. If parents cannot be positive, optimistic, and encouraging during matches, they should clearly stay away. By looking nervous or negative, they are simply adding more performance problems to their children's world. If parents cannot look supportive and unconcerned on the sideline, no matter how they feel inside, they should find some other way to spend their time. The only exception to this rule is if a child's behavior has become unacceptable in terms of cheating, temper, or negativism. In such cases, it is most important that parents play an active role, projecting disapproval and even threatening behavior at times. If the situation is not corrected, it may be necessary for parents to remove their young players from the match altogether.

• Help parents understand the risk involved in coaching their own children. In most instances, parents who get involved in coaching sons or daughters are significantly complicating their roles. Being a parent is tough enough; being a parent and a coach is simply too tough for most. Remember, the real cost is to the child, not to the parent.

• Discourage parents from going to lessons and practice sessions and taking notes, videotaping the activities, and the like. Even though a child may tell a parent that such practice is helpful, in the long run it is likely to undermine the coach's role. Experience has repeatedly shown that coaching should be left to coaches and parenting left to parents. Parents may think they are helping, but you must help them understand how these seemingly harmless practices often create more performance problems for their kids.

• Encourage parents to take every opportunity to reduce the pressures to win. Spend time with parents and help them understand how the ideal emotional climate for performing in competition is essentially pressure free. Give examples to parents of how youngsters with great talent have had their spirits broken by parents who exerted too much pressure. Help parents clearly understand the role they should be playing. Regardless of the circumstances, they should attempt at all times to be supportive, encouraging, caring, and positive. Parents provide the emotional and financial support to make things happen. They should do whatever they can to make the tennis experience healthy and positive for their child, no matter how far the youngster goes in the competitive arena.

• Help parents understand how important it is that their child not feel that his or her self-worth is on the line during competition. When winning or losing becomes closely interwoven with a youngster's identity as a person, pressures quickly become overwhelming. Parents need to be educated in the pitfalls of this whole area. They need to work hard to insure that their children do not feel less loved, less valued, or less important to them simply because they lost. This negative kind of attitude is communicated very subtly by parents when they become angry with the child for losing.

• Attitude is the one area where parents should play an active role. Encourage parents to get tough when it comes to cheating, temper, and foul language. This is, after all, a legitimate area for parenting. Parents need to keep off the pressure to win, but put on the pressure for their children to control their behavior and respond with good sportsmanship in all situations. Parents certainly do children no favor by overlooking negative behavior on the court. Lost temper, cheating, and the like are likely to escalate if left unchecked.

• Coaches realize how tough losing can be on the egos of young players. From the youngster's perspective, a loss can take on overwhelming proportions. Kids can suffer tremendous guilt, self-condemnation, and shame in response to losses. The most important time for parents to be involved is when their children suffer heart-breaking losses. At this time, parents need to provide support, care, and encouragement.

• Parents often wonder why their children did not win when they were clearly better than the opposition. Coaches need to help them understand that if their children could have won, they would have. Kids do not suffer embarrassing losses because they want to. They suffer them because at the time they were unavoidable. Parents must understand that winning and losing are beyond their children's direct control.

• Help parents understand how the competitive sport experience, specifically junior tennis, can be important in the development of youngsters. In many respects, sport is a microcosm of life. As players learn to be good problem-solvers on the court, as they learn to handle crisis and adversity constructively, they will become more effective, more complete human beings in general. Parents must realize how the crazy world of competitive junior tennis can be a valuable learning experience for their kids. They must make certain that the experience itself does not become overly negative and that it does not cause the youngsters to doubt themselves or lose confidence in themselves as people.

• Give guidelines to parents that they can use to judge the correctness or incorrectness of their actions as parents of young athletes. Help them define what is appropriate or inappropriate behavior for them. Help them see themselves as performers in much the same way their children are performers. They have a role to play just as the coach and the young athletes do. When all play their roles properly, the children have the greatest opportunity for competitive success. It is very easy for parents to get caught up in the race to be number one and in the lure of the big dollar, but that should never be the reason they are involved. The real objective of competitive junior tennis is to provide a learning experience to help young players become stronger, healthier persons. Parents and coaches should always judge the impact of the sport experience on young players in terms of the overall effect it has on them.

CHAPTER 18

Implementing a
Mental-Training
Program

This chapter sets forth a basic framework for starting an effective mental-training program for tennis players. Regardless of the nature of the program, it must meet certain conditions to be successful.

• It must be practical. Both you and your players must see practical value in the program. If it is viewed as "far out" or exotic, no one, including yourself, will take it seriously.

• It must be easy to understand. No matter how brilliant the training system, if it cannot be communicated in simple, everyday language, players are likely to get lost. The real test of how well you understand something is how simply you can describe it. Stay away from psychological jargon. Take the time to translate things into the language of your players.

• It must be comfortable for you to teach. If you are uncomfortable or have any doubts, your players will pick it up immediately. Unless you have confidence in what you're doing, you can't expect others to follow you.

• It must fit into your normal training routine. If the mental-training program cannot be integrated into your normal physical training regimen, it will likely be short-lived. It is possible to design a mental-training system that will not cause major disruptions in your ordinary schedule.

• It must make sense. If the training in any way violates what you consider to be good common sense, stop and do some serious additional investigation. A solid mental-training program should be generally consistent with your coaching philosophy and practice.

THE OBJECTIVE OF MENTAL TRAINING

The primary objective of mental training is to improve performance consistency. As coaches, we are always attempting to help players consistently perform toward the upper range of their talents and skills. For that to happen, players must understand and control more effectively their ideal performance state (IPS). They must, in effect, become better self-regulators. Mental training in a real sense is emotional fine-tuning. Emotionally stronger players have greater self-control, which usually translates into more competitive success.

Similar to a program for physical skills, an effective mental-training program will accelerate the learning process beyond that of simple trial and error. Most athletes will acquire the mental skills prerequisite for competitive success if they spend enough time competing and do not throw in the towel somewhere along the way. Mental training can effectively shorten the learning time. It should truly be a short cut to the same mental skills that are acquired in competition. Just as a good system for teaching biomechanics will accelerate the acquisition of physical skills, so will a good mental-training system accelerate the learning of mental skills.

THE ROLE OF SELF-AWARENESS

Plain and simple, improving an athlete's ability to self-regulate in competition is directly tied to increasing his or her level of self-awareness. Self-control and self-awareness are closely connected and, as a result, any training experience that serves to increase an athlete's self-awareness should prove useful. The road to greater mental toughness is through increased self-awareness. Increasing athletes' understanding of how their mood affects their performance, of how their breathing patterns, thinking, and imaging styles affect their play, of how such things as their rituals, eye control, and intensity levels affect their concentration will generally lead to increased self-regulatory success.

KNOW THE PERSON

From a mental-training perspective, the more you know about the athlete you are trying to help, the greater the chance for success. It is very difficult, if not impossible, to help someone psychologically whom you really do not understand. Make an effort to gather as much relevant information about the person as you can. Useful information includes a detailed history of the player's competitive successes and failures (multiyear tournament records); local, regional, and national ranking history; previous coaching history; short-term, intermediate, and long-term goals; and school grades, family dynamics, parental pressure, financial pressures, general health history, and history of injuries.

Of greatest importance is developing an understanding and appreciation for the personality of the player. You cannot manage what you do not understand. The more you understand the personality of a player, the greater chance you have of designing a truly effective mental training program. Simple assignments such as having your players prepare a comprehensive written description of their personalities, or periodically writing a one-page description of the current pressures in their lives, can be most revealing. Having players fill out a self-descriptive questionnaire such as the one in Table 18.1 can give you quick and valuable information.

Another useful tool for gathering initial information about a player is a daily check sheet. By having an athlete monitor relevant areas of information for a 2-week period, important factors and patterns can be isolated. Remember, you are trying to fine-tune your players both physically and emotionally; to insure success, you must examine a wide range of potentially disruptive factors. Table 18.2 presents a sample one-week monitoring chart.

ASSESS MENTAL SKILLS

Once you have a good understanding of the personality of players, their competitive histories, and factors such as family, grades, on-court and off-court pressures, and so forth, it is now time to begin assessing their profile of skills as competitors. Coaches can watch a player and quickly profile physical strengths and weaknesses in such areas as speed, agility, endurance, footwork, ground strokes, serves, volleys, specialty shots, game strategy, and so on. Coaches need to do the same thing in respect to mental skills.

Table 18.1 Self-Descriptive Questionnaire

Name: _____

Date: _____

	Very much like me			Not at all like me	
Moody	1	2	3	4	5
Temperamental	1	2	3	4	5
Hyper	1	2	3	4	5
Negative thinker	1	2	3	4	5
Self-conscious	1	2	3	4	5
Outgoing	1	2	3	4	5
Tough-minded	1	2	3	4	5
Easygoing	1	2	3	4	5
Enthusiastic	1	2	3	4	5
Disciplined	1	2	3	4	5
Hates to lose	1	2	3	4	5
Fiercely competitive	1	2	3	4	5
Independent	1	2	3	4	5
Self-aware	1	2	3	4	5
Spacey	1	2	3	4	5
Fearful	1	2	3	4	5
Calm	1	2	3	4	5
Optimistic	1	2	3	4	5
Firey	1	2	3	4	5
Burned out	1	2	3	4	5
Easily intimidated	1	2	3	4	5
Quiet/shy	1	2	3	4	5
Emotional	1	2	3	4	5
Analytical	1	2	3	4	5
Perfectionistic	1	2	3	4	5

Table 18.2 Sample One-Week Monitoring Chart

Name _____

Date _____

	Sun	Mon	Tu	Wed	Th	Fri	Sat
Hours of sleep							
Number of meals							
Time on homework							
Sugar—no. of times							
Diet (A-F)*							
Stress level (1-5)							
Feel energized today (1-5)							
Exam day—yes/no							
Hours of drill							
Hours of match play							
Aerobic work (time)							
Speed work (time)							
Moody today, off court—yes/no							
Moody today, on court—yes/no							
My intensity on court (A-F)							
My concentration on court (A-F)							
My confidence on court (A-F)							
My motivation today (A-F)							
How well I played today (A-F)							
Parental pressure (1-5)							

*Any system of evaluation can be used. A through F with A being outstanding and F being extremely poor is one possibility. Scales of 1 to 5 or 1 to 10 can also be used.

In my own work, I have found it useful to collect information regarding mental skills according to seven general categories:

- Self-confidence
- Arousal control
- Attention control
- Visualization and imagery control
- Motivational level
- Positive energy control
- Attitude control

Without question, these seven factors critically impact players' abilities to control their IPS during play. Let us look at each factor more closely.

Self-Confidence

Self-confidence is essentially the feeling athletes have that they can do it, that they have what it takes to succeed. This simple feeling is actually one of the best predictors of competitive success. The images athletes have about what they can and cannot do in a major way determine the outcome.

Arousal Control

Arousal control is the skill that enables a player to find the right balance of relaxation, calmness, and intensity within the stressful environment of competition. Arousal control is one of the primary skills athletes rely on to insulate themselves against their biological fight-or-flight alarm response.

Attention Control

Attention control is the ability of an athlete during play to tune in what is important and tune out what is not. The ability to concentrate on the task at hand is so central to good performance it cannot be overemphasized.

Visualization and Imagery Control

Visualization is the ability to think in pictures as opposed to words. It is the constructive use of one's imaginative skills as a vehicle for self-programming. The ability to rehearse themes of success using mental images is a most important competitive skill. Additionally, performing well in competition requires that athletes shift from predominantly logical, rational, analytical styles of thinking to much more spontaneous, instinctive ones. Visualization prior to and during competition helps facilitate that shift.

Motivational Level

The motivational level of an athlete is clearly number one in importance. The erosion of desire, of an athlete's hunger to play the game, undermines everything else. Motivation is in many ways a reflection of the extent to which playing the sport meets important psychological needs of the player. Motivation is the energy of commitment and discipline, without which progress cannot be made.

Positive Energy Control

Positive energy control is the skill that enables athletes to successfully fuel intensity levels during play from their positive (rather than negative) emotions. Positive intensity must flow from emotions of challenge, inspiration, fight, determination, fun, enjoyment, and so on. Positive energy is the energy of peak performance.

Attitude Control

Attitude control reflects an athlete's ability to direct the content of his or her thoughts prior to and during play in positive and constructive directions. Positive thinkers make better competitors. The right attitude produces emotional control, poise, and positive intensity.

DESIGNING A MENTAL-TRAINING PROGRAM

Designing effective mental-training programs for athletes requires that coaches first understand players' profiles of mental strengths and weaknesses. Organizing your information and thinking according to the seven factors just described should help you categorize your assessment more coherently. There are any number of ways you can collect useful information about these factors. Examples would be personally discussing the seven factors with the players; having players write about how they perceive their profiles of strengths and weaknesses in these areas; discussing with previous coaches and with parents their perceptions; and, most important, observations of the players in practice and competition. Video analysis of players in light of these seven factors can prove invaluable. Table 18.3 is a sample rating sheet that can be used to contrast your assessments with those of the players.

Table 18.3 Mental Skill Evaluation Form

1. *Self-confidence*

1	2	3	4	5
Poor		Average		Excellent

2. *Arousal control*

1	2	3	4	5
Poor		Average		Excellent

3. *Attention control*

1	2	3	4	5
Poor		Average		Excellent

4. *Visualization and imagery control*

1	2	3	4	5
Poor		Average		Excellent

5. *Motivation*

1	2	3	4	5
Poor		Average		Excellent

6. *Positive Energy Control*

1	2	3	4	5
Poor		Average		Excellent

7. *Attitude control*

1	2	3	4	5
Poor		Average		Excellent

Note. This rating sheet can be used to contrast your assessment with those of the player.

Things to Look For

Problems in the seven mental skill areas often follow predictable patterns. Here is an extensive list of clues to watch for. Specific suggestions for dealing with these problems come later in the chapter.

Low Self-Confidence

- Plays better from behind than from ahead
- Has trouble closing out matches
- Game tends to fall apart at the first sign of failure
- Projects a very weak on-court image
- Almost always plays better in practice than in matches
- Becomes more tentative and conservative as the pressure of competition mounts

Low Arousal Control

- Often appears hyper during competition
- Looks nervous, tight, or fearful during play
- Becomes easily frustrated with mistakes
- Displays frequent temper or anger problems
- Starts slowly in matches
- Is either too fired up or not energized enough
- Starts blasting balls and going for first-ball winners under pressure
- Often observed vacillating between tanking and rage

Low Attention Control

- Easily distracted during play
- Plays lots of "loose" and "spacey" points
- Makes inappropriate shot selection
- Often has unexplainable drops in performance
- Eyes wander frequently between points
- Has trouble keeping track of score

Low Visualization and Imagery Control

- Constantly analyzing grips, strokes, footwork, etc. during play
- Play appears very deliberate and uncreative
- Rarely looks instinctive during play
- Constantly looking for logical and rational answers to everything
- Frequently appears unprepared for matches
- Does not give the appearance that he or she has worked out solutions to potential problems in advance (wind, bad calls, etc.)

Low Motivation

- Poor discipline; has trouble staying on any kind of schedule
- Chronic complaining
- Appears bored and uninspired in either practice or play
- Rarely if ever does more than is required
- Often tanks emotionally in competition
- Often a disciplinary problem
- Very unpredictable on court—never sure what will happen

Low Positive-Energy Control

- Rarely gets challenged or inspired when confronted by problems during play
- Seems to have to get angry to play well
- Rarely has fun in the competitive arena
- Looks very calm but has no fire or fight
- Seems to lose positive emotional intensity easily

Low Attitude Control

- Negative thinker during competition
- Frequent negative self-talk during play
- Projects a negative image in crisis
- Always has excuses for everything
- Is often involved with negative, pessimistic thinking off the court

Set Goals for Improvement

Coaches have become very familiar and comfortable with setting goals in the areas of stroke production and physical conditioning. We know how valuable goal setting is in accelerating the process of positive change. Goal setting helps focus the athlete's training efforts and helps keep players motivated, disciplined, and in touch with the weaknesses they must improve. It helps them establish organization in their overall training programs.

The same applies to goal setting in the area of mental training. In order to truly accelerate the acquisition of competitive mental skills, goal setting is a must. The following three principles lead to the best results:

- Design the training program around the player's mental weaknesses, not strengths. Just as in the physical area, always work to strengthen the player's areas of greatest deficiency.

• Limit your goals to two or three major training objectives. Don't go after everything at once.

• Monitor training activities on a daily basis.

Consider a theoretical example. As John Smith's coach, you have determined from extensive study and observation that John's greatest areas of mental weakness are concentration, arousal control, and self-confidence. Possible training activities for John might include the following (specific training activities for various mental skill deficiencies are covered later in this chapter):

• Reduce negative self-talk during play.

• Use the "only the ball" technique between points during match play. John is simply to repeat the phrase to himself over and over again between points. This is done to improve concentration and stabilize arousal levels.

• Increase positive energy (intensity) investment during practice and play.

• Prior to serve and serve return, John is to vividly visualize what he wants to happen.

• Practice muscle relaxation exercises for 10 to 15 minutes daily.

• Set aside a 30-minute quiet time prior to match play and a 10-minute quiet time prior to practice. During this time, John is to rehearse how he wants to perform that day and specifically how he intends to respond emotionally to whatever happens.

This example shows how a coach can help players set goals that will help them address areas of emotional weakness. A good way to approach the broad area of mental training is to categorize it into on-court and off-court training.

CATEGORIES OF ON-COURT MENTAL TRAINING

There are several things to look for while your players are on the court. Each of the following items indicate mental preparedness of players.

Eye Control

When players are performing and concentrating well, their eyes are generally very controlled both between and during points. There is a close correlation between visual focus and mental focus. The more players' eyes wander during play, the more likely their mental focus will wander as well. Have players train to keep their eyes in one of three places during play: on the ball, on the strings, or on the ground. The more precise the visual focus, the more precise the mental focus.

Rituals

Players who do not have well-defined mental and physical rituals prior to serve and serve return are at a distinct disadvantage. Rituals serve to deepen concentration, trigger appropriate relaxation, and raise intensity levels prior to the start of each point. Our most ritualistic players tend to hole up best under pressure. Rituals should be basically the same each time and, most importantly, should be carried out in pressure situations.

Pace

Every great competitor has a characteristic sense of pace. Good competitors stay with their pace under pressure. They resist the temptation to rush, to speed up and short-circuit their natural rhythm. Players should train to maintain their best sense of pace during match play, especially when the pressure is on.

Breathing

Breathing is a window to our emotions, and it is one of the best vehicles we have for regulating our physiology. As consistently demonstrated by top players, coordinating one's exhalation with the precise moment of ball/racket contact increases one's sense of rhythm, timing, and muscle relaxation. When breathing and hitting become synchronized in this fashion, players' strokes become fuller and they are less likely to choke. The longer and more extended the exhalations, the better. One need not grunt to achieve the desired effects. In fact, experience has shown that a quiet, extended out-breath is superior to a loud grunt.

Breath control between points is equally important. Deep diaphragmatic breaths (breathing from the lower stomach) prior to serve and serve returns during difficult situations is invaluable.

High Positive Intensity

Projecting high positive intensity during play is essential for sustained competitive success. It is always a good training goal to have your athletes play and practice with the same intensity. During match play, players should project high positive intensity at all times, even if they don't feel it. The rule is, if they don't feel it, they are to *fake it*. They are to look as if they feel positively pumped, alive, and combative.

Project Relaxation and Calm

Competitive success requires that athletes remain relaxed and calm during crisis situations. Looking relaxed and calm is 50% of the battle. One effective way for athletes to learn relaxation and calmness is to project these qualities outwardly during play.

Mistake Management

When players are performing well, they typically respond to errors in a very specific way. They simply turn and walk away. The goal is to learn to *always* respond to errors in this way. The more athletes become emotionally involved with mistakes, the less likely they are to perform well. Players score high in this category if it is difficult to tell from their outward responses if their shot was in or out.

Confident Fighter Image

Success in competition requires a strong and powerful on-court presence. Experience has shown that our toughest competitors generally project two intense feelings during competition—high self-confidence and fight. These are communicated by the way they carry their head and shoulders, by the way they walk, smile, and talk, even by the way they dress and carry their rackets. Players should constantly train to project the image of a confident fighter.

Negative Self-Talk

When players are performing well, they rarely get caught up in a lot of negative and self-defeating self-talk during play. Players should regularly train to eliminate this. Negative self-talk is negative self-programming and, as such, can have significant short-term and long-term negative effects on performance.

Positive Attitude

Positive thinkers make the best competitors. You can often tell whether a person is thinking positively or negatively during play by simply observing external reactions. The common response to crisis and adversity is negative thinking. Success in competition requires the uncommon response—rather than become negative when things get rough, players must try to get challenged and inspired.

Table 18.4 is a form to help coaches evaluate players in the on-court categories of mental training.

Table 18.4 Sample On-Court Rating Form

	Excellent				Poor
1. Eyes controlled	1	2	3	4	5
2. Rituals—serve	1	2	3	4	5
—serve return	1	2	3	4	5
3. Pace	1	2	3	4	5
4. Breathing—during points	1	2	3	4	5
—between points	1	2	3	4	5
5. High positive intensity	1	2	3	4	5
6. Project relaxation/calmness	1	2	3	4	5
7. Mistake management	1	2	3	4	5
8. Confident fighter image	1	2	3	4	5
9. Limits negative self-talk	1	2	3	4	5
10. Positive attitude	1	2	3	4	5

CATEGORIES OF
OFF-COURT MENTAL TRAINING

There are a variety of tactics that you can use off the court to help your players be better mentally prepared. The following exercises are excellent.

Muscle-Relaxation Exercises

The ability to appropriately trigger muscle relaxation during competition is an acquired skill and can be learned through a wide range of off-court training strategies. One of the most widely practiced muscle-relaxation exercises is the Jacobson System, which involves the alternate tensing and relaxing of muscles, starting with those of the forehead and gradually extending to the feet. The objective of this system is twofold: to learn to differentiate increases and decreases in muscle tension, and to learn to relax specific muscle groups upon command.

Other strategies include listening to relaxation tapes, physical exercise such as running or jogging prior to match play, stretching, practicing yoga, and massage. All these are simply different methods of attaining the same goal.

Calming Exercises

Accelerating athletes' abilities to sustain a sense of calmness and mental quiet during competition is an important mental-training objective. Various forms of meditation have been used to achieve this training objective. Practitioners frequently report that regular meditation facilitates concentration and muscle-relaxation skills as well. A variety of books are available on the topic of learning how to meditate. One of the best is Herbert Bensen's *The Relaxation Response.*

Breath-Control Exercises

Practicing breath control off court can significantly enhance breath-control skills on court. Learning to identify thoracic breathing patterns (short, shallow, jerky) and how to quickly change them to diaphragmatic patterns (deep, regular, and full) can be very helpful to performing athletes. Numerous opportunities exist throughout the day to short-circuit the stress response or anger/temper response by controlling breathing patterns.

Visualization and Imagery Exercises

The regular practice of off-court visualization has proven invaluable to many tennis players. Mentally rehearsing match strategy, how one will respond emotionally and physically in various crisis situations, temper control, match goals, and even stroke mechanics is often very useful. Visualization involves thinking in pictures rather than words and is most effective when the images are vivid, detailed, and enhanced through the use of all five senses. Visualization can be a powerful vehicle for effective self-programming.

Goal Setting

Goal setting has long been recognized as a valuable mental-training strategy. Goals help players stay more motivated, focused, and disciplined in regard to training and match play. Setting realistic but challenging long-term, intermediate, and short-term goals is very important. Prior to match play, establishing clear and concise match goals, over which the player can exercise definite control (e.g., effort, attitude, fight, etc.), is nearly always beneficial.

Establishing Disciplined Off-Court Training Rituals

Improved self-discipline nearly always leads to increased self-confidence. The more athletes develop and adhere to definite training rituals in the areas of diet, exercise, sleep, homework, time management, and so forth, the mentally stronger they are likely to become during match play.

Establishing Definite Prematch Preparation Routines

Many players have no consistent method of prematch preparation. They simply show up and play. A good prematch training routine should include the following:

- When to go to bed and when to get up
- When and what to eat
- Workout schedule before the match (when, where, with whom)
- Prematch goal setting
- Crisis rehearsal (visualization)
- 30-minute prematch quiet time

Appendix C is a detailed list of specific mental-training suggestions.

CHAPTER 19

Tips for Coaching Psychological Skills

What makes a great coach from the psychological perspective? This chapter intends to synthesize those psychological factors that have proven to be important in successful coaching in a set of guidelines that you should find concrete, practical, and helpful.

PERCEIVE YOURSELF AS A PERFORMER

Just as your players are performers, so are you, their coach. Just as tennis players must constantly seek to understand those factors that bring out the best in them, so must you. You must strive to achieve the highest possible levels of coaching excellence. Your ultimate goal must be, as it is for competing players, to perform as consistently as you can toward the upper range of your talent and skill. When it comes to the importance of mental toughness, you are no different from your players. To achieve success, coaches must learn and use the same psychological skills that their players must.

LEARN TO CONTROL
YOUR IDEAL PERFORMANCE STATE

The ideal emotional climate for coaching is no different from the ideal emotional climate for competition. To be at your best you must learn to be relaxed and calm in the midst of crisis. You must learn how to take the pressure off regardless of how crazy or pressurized external events may seem. You must be able to generate within yourself the feelings of high energy that stem almost exclusively from your positive emotions. Just as an athlete gets pumped for performances, so must you. You must minimize negative energy stemming from negative emotions. If you want to perform at your best, you must train hard to develop an optimistic and positive attitude. It is no surprise that, just as athletes must come to enjoy the battle to be truly good at it, you must learn to have fun at what you do; it is impossible for you to attain your best if you are not deriving personal enjoyment.

Obviously feelings of confidence, alertness, control, and focus are also important. Every time you step into the coaching arena you should try to trigger this ideal balance of feelings. Rather than becoming negative when confronted with problems, you must get more challenged, channel more positive intensity to the task at hand. With time you will find your own psychological skills dramatically improved. Remember, the real test of great performers is what happens to them in adversity and crisis. This is what separates the few that make it to the top from the many who do not. Practice your psychological skills in precisely the way you would have your players practice theirs.

MODEL WHAT YOU WANT TO TEACH

There is no more powerful way to teach psychological skills than to model them. Coaches are often shocked when they realize just how powerful their influence can be on players, both from a positive and negative perspective. You are a powerful person in your players' lives; they are learning from you all the time, even when you may not be actively teaching. If you are acting in ways that reflect excessive pressure, if you have little energy and positive intensity yourself, or if you are a negative thinker, your players sense that you do not enjoy what you are doing and that you have little confidence or emotional control. Once you fully comprehend that your players are learning from you every moment you are with them, you will more effectively use every valuable minute to model the behavior you wish them to learn.

DEVELOP YOUR OWN PERFORMANCE RITUALS

Find out what rituals help you perform consistently toward the upper range of your abilities. These might include sleep patterns, regular diet and eating times, and specific mental preparations you make before starting your day. The better you know and follow the rituals that contribute to your coaching performance, the greater your chances of becoming a successful coach. Establishing a balance in your life with work, family, leisure time, and all the rest is critical, just as it is for the performing athlete. Know and follow your rituals.

TRAIN YOURSELF TO BE ORGANIZED AND DISCIPLINED

Disorganization and the lack of discipline are two of the most common reasons individuals fall short of their potential. These are goals that should never be ignored. Make a commitment to yourself each day that you will get better and better with time. Whether it means preparing a daily list of things to do, getting up a half hour earlier, or taking every hour of each day and planning for its best possible use, you must take such steps. Constantly explore ways to improve your organizational and self-disciplinary skills. As you do, you will find that your self-confidence will steadily climb. Self-discipline, self-confidence, and self-control are closely interrelated.

MAINTAIN YOUR GENERAL HEALTH

Like your athletes, you need to be physically fit to achieve optimal performance levels. We are learning that as we become fitter we become emotionally stronger. We feel better about ourselves and handle crisis and conflict more successfully. Overweight coaches who smoke and eat the wrong foods have poor physical fitness and are bad models for their players. Put yourself on a good physical training program and you will automatically get stronger mentally. You will also be modeling what you want to teach.

PACE YOURSELF

Coaching can be very stressful. The time demands and psychological pressures can quickly produce burnout. Coaches must learn to pace themselves—to take breaks and schedule time off. Doing so is an important part of being able to summon the best in you when you need it most. All too often we find ourselves pushing too hard and too long with the end result being burnout.

TRAIN TO BECOME POSITIVE

Just as positive thinkers make better competitors, so they make better coaches. Positive thinking is a habit acquired through diligent persistence; it is much easier to become negative and pessimistic as the pressures mount. Coaches know how important positive thinking is, but all too often they lose sight of its application to their own lives and performance levels. Avoid this mistake. Constantly train to think like the champions that you are trying to get your athletes to become.

WHEN YOU DON'T FEEL IT, ACT AS IF YOU DO

Sometimes we have considerable difficulty triggering our ideal performance state in front of our players. In such cases we should demand of ourselves no less than we demand of our players: Fake it. If you do not feel energized or relaxed or positive or enthusiastic, simply act as if you do. Project the same feeling that you wish to feel. To let yourself act the way you feel in front of your players— negative, pessimistic, listless, and critical—is to do them a real disservice.

MAKE SURE YOUR COACHING
PHILOSOPHY IS SOLID

Although the win-at-all-cost philosophy in junior tennis can have devastating consequences, it is the model basically prevalent in professional sports: "Winning isn't everything—it's the only thing." Unfortunately, when this attitude is allowed to permeate junior sport, it takes precedence over the personal development of the players. Junior sport exists for the players—not for the fans, the parents, or the coaches. Junior athletics serves the purpose of developing players as persons and as athletes. This must be the first and foremost objective of any junior program. The most important thing a coach can do for young athletes is to get them to believe in themselves and their abilities. Each individual must feel there is hope for improvement, for achievement, for success. When the primary goal is winning, it is very easy to lose sight of these valuable priorities.

If coaches do not have clearly defined principles to guide their actions, it is easy for them to get caught up in the obsession to win. Our society makes it very difficult to focus on anything else in tennis. As coaches become increasingly obsessed with winning, the behavior of their students changes predictably. Young athletes begin to define their worth in terms of winning or losing; the more they lose, the less valuable they feel as persons.

In a draw of 64 there is only one winner; somewhere along the line, everyone else loses. If winning is equated with success and losing with failure, there will be 63 failures. We see many casualties in junior tennis today because we create enormous psychological pressures. Even at the highest levels of the game there are a lot of casualties, and these players are supposed to represent the success of the system.

There are real risks to young players when coaches lose their philosophical sense of direction. Vince Lombardi's often-misquoted line actually was, "Winning isn't everything, but striving to win is." The real triumph, or tragedy, of junior tennis is what happens to the individual as a result of the experience. As we have pointed out, tennis in the proper context is an invaluable vehicle for teaching life skills to youngsters. In many ways, the analogy of tennis as a microcosm of life is apt. One must face the world alone, and the world is a tough opponent. When things go badly there are no substitute players and no time-outs. One is faced with a continuing series of problems and challenges. Finding one's way through the maze and producing the right solutions at the right time demands great self-control and self-belief.

Acquired skills in positive thinking, discipline, stress management, and self-regulation are indispensable to life's journey. There are few shortcuts. The real battle for winning or losing is waged internally; those who vanquish their own weaknesses find themselves positively transformed in the process. The experience leaves them feeling more complete, more alive, and more fully functioning. That is precisely what junior tennis should be all about, and coaches should not forget it.

LEARN TO MANAGE MISTAKES

One of the greatest obstacles athletes face in their pursuit of excellence is the management of mistakes. In tennis, a player can commit scores of mistakes in a relatively short time. The inability to manage mistakes well proves to be the downfall of many players regardless of their talent. The frustration, the anger, the loss of confidence can at times overwhelm them. Coaches must constantly work to help players in this area and try to be excellent models of mistake management in their personal and professional lives.

BE INVOLVED AND CARE

A number of research efforts have examined what athletes feel was the single most important trait of their best coaches. The same trait surfaced repeatedly. Those coaches who affected their players most were not necessarily the ones with the most knowledge or degrees. The single most important attribute was the perception on the part of the players that the coach really cared about them.

Coaches must invest a great deal of dedication, time, and emotional energy in players at the junior level. According to the research, if you really want to have a positive impact on the lives of your players, you must get personally involved—and care.

REINFORCE THE POSITIVE

From a learning as well as from a motivational perspective, players are better off when we reinforce the positive aspects of their play as opposed to punishing the negative. It is often easier for coaches to spot errors than it is to identify the positive aspects of a player's efforts. We must constantly train to look for positive things to reinforce. The learning process presents a continuous opportunity for focusing on both the positive and the negative parts of learning. The general rule is to provide feedback quickly and accurately and to make the feedback positive rather than negative. Consider the following important guidelines:

• Positively reinforce specific match behavior rather than simply the outcome of matches. Simply reinforcing winning is of dubious value.

• Reward learning in both the physical and psychological areas. Coaches have a tendency to reward the things they are most comfortable with, such as strokes and mechanics. Never overlook psychological and emotional successes of your players.

• Break success into gradual steps. Major success is achieved by reinforcing the little things that lead to it.

• Reward effort more than any other single factor, and always over outcome.

• Your positive reward should occur as close in time as possible to the occurrence of the behavior you wish to encourage. If you wait too long, the reinforcing effects are diminished.

• The more you can get your athletes to understand that intrinsic rewards are the most powerful driving forces in performance behavior, the better.

BE TOUGH ON TEMPER, TANKING, AND BEHAVIOR PROBLEMS

Coaches need to establish firm limits regarding bad habits and behavior problems and set appropriate disciplinary consequences. Coaches who allow attitude and behavior problems to go unchecked are actually encouraging their frequency. To a certain extent all players have a tendency to openly express their disappointments and frustrations. Players need to learn to channel negative energy. As long as they are able to express it openly during play, they will likely never learn the self-control that is essential to future competitive success.

Coaches often find it difficult to decide how to handle players with behavior problems. They are afraid that if they get too tough with these players they might lose the opportunity to coach them. Another common reason for indecisiveness is that coaches have not defined firm policies and clear consequences for violations. It is important once limits are set that they be consistently enforced. Penalties for poor court behavior can include withholding players from tournaments, denying them lessons the following week, or not allowing them to play for an extended period. Obviously, such action must be taken with the full knowledge and support of the parents. In most cases, parents will support your action if the policy is defined openly and responsibly.

WORK WITH PARENTS

As indicated in the previous chapter, coaches are frequently beset with problems from parents. Many of these problems can be avoided if a coach takes the time to train the parents. When you take on the responsibility of coaching a youngster, you should make up your mind to work with the parents as well. Parents play a critical role in a youngster's learning process; to leave them out of the picture is to invite future problems both for yourself and, more crucially, for the young player.

Conduct regular training sessions for parents (refer to them as something else!). Problems materialize when they are left in the dark about what is happening; they must feel included in the process, or they will likely become a source of trouble. Keep them informed of the progress you are making or not making with their son or daughter, and make sure that they are adhering to the overall game plan you have worked out for them. It is extremely unlikely that parents will stay on target in this area without some guidelines to follow. Most parents, however, will do whatever seems helpful and reasonable.

DEMAND INTENSITY

One of the most important training practices you can implement is to require that your players learn how to channel intensity into constructive activities. Allowing players to practice with low intensity is to deny them the opportunity to improve their activation skills. Players should practice the way they want to play. In my own work and research, intensity has consistently surfaced as the number one factor in importance. Coaches should take every opportunity to help players learn how to more effectively control intensity levels.

BE CREATIVE AND STIMULATING IN PRACTICE

Boring, uninspired practices breed poor physical and psychological habits. Coaches who insist on the same routine day after day and week after week create a formidable obstacle to interest and stimulation. Players learn much more when they are really involved in what they are doing. Coaches should try to challenge and inspire players to push themselves, to go beyond their ordinary limits, and to constantly reach out for higher accomplishments. This challenges coaches to be creative.

There are any number of ways to train to meet fixed training objectives. Use as much variety and innovation as possible to achieve your practice objectives. Request suggestions from your players about ways to improve practice routines. Something as simple as adding music to the drills might help to provide stimulation. Change routines often. Repeatedly devoting extended time to certain drill routines breeds motivational and attitudinal problems. Part of establishing interesting practice routines is simply being prepared before going out on court. Taking 15 minutes at the start of the day to plan activities that help you meet the day's training objectives can make all the difference.

USE VIDEO FOR PSYCHOLOGICAL TRAINING

One of the most valuable tools to facilitate the learning of psychological skills is the use of video. Showing players how they look during competition when they are relaxed, calm, and projecting high intensity, as opposed to how they look when tight, nervous, or negative, has immeasurable value. Just as video can significantly enhance the learning of physical skills, it can help athletes see what happens to them in crisis and adversity. To see such things as the level of confidence they project during a match and the way they manage mistakes helps them develop a clear sense of their court presence.

The cost of video equipment today is generally within reach of most coaching budgets and is well worth the investment. Players should have regular opportunities to discover what positive changes are occurring in psychological areas. Key point: When videotaping for psychological purposes, the most important time during a match to capture the player is *between points*. It is generally most helpful to keep the camera on the player throughout the match. Rather than following the ball, follow the player—especially between points.

MONITOR ANYTHING YOU WANT TO CHANGE

Whether you are talking about changing attitudes, improving intensity control, or eliminating temper problems; whether you are working on pace, confidence, or breath control—if you regularly monitor a particular activity, you will generally see improvement. By requiring players to keep regular records in the areas in which they want to improve, you force them to give attention to the learning on a regular basis. Coaches often fail to take advantage of this simple principle. Players can use any system of monitoring and evaluation they choose. Their daily objective is to seek to do the best they can and then evaluate how they think they did.

SET GOALS FOR YOURSELF

Coaches are constantly talking about goal setting for their players. Most insist that their players commit their goals to writing. It is always interesting to ask coaches how important they think this area is. Invariably, they feel it is fundamentally important for the players. When asked, however, if they set goals for themselves, the answer is frequently no. What holds true in the area of goal setting for your players holds true for you.

What is your dream? What do you hope to accomplish with your life in coaching? If you have not given these questions much thought, you should do so, as this is the essence of motivation. What are your intermediate goals? What must you accomplish over the next several years to achieve your long-term goal? These plans should be realistic and well thought out.

What are your daily goals? I firmly believe you should be on a training program similar to the one you put your players on. The point is, you should be constantly moving toward important goals yourself. Doing so will help you be more organized and feel that you are moving in a direction that is important for you. A lot of people are expecting to be motivated and inspired by your enthusiasm, dedication, and commitment. When you have an inadequate personal sense of motivation and drive, you can have a powerfully negative impact on those around you.

AVOID FEAR, THREAT, AND PUNISHMENT

It is true that negative strategies often get results. Charged negative emotions can get players off dead center and get them doing amazing things. Experience has proven, however, that continued use of negative reinforcers typically has long-term negative consequences. These negative consequences affect the most vital aspect of players' psychology—their self-motivation.

KEEP GOOD RECORDS

Keep records of everything. You should have a detailed file on all players you work with that includes everything from their workout schedules to tournament results. The more you know about players, the better you can structure their training routines to produce constructive change. Records also help to chart the progress players are making in a detailed, visible way. So often athletes become discouraged because they feel they are not going anywhere. Progress charts drawn from accurate records will help players through these difficult times with good effect. Keeping track of successes and genuine signs of progress enables coaches to help players with regular, positive feedback during their journey through the maze of problems, crises, and grueling practices.

COMMON PSYCHOLOGICAL PITFALLS OF COACHING

As a coach, you must be aware of common misconceptions about your position and your actions. Those listed here frequently occur.

• Thinking that because you are the coach, players will automatically respect you. Respect must be earned. This will occur over time in direct proportion to such things as your dedication, integrity, honesty, and overall coaching skills.

• Becoming increasingly negative, critical, and hostile with your players as pressures mount. Coaching is unquestionably stressful and can at times be threatening and embarrassing. We all have a strong tendency to defend ourselves by becoming critical, projecting our own inadequacies and frustrations onto those with whom we work. Coaches must avoid this pitfall as it serves to undermine their credibility and creates a host of complicating psychological problems for their players.

• Failing to establish consistent policies. Consistency in performance, as we have repeatedly shown, is one of the primary indicators of excellence in an athlete. The same is true of coaches. Inconsistency in policy, in practice schedules, in being on time, in keeping appointments, and so on undermines everything the coach is attempting to do.

• Blaming rather than teaching. Coaches often fall into the trap of blaming players for things that go wrong rather than teaching players what to do about them. When things go badly, we tend to look for a target at which to direct our pent-up negative emotions. Simply pointing out that a player lost because he or she is out of shape, has not been coming to practice, or has a poor attitude does very little good. However, helping the player to understand how losses are connected to certain factors that must be changed in positive directions is a valuable coaching activity. A fine line exists between blaming and constructively pointing out what must be done for the future, and coaches must walk that line. This is the line that parents are often unable to navigate.

• Talking too much and not enough listening. Coaches often talk too much. Players need to feel they are understood. From a psychological perspective, coaches must tune in to how players are feeling, to what is going through their minds and hearts. This is possible only when coaches ask questions and then genuinely listen. Coaches often feel more comfortable giving messages than receiving them. But a balance must be struck between giving advice and direction and listening to the inner concerns of your players.

• Communicating poorly with your players. Coaches must work to constantly improve their ability to communicate powerfully, honestly, and effectively. Successful teaching and coaching demands excellent communication. Coaches should constantly strive to improve their overall facility for sending and receiving accurate, clear messages.

• Failing to do your homework to stay current. The science of coaching is changing rapidly. The advances made in the past few years in nearly all areas of sport science are impressive. To be fully professional and do the best job you possibly can requires that you continually seek new training and education. Research in the area of sport psychology can be of tremendous value to coaches in improving the mental aspects of their coaching. To avoid falling behind in the knowledge curve, read everything you can get your hands on that relates to your work as a coach.

• Becoming stale and burned out. Any profession as demanding and stressful as coaching has a relatively high risk of burnout. There are various forms of burnout, some obvious, some subtle. Subtle forms are reflected in lower energy levels, reduced tolerance for frustration and uncertainties, a tendency to be irritable, and a general absence of enthusiasm and fire in your work. There is no mistaking the not-so-subtle signs of burnout. Your work brings you little if any satisfaction or enjoyment. You find it hard to get up in the morning to address the things that are necessary for success. Days go by and you have a nagging sense of incompleteness and inadequacy about what you are doing. There is rarely a sense of challenge or satisfaction; your attitude becomes cynical and hypercritical.

Burnout is the result of too much stress and pressure and not enough fun and relaxation. Without deliberately building into your schedule some variety, stimulation, and change, you are likely to find yourself slipping ever closer to the reality of burnout. The combination of boredom and high negative stress is lethal. Take the time to structure your world to minimize the probability of burnout. You can do this by programming considerable variety into your schedule, by taking regular breaks from the action, and by improving your stress- and time-management skills.

Afterword

A comparison of the top five men and women on the pro tour reveals different game styles, personalities, athletic abilities, nutritional habits, and so on. On every level, different and flexible teaching approaches must be taken with athletes on an individual basis. Coaching style depends to some extent on your personality, but it is crucial to realize that it must also be governed by the personalities of your athletes.

The development of quality tennis players requires extensive scientific knowledge and depends on many intangibles. Motivation is one of the most important intangibles. Some believe that coaching is one-half instruction and one-half motivation.

Actually, the proper ratio varies with the make-up of each individual. Younger athletes often possess plenty of natural enthusiasm. Depending on their backgrounds and personalities, more-experienced athletes might need less motivation. Frequently it is those who are stuck on a skill plateau, or are struggling to recover from a decrement in performance while changing a stroke technique, who most need encouragement and motivation.

In any case, successful motivational programs begin with the coach. Your own motivational level sets the top limit for everyone else. Set it high enough so that there is ample room for assistant coaches and less-motivated players to reach for and attain a level of enthusiasm conducive to success. Common motivational methods —pep talks to psych up a player—help individuals play better in the short term, but lose effectiveness over the course of a year or more.

The ultimate goal is to produce an entirely self-motivated athlete who approaches each match so thoroughly prepared that all the coach needs to do is to fill out the entry forms. There is no "cookbook" recipe delineating the process by which athletes become self-motivated. Certainly one of the most successful methods is the systematic setting of realistic expectations and goals—short-term, intermediate, and long-term. As you coach your athletes toward the goals they have (with your guidance) set, make optimal use of the time you have together—make it *quality* time.

Remember also that tennis is a game of pauses and breaks. As Dr. Loehr suggests, utilize your coaching energy efficiently—store it, expend it, and conserve it, pacing yourself. We concern ourselves that athletes who are in a constant state of high anxiety will run out of gas. The threat of burnout over the course of a coaching career is an equivalent concern.

Whereas some coaches attempt to be all things to their players, an important goal of the effective coach must be to develop players who are independent thinkers on the court. You want to develop athletes who know how and when to change a game strategy, how to handle stress during a match. When your player looks at you to verify if a ball was in or out, it is an obvious sign of dependence and sometimes a call for help. Winners handle on-court psychological pressures; their stroke production and movement mechanics change very little under stress, and, when the chips are down, they respond positively and aggressively.

As we said at the outset, no book can provide an all-purpose formula for magically creating world-class tennis players. We hope we have convinced you that a comprehensive sport science approach to coaching is the most effective way to develop technically skilled, independent-thinking, self-motivated players. Good luck in your efforts to mold a Wimbledon champion.

Jack L. Groppel, PhD

Tennis Fitness Evaluation Form

Name: _____   Ranking: _____

Test: _____   Dates: _____   _____

Agility, dynamic balance, and response time

Modified Semo agility test _____   _____

Quinn agility, dynamic balance, and
   response-time test _____   _____

Speed

20-meter dash _____   _____

Baseline-service line dash
   (speed/response) _____   _____

Power

Vertical-jump test _____   _____

Cardiovascular endurance

12-minute run _____   _____

1-1/2-mile run _____   _____

Muscular endurance
Sit-up test   _____   _____
Push-up test   _____   _____

Flexibility
Sit-and-reach test   _____   _____
Trunk-extension test   _____   _____

Strength
Grip-strength test   _____   _____

Physical characteristics
Height   _____   _____
Weight   _____   _____
Percent body fat   _____   _____

Coach's subjective evaluation and recommendations

Strengths

Weaknesses

Sample Fitness Training Program for Junior Players

This program is an example of a one-week plan for a junior player. Apart from the daily schedules described, warm-up, flexibility exercises, and cool-down are assumed as routine daily activities. Explanations of the various training drills can be found in their respective sections of chapter 14.

Monday
All-direction line sprint
Forward/backward line sprint
Diagonal court sprints
Roll-ball routines: 4 sets of 25 balls
Volley drill × 50
Ball-recovery drill × 2

Tuesday
Fartlek run—30 to 40 minutes
Stretching—30 minutes

Wednesday
Circuit training × 3
On court: baseline, serve, and volley reaction drills

Thursday

Interval training: 4 laps easy warm-up; 8 × 40 meters; 6 × 75 meters; 4 × 100 meters; 2 × 150 meters; 4 × 100 meters; 6 × 75 meters; 8 × 40 meters; 4 laps cool-down

Friday

Stair running—20 minutes

Across-the-court runs: forward, backward, sideways right and left. Do this across six courts, or repeat six times if only one court

"W" drill × 2

Shadow drills with weighted racket, following a partner, for 15 minutes

Saturday

Jump rope—20 minutes

Aerobics—40 minutes

Sunday

Day off. Enjoy!

APPENDIX C

Training Suggestions for Various Mental-Skill Deficiencies

LOW SELF-CONFIDENCE

• Increase self-discipline throughout all phases of the player's training. Better self-discipline invariably leads to higher self-confidence.

• Increase the overall fitness and endurance of the player. Improved fitness automatically translates into greater self-confidence.

• Prescribe a daily diet of success. When confidence is low, winning is seldom possible. Success must be broken down into achievable daily building blocks. Establish daily goal setting in areas the athlete can control (attitude, effort, etc.).

• Review film of best matches. If film is available, this can serve to powerfully instill renewed confidence.

• Get the player to repeatedly visualize themes of success. "Seeing" is believing. The more you can get an athlete to visualize being confident, breaking through, playing well, and winning, the sooner it will start to happen.

• Get the player to constantly use positive affirmations. Repeated use of positive affirmations such as "I can do it," "I'm getting tougher," and "My confidence is growing" builds positive response expectancy. Such positive self-programming can have highly desirable performance effects.

• Get the player to act *as if*. Although players do not feel confident or self-assured, they are to act as if they do. They are to *fake it*. Acting confident, strong, and in control paves the way for being so.

LOW AROUSAL CONTROL

• Increase players' general awareness. The more aware the athletes are of how different states of activation and arousal affect their performance, the greater the chance of control. Have players frequently rate their levels of intensity on a scale of 1 to 10; then rate the extent to which the intensity is generated from their positive or negative emotions.

• Give players specific time limits to become optimally activated. In match play, only 5 minutes of warm-up time is allowed. Players must learn to raise intensity and activation levels very quickly. It is a helpful training strategy to allow only the same 5 minutes in practice for warm-up. Players then get daily practice going from low intensity to optimal levels within typical match time limits.

• Train players in breath control. Teaching players to regulate arousal levels through breath control is generally very useful. Developing specific breathing patterns for all aspects of play—prior to serve, during serve, between points—may be necessary for some players.

• Develop clear and concise action plans for choking or temper problems. The more specific a plan of action athletes have to call upon in crisis, the better they are likely to do. An example of a plan for choking might be as follows:

As soon as the player is aware of nervousness or panic, he or she should

1. take more time doing everything,
2. become very ritualistic,
3. resist the temptation to "push" or go for first-ball winners,
4. mentally focus on hitting the ball *early* and *seeing it all the way in*, and
5. play high-percentage aggressive tennis.

• Take off the pressure to win. Excessive pressure to win can quickly lead to arousal-control problems. Put pressure on players to control those things they can, but reduce the pressure to win, which is clearly beyond their control.

• Improve players' rituals. Better rituals generally lead to better arousal control. Rituals should have both a mental and physical component. The more precise and detailed, the better.

• Improve players' sense of pace. Players with arousal-control problems frequently find their pace changing as their emotional state changes. Helping players maintain a consistent match pace regardless of how they are feeling can substantially aid in reestablishing emotional control.

• Improve mistake management. This is a most-important area for mental training. Helping players to emotionally respond to mistakes so that intensity levels are not adversely affected requires considerable work. This is where many players never make it mentally.

• Improve relaxation and calming skills. Use whatever seems to work here—muscle-relaxation exercises, meditation, hypnosis tapes, relaxation tapes, and so on. Each player has his or her own preferences. Fit the technique to the player.

• Monitor food intake—particularly sugar. Some arousal-control problems can be linked directly to food sensitivities, particularly simple carbohydrates. Always explore diet as a possible factor.

• Monitor sleep patterns. Most athletes require 8 to 9 hours of sleep daily. Experience has repeatedly shown that as athletes get less sleep, their ability to hold up under pressure, to control temper, and to concentrate diminishes accordingly.

LOW ATTENTION CONTROL

• Improve eye control between points. Get your players to keep their eyes controlled between points on the ball, on the strings, or on the ground. A close correlation exists between visual focus and mental focus.

• Increase positive intensity. Increasing the flow of positive intensity will nearly always lead to increased attention control. When a player's intensity is right, concentration occurs very naturally.

• Improve calming and quieting skills. Helping your players remain calm and positive in crisis will substantially improve their concentration success. To improve attention control, players should train to increase their control over the feeling of calmness in the presence of high intensity.

• Practice meditation. Meditation is actually a form of concentration practice. A variety of meditational strategies involve focusing one's attention on a specific target and holding it there. It is practice in tuning in what is important and tuning out what is not.

• Invoke the "only the ball" technique during play. Repeating silently between points the phrase *only the ball* helps keep wandering eyes and wandering focus under control.

• Concentrate in practice. Players should be made to work extra hard in practice to maintain good concentration. Athletes perform as they practice—both mentally and physically.

• Help players develop simple cognitive cues for getting refocused. Cues that often help in reestablishing concentration are thoughts such as *contact the ball early, quick feet,* and *see the ball all the way to contact.*

LOW VISUALIZATION AND IMAGERY

• Encourage your players to practice visualization daily. Get them feeling comfortable thinking in pictures rather than words. They should try to enhance the vividness of the imagery by using all five senses. Practice sessions should be short—3 to 5 minutes— and goal directed.

• Best effects are produced when the athlete is calm and relaxed. Visualizing playing well, overcoming obstacles, succeeding, and so on is facilitated by a relaxed, quiet atmosphere.

• Have your players visualize stroke production and strategy. Visualization facilitates the learning of both stroke mechanics and game strategy as long as the player has a clear concept of what should be practiced.

• Use video, photographs, mirrors, or film to enhance visualization. These can substantially help players to visualize more accurately and vividly.

• Mentally rehearse tough situations in advance. An athlete who is surprised is in trouble. Mentally rehearsing how one wishes to respond to potential problematic situations in advance generally means more self-control.

• Have players visualize *during* play. The dictum is, "Visualize during play—don't verbalize or analyze." Players should be taught to visualize prior to serving and returning serve as part of their normal ritual.

LOW SELF-MOTIVATION

• Have your players identify their long-term goals. What is their dream? This becomes the most important core of self-motivation.

• Have players set realistic intermediate goals to serve as stepping stones to major accomplishments. Players need to know what specific steps they must take to successfully arrive at their long-term goals.

• Have players set daily short-term goals. For many players, success at these is the most important vehicle. Daily goal setting virtually guarantees a steady diet of success. Perceived success is the key to motivation, and this is the way to make it happen.

• Players should commit their goals to writing and set a date for completion. Committing things to writing makes them become more real. It also helps to focus thinking and training on a daily basis.

• Have players keep a daily log of their successes. When the going gets tough, having a record of where they've been and where they're going is invaluable.

• When motivation starts to fade, change the training routine. Keep your practices stimulating and challenging. If practice is boring, find ways to reintroduce learning in a more stimulating manner. Be creative.

• Build in regular breaks in the action. One way to ensure your players do not overdo and burn out is to require regular breaks in their training. Do everything you can to keep your players fresh and excited about playing.

• Display enthusiasm and enjoyment yourself. Motivation is contagious. If you are excited and enthused, your players are likely to draw motivation from your example. The converse is equally true: If you are bored and uninspired, your players will have a much tougher time motivationally.

LOW POSITIVE ENERGY

• Increase awareness of positive versus negative intensity. Get your players to improve their ability to detect changing energy states. Players must be able to recognize their own energy states and the effects of these on their performance levels.

• Get your players to act *as if*. Players should strive to project high positive intensity regardless of how they feel. Showing intensity paves the way for genuinely feeling it.

• Study intensity changes on film. When reviewing film or video of match play, make note of the number of times the player's intensity noticeably drops as well as the number of times it went from positive to negative.

• Get your players to think *challenge*. If you can get them to think *challenge* every time adversity strikes, their positive-energy control will improve dramatically.

• Never let your players run out of options. Players should never lose a match—they simply run out of time. They are always trying to figure out a way to win; they always have another option. This approach has a powerful impact on positive energy flow.

• Insist on 100% effort. There are lots of things your players cannot control during a match, but one thing they can always control is their effort. As long as players have the option of tanking (emotionally giving up), they are not likely to make much progress with their positive-energy control. Always demand total effort regardless of the outcome.

• Develop positive-energy triggers. Energy follows thought and images. Get your players to identify the thinking and imaging patterns that most powerfully trigger positive energy.

• Get your players feeling better about themselves. The better they feel about themselves, the more positive energy they will have to invest in tennis. Increased self-discipline, better use of time, and healthier personal relationships generally translate into more available positive energy.

• Demand high fitness levels. Many players are incapable of sustaining high positive intensity throughout the duration of a match because of inadequate physical fitness. Playing with high intensity demands high fitness levels. Exercising and eating right translates into more available physical energy, which in turn means more mental energy.

LOW ATTITUDE CONTROL

- Get your players to think like champions. The popular saying, "Attitude is the stuff of which champions are made," is absolutely true. Constantly model and discuss how your players are to think in various situations, particularly in crisis. The right habits of thought repeated over and over lead to powerful belief systems. These core beliefs ultimately separate winners from losers.

- Never stop emphasizing the importance of a positive attitude. Good examples of how attitude makes the difference appear nearly every day in the sports page. Be relentless here.

- Identify positive and negative attitudes. Have your players make up a list of their attitudes that hurt them and those that help. Examples would be how they think about the wind, cheaters, early morning matches, mistakes, "pushers," bad line calls, and so on. Help your players see how their negative thoughts get them into trouble.

- Identify the most important attitudes you want your players to have. What do you believe in as a coach? What are your core beliefs regarding the making of a champion? Make sure that your players never stop rehearsing those habits of thought.

- Get your players to say "Stop." Every time players realize they are involved in negative or destructive thinking, get them to say "Stop" and quickly generate positive thinking.

- Get your players to read and listen. The more players read about positive attitudes, the better. Constantly reinforce the right attitudes by having your players read the life stories, the struggles, the triumphs of great athletes. Have them read all the positive-thinking books, articles, and magazines they can. Having your players listen to audio tapes dealing with attitudes, motivation, and so on is very worthwhile.

- Be a model of positive thinking yourself. There is nothing more powerful as a learning force. Always model the mental skills you want players to learn.

ABOUT THE AUTHORS

Jack Groppel is Director of Player Development for Harry Hopman/Saddlebrook International Tennis and was selected 1987 Professional of the Year by the U.S. Professional Tennis Association. A sport science advisor to the United States Tennis Association and an instructional editor for *Tennis* magazine, he is also the author of *Tennis for Advanced Players: And Those Who Would Like To Be*. He has advised such players as John McEnroe and Stan Smith.

James Loehr is Director of Sport Science for the United States Tennis Association. A regular columnist for *World Tennis* magazine, he is the author of *Mentally Tough*, *Net Results: Training the Tennis Parent for Competition*, and *Mental Toughness Training for Sport* and has worked with over 40 of the world's best players.

Scott Melville is an associate professor in the Health, Physical Education, and Athletic Department of Eastern Washington University. In addition to having coached both men's and women's collegiate tennis teams, he has extensive experience working with young children in the areas of motor learning and physical education.

Ann Quinn is an Australian sport science consultant who works with elite and professional athletes. She serves as trainer for 1987 Wimbledon champion Pat Cash and has advised many other tennis champions, including Hana Mandlikova and numerous world class juniors from various countries. Ms. Quinn serves the U.S. Tennis Association as clinician and consultant.

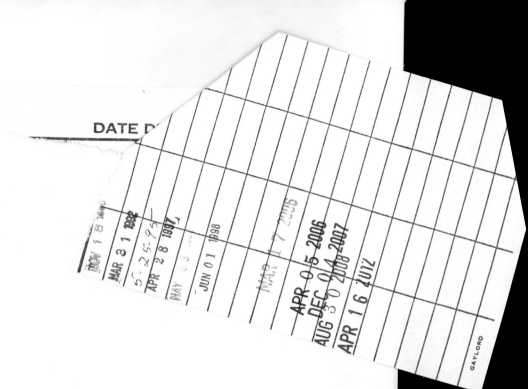